THE BLIND HORN'S HATE

The above painting (also reproduced on dust jacket) of the foundering off Cape Horn of the *Oxnard* of Boston, a ship of 142 feet, 6 inches length, with a depth of 22 feet, 9 inches, weighing something close to 596 tons, was executed by the artist James G. Evans.

RICHARD HOUGH

The Blind Horn's Hate

'It's north you may run to the rime-ringed sun,
or south to the blind horn's hate...'
Rudyard Kipling, *The Long Trail*

W · W · NORTON & COMPANY · INC · *NEW YORK*

SBN   393   05429   2

Library of Congress Catalog Card No. 76–116102

Published in Great Britain 1971 by Hutchinson & Co. (*Publishers*) Ltd.

PRINTED IN THE UNITED STATES OF AMERICA

1 2 3 4 5 6 7 8 9 0

Contents

Illustrations

For permission to reproduce illustrations, thanks must be given to *The National Maritime Museum, Greenwich* for the illustrations on pages 18, 24, 28, 50, 87, 92, 103, 155, 158, 159, 163, 178, 193, 240, 283, 303; to the *Radio Times Hulton Picture Library*, pages 33, 37, 62, 71, 72, 76, 107, 145, 162, 164, 169, 188, 195, 236, 245, 305; to *The Royal Geographical Society*, pages 66, 117, 161, 177, 246, 260, 266, 299(2), 300, 302(2); *National Portrait Gallery*, pages 83, 183, and the portrait of Sir Francis Drake. The photographs on pages 34, 118, 135, 202, 219, 270, 287 were taken by the author.

MAPS

To Capitan de Fragata Reinaldo Rivas of the Chilean Navy who navigated us so safely through the Fuegian channels and beyond, and was such an informative and delightful companion.

Introduction

The southernmost area of South America, from the tip of Cape Horn to the northern shore of the Magellan Strait, is one of the least known, the most hostile and yet most beautiful areas in the world. Its history and its geography are untidy, stark and violent. This is Tierra del Fuego. Until 1520 it was believed that the newly discovered American continent continued unbroken from the north to *Terra Australis*, the great apocryphal southern land mass. Ferdinand Magellan found a way through; but another sixty years passed before Francis Drake—that wicked pirate Francisco Draquez, his Spanish victims called him— discovered that America had an end, that 'The Atlantic Ocean and the South Sea meet in a large and free scope'.

Magellan and Drake were only two of many voyagers who plotted and suffered to find a short sea route to the spices and silks, the 'diamonds, emeralds, amethysts, topazes, and cinnamon, and gold moidores' of the East, and the rich minerals of Peru and Chile. Many of them died in their attempts to reach the golden *Mar del Sur*, the Pacific Ocean. They died from drowning or the scurvy, or from mutiny at the hands of their shipmates. Many more were hurled back into the Atlantic, for there are no gales in the world with the endurance and the punching force of Fuegian gales, and, under a jury rig, limped up the coast to the River Plate or Brazil. It took sublime seamanship, instinctive navigation, uncanny tenacity, and the gambling spirit—with luck on your side—to break through from the Atlantic to the Pacific. Then the rewards could be almost beyond calculation.

About this region of strange guanacos, burrowing penguins, of giant men, and women who fished naked with their dogs in freezing seas, of eternal snow-capped peaks and glaciers, fruit that could kill, or cure scurvy—and above all a region of hostile natives and weather—there grew up a fearful and superstitious reputation. Then the boldest captains kept clear of the uttermost south, and for centuries most of the ships which attempted to force the passage from ocean to ocean were manned by impressed crews. They left behind crosses on clifftops, wreckage among the rocks, and gibbets where treachery had been avenged.

Little by little these explorers and exploiters learned more of the nature and shape of this southerly land, its hellish climate, its insane configuration, its birds and animals, its human life living nomadically at the lowest level of primitiveness. In turn, those who survived the passage through, or round Cape Horn, plotted the numberless islands between sleet squalls, learned to live off crustaceans, wild dog or penguin flesh, and attempted to acquire some sort of relationship with the natives.

Today the storms still lash the shores from Desolation Island to Deceit Rocks, but claim no victims. On these rocky island shores there are no longer to be seen little gatherings of natives—anxious, fretful, opportunistic—their seal oil-soaked bodies glistening, screaming their demands before scuttling off to their canoes or the security of the forests. Civilised diseases, and the attentions of over-assiduous missionaries, have finished them off for ever.

Today you can travel the fiord-like channels for days on end, past a hundred dead, beautiful islands, whose dark, tree-rotted lower slopes rise to spectacular white-topped silhouettes. This is like gliding slowly above a bank of blue cloud between the peaks of the Andes. Instead of natives, penguins and cormorants on rocky promontories stare out incuriously at you. Only the air and the sea are alive, and are driven to an ornithological frenzy as your prow cuts through the water—terns, great skuas, steamer ducks, Magellanic gulls by the million, fishing and scavenging for all they are worth.

For days on end, summer or winter, drizzle, sleet or snow obscure everything, and the wind screams between the antarctic beeches and the crags. The days are worth enduring for the hours when the skies open up and a chill sun flashes on the snow and the glaciers, the glinting green forests and the kelp-draped rocks of the coastline. There is no spectacle in the world to surpass this for lonely scenic grandeur.

But go ashore onto one of these islands, walk across the grass of the hinterland (as welcoming as a Sussex meadow and sweet with flowers in the Spring), then strike into the forest. There are lifeless swamps, cold rocks, a near-impenetrable tangle of fallen trees that—like everything else in this cold climate—take too long to rot away. Nothing stirs in the dark pools or beneath the boulders and tree stumps. As shipwrecked Spanish explorers and colonists, stranded Dutch seamen and British missionaries have discovered, these beautiful islands were never intended by God to support human life: perhaps they should always have been as they are today.

You can feel the beat of the Pacific as the channels near the sea, and once out of their shelter the violence is a welcome reminder of reality—unless, of course, you are a Spanish *marinero* sick with scurvy and touched with frostbite, six months out of Cadiz in a battered caravel.

I have attempted to shape the history and spirit of this empty tip of a continent by singling out episodes in the lives, and sometimes the deaths, of a handful of men whose triumphs and tragedies were bound up in their experiences in 'the uttermost south': those who were driven there by a spirit of ambition and greed, or scientific curiosity or evangelical zeal. Some only glimpsed the towering black face of Cape Horn through sleet squalls as they fought their way round from ocean to ocean, others became trapped for weeks among the islands of the Fuegian archipelago. All these sailors, and those who later came to chart and study and civilize the place, left thankfully. For even in its mildest moods the uttermost south is untrustworthy, and the hate of the blind Horn has a special satanic quality unsurpassed anywhere in the world.

I

Ferdinand Magellan

'No fear, no danger shall his toils controul.
Along these regions from the burning zone
To deepest south he dares the course unknown.
While to the kingdoms of the rising day,
To rival thee he holds the western way,
A land of giants shall his eyes behold,
Of camel strength, surpassing human mould:
And onward still, thy fame, his proud heart's guide,
Haunting him unappeased, the dreary tide
Beneath the southern star's cold gleam he braves,
And stems the whirls of land-surrounded waves.
FOR EVER SACRED TO THE HERO'S FAME
THESE FOAMING STRAITS SHALL BEAR HIS
  DEATHLESS NAME.'

Luis de Camoens

A year and a day had passed since the armada of Ferdinand Magellan had left the port of San Lucar in southern Spain, its departure accompanied by the sounds of lamentation and the farewell boom of cannon; the one signalling the grief of wives and-children, the other the expectations of those who hoped to gain great riches if the ships ever returned.

Now it was 21 October 1520, an early spring day in the sub-Antarctic, although Magellan's mariners had not felt any touch of warmth against their faces nor seen a hint of green on the shoreline they had been following. For some eight months they had been searching for the *paso*, the legendary short cut to the riches of the East, or had been wintering in a bleak, chill anchorage two hundred miles farther north. They had suffered storms and tropical becalming, short rations, shipwreck, and the fury and bloodshed of a mutiny. Their hopes, like one of their *naos* in the South Atlantic swell, had lifted, held momentarily high, and fallen again into a deep trough with the exploration of every estuary, inlet and bay, from Brazil to southern Patagonia, which might lead them to the *Mar del Sur*.

They knew this ocean was there, somewhere to the east beyond this great Continent. Seven years earlier, Nunez de Balboa had seen it from the isthmus of Panama, seemingly limitless in its blue vastness. Only the faith and zeal, the discipline and single-mindedness of Captain-General Magellan had kept the helms of the four surviving ships on a southerly course, always searching for the passage. As to the rest—the carpenters and the priest, the caulkers and coupers, the pilots and pursers, the common seamen (*marineros* and *grumetes*) and their treacherous Spanish captains— all favoured, secretly or openly, an immediate return to their homeland, or a course eastwards to join the known route round Africa, across the Indian Ocean to Calicut and Malacca: the long route, the safe route to the other side of the world.

It is said that Magellan himself was the first to sight the cape, the only distinctive landmark they had seen for so long, and it was certainly he who named it, on St. Ursula's Day, the Cape of the Eleven Thousand Virgins, which lies 250 miles north of Cape Horn. Beyond the sandy spit and the cape of low white rock cliff and flat hinterland 'we saw an opening like unto a bay', observed Francisco Alvo of the flagship *Trinidad*. This bay was of uncommonly black water, wind-torn and eerie. Everyone noted this, even the least superstitious, and experienced a sense of unease and 'looked dubiously at the dark inlet'. On the southern shore the

Cape of the Eleven Thousand Virgins. From the original drawing by Lieutenant Brett R.N. on Anson's circumnavigation

cliffs were as white as the water was black. They were also higher and broken, and there was a new angularity to the horizon, which was in sharp contrast with the flat characterless land which had kept their spirits low since the previous March.

Beyond the cliffs there appeared to be dense forests and the land rose rapidly and at last to distant snow-capped peaks. (They were looking towards the heart of the main island of Tierra del Fuego.) The south side was also especially sheltered, and it was to a bay within the greater bay that Magellan directed his four ships. Two were to anchor here while the *San Antonio* and *Concepción* were to continue at once on a reconnaissance of the bay, although they all agreed that there was little chance of discovering an outlet from the west side of this black stretch of water. How could a place so doom-laden lead them to Balboa's sun-drenched ocean?

That night a storm arose and as a north-east gale threatened to hurl the *Trinidad* and the little *Victoria* onto the rocky shore, Magellan ordered anchors to be raised and they stood out to sea. The night, Magellan knew, would be even more hazardous for the *San Antonio* and *Concepción*, now deep within the bay. There was a special quality of fury and viciousness to this gale as if already the Antarctic was giving a first warning of what lay ahead for them should they penetrate farther south. And yet they were only at 52 degrees, and Magellan had told his captains that he would search for the end of this Continent, or a way through to the *Mar del Sur*, to 75 degrees if necessary.

The storm abated the next day at noon, and Magellan brought his flagship and the *Victoria* back to their anchorage. There was no sign of the other two vessels and he feared for them. Three more days passed. The loss of the *San Antonio* would be especially serious for she carried on board the greater part of their supplies, and without her Magellan knew that he might be forced to return to Spain.

A cry from the *Trinidad*'s look-out heralded the news not only that their consorts were safe, but that a passage to the *Mar del Sur* had surely been found. Every aspect of the bearing of the two *naos* told of success. Their pace was dramatic. They had crowded on all sails for a following wind, and were driven faster still by a strong tide that thrust across the bay from the west. Many-coloured ensigns were spread and as they came near Magellan saw puffs of grey-black smoke spout from their gunports and heard the crash of the firing bombards.

It was an epoch-making salute. It told Magellan that his belief was confirmed and that his search for a *paso* through the newly-discovered continent of America was over at last. There was, then, a shorter way to the East. And the earth must therefore be circumnavigable.

Beyond this bay was another, Magellan soon learned from his captains. The *San Antonio* and *Concepción* had been thrust willy-nilly by the force of the gale down a narrow concealed passage and into this second bay. From here a second narrow channel led to an inland sea. Here the tide ebbed and flowed as strongly as ever, and the water was as saline as the Atlantic's. Another ocean, the Southern Sea itself, must lie beyond: there could no longer be any doubt of that 'and we were very joyous and saluted them with artillery and shouts', wrote the *Trinidad*'s diarist.

The Lure of Spices

The man who was to lead the first circumnavigators was a proud, professional free-lance adventurer, a man of vast courage but uncertain loyalties, and with a predilection for getting into impossible situations. All through his life he had been prone to accident. These would have been fewer if he had been more judicious, less impulsive, and less actively defiant against the pricks of caste and fate. It was typical of the man that, before his discovery of the strait, he should have found himself in this fearful, chill, part of the world, a Portuguese of indifferent breeding in command of a Spanish expedition, officered mainly by Spanish aristocrats who despised and distrusted him, and were determined that he should never get back to Spain to collect his kudos and rewards.

Magellan's childhood and young manhood spanned the most remarkable age of exploration and exploitation in history. In the forty years from the date of his birth the American Continent was touched from as far north as Newfoundland and as far south as the estuary of the River Plate. The *Mar del Sur* had been located by Balboa, and the South Atlantic had become a busy shipping lane for the carracks and caravels *en route* to Malacca and Calicut. When he was five no chart marked the end of the African continent. By Magellan's eighteenth birthday Vasco da Gama was sailing off the Malabar coast, and soon Portuguese ships were trading at Canton. The coastline of Brazil was roughly mapped by 1515, and if no way could be found round or through the South American sub-continent, a Panama Canal might be cut; for this was already under serious discussion before Magellan left San Lucar with his armada.

The motive behind this new restless exploration was as old as trading; the riches of the East was the goal. Only in the East, from Arabia to the Moluccas and north to China, could the profitable luxuries be found—and they were in ever-increasing demand during the 15th and 16th centuries: musk and ambergris, diamonds and pearls and silk to scent and beautify; camphor and opium to ease the pains of the ever increasing numbers who could afford the services of an apothecary; ginger and pepper, cinnamon and nutmeg and cloves to give taste to the dull European diet, especially in winter. Pepper was a priceless preservative and a medicament: given in wine it was considered an effective cure against colds in lungs and chest, mixed with oil it made an ointment for many diseases of the skin, mixed with laurel leaves it was a remedy against venomous stings. Spiced food and spice-warmed drinks added cheer to men's lives.

Among the most rare and precious of spices were cloves. Like pepper, they had many uses. Their sharp odour and taste camouflaged the taste and smell of bad meat—and much bad meat had to be eaten in the winter months—and made a fine seasoning, with medicinal virtues. 'Their virtues are manifold', a contemporary encyclopedia describes them. 'This spice is good for stomach, liver and heart: it comforteth the brain, and is a remedy against headaches . . . mixed with wine it sharpens the sight, it is good against inflammation and redness of the eyes. It helps against failing of the heart and against indigestion.' In the 15th or 16th centuries, when an English labourer might earn 4d. a day, he would have to work for 64 days to buy one pound of cloves.

A tree of cloves was as valuable as a rich seam of gold; and the sight of a fully-grown tree, an evergreen of some forty feet high, rich in flower buds, was said to move men to tears. But the official narrator of Magellan's expedition was as coolly factual and informative as a present day John Gunther—although he was one of the first Europeans to see the *Eugenia caryophyllata* in flower.

The same day I went on shore to see how the cloves grow, and this is what I observed. The tree from which they are gathered is high, and its trunk is as thick as a man's body, more or less, according to the age of the plant. Its branches spread out somewhat in the middle of the tree, but near the top they form a pyramid. The bark is of an olive colour, and the leaves very like those of the laurel. The cloves grow at the end of little branches in bunches of ten or twenty. These trees always bear more fruit on one side than on the other, according to the seasons. The cloves are white when they first sprout, they get red as they ripen, and blacken when dry. They are gathered twice in the year, once about Christmas and the other time about St. John's day, when the air in these countries is milder, and it is still more so in December. When the year is rather hot, and there is a little rain, they gather in each of these islands from three to four hundred bahars of cloves. The clove tree does not live except in the mountains, and if it is transferred to the plain it dies there. The leaf, the bark, and the wood, as long as they are green, have the strength and fragrance of the fruit itself. If these are not gathered when just ripe they get so large and hard that nothing of them remains good except the rind. It is said that the mist renders them perfect, and indeed we saw almost every day a mist descend and surround one or other of the above-mentioned mountains. Among these people everyone possesses some of these trees, and each man watches over his own trees and gathers their fruit, but does not do any work round them to cultivate them. This tree does not grow except in the five mountains of the five Molucca islands.

As Magellan's narrator noted, cloves were known to grow only in the Moluccas, that group of spice islands west of New Guinea, which had become the goal of avaricious Portuguese traders since the time of Vasco da Gama, and was Ferdinand Magellan's destination—by the shorter, western route through the American continent. Possession of the Moluccas and a monopoly of cloves would produce riches beyond the wildest dreams of the Kings of Portugal and Spain. Magellan intended to grasp that monopoly, and become the most famous as well as one of the richest men in the world.

The New Era of Reconnaissance

Maritime ambitions on the scale of Magellan's could not even have been considered at the time of his childhood. To achieve conquest as a sea power required the revival of arts and crafts neglected since the downfall of the Roman Empire. Astronomy, map-making, navigation, cosmography, ship design and ship building, all required special skills which had been unexercised by Western man for centuries. A spiritual revolution was needed to transform a parochial and incurious people to a condition of enterprise, with ambitious eyes focused on the horizon. It fell upon the small nation of Portugal to lead this revolution, which was to reshape the world and to leave as mid-twentieth century witnesses the last tangible vestiges of its power and extent at Macao, Goa and Portuguese West Africa.

At the beginning of the fifteenth century the Portuguese people, when they considered the sea, viewed it mainly with fear and hostility. Seafaring was limited to fishing in the river estuaries or along the coastline in undecked little *caravela*, while only a handful of intrepid souls ventured farther into deep seas. True tales of storms and piracy and apocryphal tales based on superstition turned men's eyes away from the ocean to the reassuring and comforting sight of the olive groves and vineyards of Alemtejo.

The man who created this Iberian revolution and the new race of imperialists, who revived the long-dormant European will to conquer and possess beyond the seas, and caused, no less, the world to be reshaped, was the Infante Enrique, Prince Henry of Portugal, son of King John I, grandson of John of Gaunt. Impelled by ambition and patriotism and religious zeal (for the spirit of the Crusades still lived), blessed by immense riches and the powers of a visionary, and encouraged by the predictions of his horoscope which bade him 'to engage in great and noble conquests . . . and attempt the discovery of things which are hidden from other men', Prince Henry, with business-like enthusiasm, set about the task of laying the foundations of an empire, and justifying the name he was soon to acquire—Henry the Navigator. In 1419 he began constructing a castle-headquarters and observatory at the seaport of Sagres at the south-westerly tip of Portugal, overlooking the route his Captains must steer on their first explorations.

Gradually over the succeeding years, Prince Henry's inspiration spread and science and enterprise cast out superstition and timorousness. Every sea Captain who called at Sagres was summoned to the castle and interrogated, and in turn was offered information. The reservoir of knowledge increased year by year. Prince Henry began to finance his own expeditions, and soon his ships were creeping farther down the African coast, far beyond the range of the Atlantic islands Spain and Portugal had already acquired. The Prince listened to anyone and read everything, discriminating between legend and probable fact. He shocked his geographers by reading, and believing, the tales of Marco Polo. Tales of tropical heat that would incinerate every crew member and ignite the ships themselves he ignored; but he was

l'Infant Don Henri.

Duc de Viseü, G.^d Me de Christ, prem. moteur des Découvertes.

ready to credit the truth of Herodotus's legend of the Phoenician
fleet at the time of the Pharoahs which had sailed south down the
Red Sea and was at length given up for lost, only to return home
from the west two years later by way of the Pillars of Hercules.
Prince Henry, the navigator who never captained a fleet, or even

a ship, the theoretician who yet possessed the imagination of a romantic poet and the patriotic fervour of King Alfred, knew that the greatness of Portugal lay in the East, that there was a way to it round Africa, bypassing the Muslim empires. Not just a trade monopoly in the bottoms of Portuguese ships but eventual possession was the ambition of this scientist-prophet.

At the time of Prince Henry's death in 1460 there was still little to show for his labours. The structure of the great Portuguese empire had to be built on the foundations he had laid and with the tools and materials he had made available. The master-craftsmen he had inspired were Gil Yanez, who rounded Cape Non and discovered Guinea, Diogo Cam who found the mouth of the Congo and comfortably survived the heat of the tropics, and Bartholomeu Dias, who two years later in 1486, announced to the world that he had discovered the end of the African continent and rounded it. Then on 20 May 1498 strange, tubby vessels, carrying great masts and great guns appeared off Calicut, and 'there a multitude of people flocked to the beach, all dark and naked . . . much amazed at seeing what they had never seen before'. Vasco da Gama's arrival in the East and his return sixteen months later loaded with priceless cinnamon and pepper and mace, signalled the end of the first stage of the era of reconnaissance.

Other fleets followed that of da Gama, and the riches flowed ever faster into the warehouses of Lisbon. Trading was not always a peaceful business. There were struggles with Chinese traders, disputes with native chieftains, full scale battles with rulers over trading rights. A naval base was set up at Goa and from here some sort of protection was offered to the numerous trading posts established from Macao to Malacca. Losses from local pirates, and from storms on the long and hazardous voyage back around the Cape, were appalling. Yet so high was the value in Europe of the spices and silks and diamonds of the East, that one ship safely returned of a fleet of five gave a profitable return to the Crown.

While many of the great powers of Europe squandered their strength in futile wars, the little kingdom of Portugal, poised on the edge of the strife-torn continent, became heir to half the world. This fact was even underwritten by Papal decree. The sagacious Prince Henry had obtained from the Vatican a charter which legally conferred on Portugal all lands, seas and islands east of Cape Bojador on the west coast of Africa. It was the most sweepingly generous document ever drawn up. It also had the effect of

conferring on Portugal a sense of magnificent God-given security
and superiority.

Then in 1493 an obscure Genoese navigator arrived at the
court of King John II in Lisbon with the radical and disturbing
idea that the Indies could be reached more cheaply and more
quickly from the west. The royal cosmographers doubted it and
the King's political aides advised against it. Their present route
was established and flourishing; and besides, the Papal Charter
might not be stretched to include all territory to the west as well
as the east of the agreed line. There could be some limit even to
the Pope's generosity. So Christopher Columbus's request for a
fleet was politely declined, and the Genoese made his way across
the frontier to Seville, where his proposal was more favourably
received.

Columbus returned from his first historic voyage west on 15
March 1493. He had taken little more than a month to cross the
Atlantic Ocean to 'Hispaniola'. But it was no new continent that
he had found, merely some islands beyond which, he was convinced, there lay the mouth of the Ganges. From Hispaniola the
mainland of Asia was only a few days' sailing away.

There seemed to be every good reason for the instant and acute
Portuguese alarm. Within a few weeks they were at the conference
table with their Spanish rivals and the Vatican's delegates, and
by 4 May 1493 everything was settled. A new Bull of Demarcation
decreed that the Portuguese could keep the East, the Spaniards
could have the West—to the exclusion of everyone else. In the
western hemisphere the line was clear. It passed north to south
one hundred leagues west of the Cape Verde Islands. Where 'the
twain shall meet' in the eastern hemisphere was another matter.
Nobody could tell until the world was circumnavigated; and
meanwhile the centres of the eastern riches remained in a kind of
limbo for mutual exploitation. The Portuguese had already gained
the ascendancy in many areas of spice trade and production. But
the richest region of all, where the prized clove thrived as nowhere
else, were the Moluccas, the near-legendary spice Eldorado, half
hidden, on navigators' charts and the minds of acquisitive
merchants alike, by a haze of tantalising uncertainty. He who
held the Moluccas held the greatest prize on earth.

Besides being one of the most arbitrary documents in history
the Bull of Demarcation acted as a new stimulus to exploration,
and especially to Spanish exploration. Under the Treaty of
Tordesillas, signed a year later, on 7 June 1494, the line was

moved another 270 leagues west, which conveniently gave Brazil to Portugal when the coastline was first reached six years after. Now Spanish navigators had to sail westward for many weeks before crossing into their zone. They did so, time and again, over the following years. Great navigators like Amerigo Vespucci and Yanez Pinzon, Ponce de Leon and Rodrigo de Bastidas, ventured beyond the outlying islands which Columbus believed—and continued to believe until his death—marked the beginning of the Asian continent. They found instead new land, vast in its extent, rich in its potential, varied in its climate and vegetation, from the frozen wastes of Labrador to the sunny splendour of Florida, discovered by Ponce de Leon in 1513. It was all theirs, by Papal decree, to explore and exploit. One expedition after another sailed from Seville, charting the coastline, exploring every bay.

They believed that there must be a way through to another ocean, across which would lie the source of all the riches their Portuguese rivals were bringing back to the Tagus. South of Florida the coast shaped west, cutting deep into the land. For a while it appeared certain that they would soon discover a *paso* through, or the end of the Continent. But no break could be found. The coast swung east again, and appeared to go on forever.

The Portuguese heard with relief of this vast land mass barrier to the East. God and the Pope were on their side. The Spaniards could have this new Continent, except for Brazil of course for that was in their zone. Meanwhile they had many difficulties and dangers to contend with themselves. Their eastern empire required taming, consolidating, fortifying and settling, and the old heathen trade arteries to Cairo and the Levant had finally to be severed. During the first years of the 16th century the nature of Portuguese activity in the East changed rapidly from exploration and trading to armed reconnaissance and then to conquest and enforced trade. In 1504 two great armadas, one of thirteen ships under the command of Lope Soarez d'Alvarenga, sailed down the Tagus for India to establish trading posts, protected by fortresses, and to show the Portuguese flag. Like those who had preceded them, they would suffer extreme dangers and casualties, but the rewards would be immense, and new impetus would be added to the freshly bounding vigour of the nation. The spirit of enterprise and adventure affected every class. So did the new affluence. Ambitious young men from the foothills of the Serra d'Estrella, the coastal plains of Estremadura and the acorn forests of the Monchique and Guadalupe mountain ranges flocked into Lisbon to volunteer as crew members; and shipwrights and sailmakers worked for longer hours and in ever increasing numbers to complete the new caravels and carracks in which they would sail.

Ferdinand Magellan

The Beginning of the Dream

Ferdinand Magellan, then aged some twenty-three years, was one of the many young men who watched the fitting out of these fleets, the loading of the pipes of wine, the barrels of biscuit and salted meat and fish; the coloured cloths and brass bracelets, the bells and knives and looking glasses for trading; the culverins falconets and bombards, the arquebuses and gunpowder and the moulds for making cannon balls; and the supplies of flags for raising over newly conquered lands. 'We can imagine', wrote Magellan's biographer, Guillemard, 'the effect that experiences such as these must have had upon one so adventurous as Magellan. At such a time, when all around him were up and doing, it was impossible that he should remain a mere spectator.'

Almost total obscurity surrounds the early life of Ferdinand Magellan. The year of his birth was probably 1480. Even the place of his birth is doubtful. Some say Oporto, others Sabrosa, near Chaves, the gloomiest and most intractible province of Portugal. His family was noble, but only just so, being of the fourth grade, the *Fidalgos de cota de armas*. His father died when he was young, and as eldest son he inherited the family estates, which seem to have consisted of two properties, the Quinta de Souta and the Casa de Pereira, both at Sabrosa. He then served at court, in a comparatively humble capacity, probably as a page. And that is about all.

Towards the end of 1504, Magellan obtained court permission to volunteer for service with a new armada being prepared for service in India and the Far East. This was intended to set the seal, formally and indisputably, on the new Portuguese eastern empire; and should there be any difficulties there would be several hundred cannon and some 1500 brave, resourceful and superbly equipped infantry to confirm the claim of King Manoel of Portugal. Magellan suffered the first of his many wounds at Cannanore, the most fierce, bloody and decisive of the many battles which brought the Eastern rulers—in this case the Zamorin of Calicut—to heel and temporarily strangled the Hindu and Moslem trade monopoly. He was shipped back first to Africa with the other wounded, now deeply imbued with the contemporary lust for adventure, exploration, combat and riches.

Magellan was back in the Indies in 1509, still in the most humble rank, as one of the crew of four ships sent to reconnoitre the Malacca Straits, the funnel through which for centuries the riches of China and Japan and the Malaysian archipelago had passed. The town of Malacca, the mecca, the greatest and richest trading post of them all, was their destination. Here, so it was told, rubies from Ceylon were traded with the silks and porcelain of China, sandal wood from the shores of the Timor Sea with pepper from the Malabar coast. In the waters of Malacca harbour there would be at any time junks and prahus and barks, and on the waterfront seamen and traders of a dozen nationalities and of as many shades of skin. Above all, to Malacca came the priceless riches of the Moluccas.

When this Portuguese squadron sailed into Malacca harbour on 11 September 1509, the first European ships ever seen in these parts, Magellan and his fellow crew members saw at once that the tales they had heard had not been over-coloured. This was the pearl of the East, a spread of water richly threaded with a hundred laden ships, and dominated by the magnificent palace of the Sultan. Here, before their prows, was everything the acquisitive and warlike Portuguese could aspire to: the summation of all Henry the Navigator's dreams of wealth and power for his country.

Tales of Cannanore, of other battles and depredations, conquests and cruelties, had long before reached Malacca, and the fearful Sultan quickly plotted to massacre these uncircumcised, bearded white men who had certainly come to plunder and not to trade. It has been told that Magellan first brought warning to his Admiral when brown figures were later seen to swarm over the gunwales of the flagship in too great numbers for friendly purposes. In the fierce engagement that followed many of the Portuguese mariners stranded ashore were massacred. Among the few who were seen to have escaped, but already hard-pressed by knife-carrying Malays, was one Francisco Serrano, a cousin and close friend of Magellan. Magellan rowed rapidly ashore and drove off Serrano's assailants at the point of the sword and brought him safely away.

This rescue of this old friend was to have a greater influence on the shape of history than the main action or the massive battle for Malacca in 1511, when the Portuguese returned and conquered. For, by a strange series of adventures, Serrano was later cast on the shores of Ternate, one of the richest of the Molucca Islands, and, opting for hedonism after a surfeit of violence, settled down peacefully with a native wife and as military adviser to the King.

Francisco Serrano kept open a line of communication with the old world. By circuitous channels—through the captain of some prahu or junk loaded with cloves and bound for Malacca—he succeeded in sustaining a correspondence with the man who had saved his life. When Magellan returned home he thus became the best informed Portuguese mariner on the geography and attractions of the islands, 'giving him to understand that [Serrano] had discovered yet another new world, larger and richer than that found by Vasco da Gama'.

Unlike Serrano's, Magellan's ambitions for action, conquest and riches were not yet satisfied. This is clear from a surviving letter found among Serrano's papers after his death on Ternate. Magellan promised 'that I will be with you soon, if not by way of Portugal, by way of Spain'.

While Francisco Serrano was enjoying his last years in comfortable peace, Magellan, now an officer, was ordered to Africa to fight in the campaigns against the intransigent Moors. He hated land fighting. His eyes longed for the sweep of sea horizons and the sudden lift of new shores. He was badly wounded by a lance thrust in his knee which severed a tendon. This gave him much pain, and a limp, for the rest of his life.

It was at this time, too, in the Spring of 1514, that we see the first evidence of another side to Magellan's character. There were defiant chips on his shoulder, stemming from his low level in the nobility, his slow promotion, the small rewards he had gained from his years of campaigning. Like every officer who had survived the hazards of the early expeditions in the wake of da Gama, he had returned home to find Lisbon as never before. Everyone was suddenly rich and busy. The big merchants and a select few senior officers favoured at court had gained by far the greatest wealth, at the cost of the sufferings and losses of the seamen and soldiers and junior officers. It was the old story of the people doing the real risky work gaining the smallest reward.

It was the last straw when, while in Africa, Magellan was accused of selling some captured horses and cattle back to the Moors. This was a serious crime, and if he was found guilty he would be in for a long prison sentence. Rather than defend himself, he took the law into his own hands, and sullenly nursing his wounds and grievances, left the army and made his own way back to Lisbon to demand an audience of the King. Magellan was neither diplomat nor silver-tongued sycophant. There was an awkward cussedness in his manner and speech which did not endear him to his superior officers, let alone a King. The news of the charge preceded him and he was turned away from the court.

Report back to the High Command in Africa, he was told; and he
had to obey. The charge was never made. Instead he was given
an honourable discharge: the army had finished with him.
Magellan re-embarked, this time armed with proof of his innocence, and on his return to Lisbon tactlessly again demanded
audience of the King, this time to request an increase in his pay
and status at court.

The Curt Dismissal

By now King Manoel, tight-fisted even with those he needed
and the few he admired, was tired of this glowering, self-righteous
fellow. We can see Magellan's short, dark, limping figure advancing across the throne room and the King listening to the appeal,
delivered no doubt with the minimum deference, and then
refusing it brusquely. Magellan did not at once retire. Would his
majesty, then, hold out some hope of an appointment to command
a ship in a new expedition to the East—by way of a western route
yet to be discovered? The King shook his head immediately.
Finally, persisted Magellan, would there be any royal objection
to his seeking service in some foreign country? The King indicated
his utter indifference, and Magellan withdrew. So that was that.

Thirty-one years had passed since an earlier Portuguese
monarch had refused to support a voyage westward across the
Atlantic. Christopher Columbus instead sought Spanish sponsorship. Now the world was divided, by Papal decree. The west
belonged to the Spaniards, and they had got the worst of the
bargain—or so it seemed at that time, for they had not yet discovered the riches of Mexico and Peru.

Magellan had known well enough that he would be rebuffed,
and his plans were already as well matured as his grudges. 'By
way of Spain . . .' meant not only passing through the Spanish
zone, but with Spanish sponsorship, reinforced with all the
geographical and astronomical knowledge Magellan could
plunder from the treasury, the libraries, the observatories and
above all the secret royal chartroom of his own land. For Magellan
did not at once leave Portugal in a huff. Instead, he remained on
his estates or at the court in Lisbon, a shadowy, discredited figure,
who could sometimes be found studying the works of the great
cosmographers, cartographers and astronomers.

During this time, Magellan learned much that was new to him.
King Manoel, he discovered, had already lent his support to, or
had actually secretly sponsored, an expedition to search for a

Manoel I

route west through the Spanish zone to the East. The great
Portuguese navigator, John of Lisbon, had led one of these, and
on 12 October 1514 had discovered far down the coast of South
America a cape, marked by three prominent hills, which he

'Strange beasts and birds' of the uttermost south
Above: The now rare Guanaco, described wonderingly by Pigafetta:
'This beast has its head and ears the size of a mule, and the neck and
body of the fashion of a camel, the legs of a deer, and the tail like that of
a horse'.
Below: The Great Skua, the subject of many superstitious tales,
photographed by the author near Cape Horn.

named Cape Saint Mary. John of Lisbon had not lingered for long because he was in territory that was nominally Spanish, though no Spaniard, nor any European, had ever before ventured so far south. But from his brief observations, he was convinced that here was a strait that must lead to the great ocean sighted by Balboa a year earlier. Three caravels had sailed from Spain the following year on the same quest and had confirmed the discovery. The commander, a Portuguese expatriate, John de Solis, had been killed and eaten by natives while exploring up this supposed strait. But the western race to the Moluccas was already well in its stride.

Also in the royal chart room Magellan was able to study charts which were based on all the accumulated wisdom of cosmographers, astronomers and the findings of the great expeditions since the early days of Henry the Navigator. On one of these was the evidence again: a strait, cutting clear across the South American sub-continent.

No further doubt remained in Magellan's mind, and the pace and enthusiasm of his researches accelerated. He received invaluable first-hand information on the tides and currents and winds of the west South Atlantic, and of the navigational hazards of the coastline, from captains who had sailed these seas, for they, hardy veterans all, were of a different breed from the effete conspirators of the court; they clung close together, and were naturally sympathetic to the wronged warrior-seaman. Magellan, after all, was one of them, and Manoel was not a loved king. There is also evidence that Magellan received first-hand information from John of Lisbon himself, who could add detail to what he had written in his reports about that remote cape and the strait beyond.

Magellan Finds His Sponsors

Magellan's navigational plans matured swiftly. But in 1517 he was still without sponsorship, and was in as weak a position as an inventor today without capital or production resources. Magellan needed an *entrepreneur*; and at length found one in a man called Duarte Barbosa, one of a family of rich Portuguese merchant-adventurers for whom—like Magellan and many others—the Portuguese court had turned sour. The disenchanted Barbosas had made for Spain, where their influence at court, with the Church, and with India House, the Spanish maritime establishment, had grown powerful. The Spaniards were always on the look-out for experienced Portuguese navigators as they had so few of their own. Duarte Barbosa was brave as a lion, a great pleasure-lover, much travelled, a shrewd merchant, and a scholar, too. He was the author of a massive work on the geography of the East. He, and his father, Diogo Barbosa, were ready to support new profitable enterprises, and men to lead them. They had conceived the idea of getting royal support and sponsorship for a voyage to make one more attempt to find the *paso* through southern South America for which John de Solis had been searching before he was killed.

Duarte heard of this fellow Portuguese, Ferdinand Magellan: here was a man with much experience in the East, a superb navigator, a fine leader, and, moreover, he had an obsessive ambition to discover this same *paso*. Duarte made his way back to Portugal and sought out this navigator.

The meeting between these men led to the discovery of the way through America, and of Tierra del Fuego, to the first circumnavigation, and to the first voyage across the Pacific Ocean.

In October 1517 Magellan left his homeland for the last time. With him he brought some experienced Portuguese pilots, and an old friend and kinsman, John Serrano, brother of Francisco Serrano, still living in luxury among the islands they hoped to reach by a new short route. Magellan wanted John Serrano as captain of one of the armada's ships: he was rather old for the job but he was marvellously experienced.

Disruption and Plotting

Almost two more years passed before Magellan at last got to sea with his armada. This seems a long time, but there were numerous difficulties to contend with. First, Portuguese alarm increased as the day for departure approached. King Manoel now wondered if he had done the right thing to send Magellan away with a sneer. He invited him to return: all would be forgiven. He complained to the King of Spain, his nephew Charles, a mere stripling of seventeen, but a youngster burning with regal lust for greater power and greater conquest for his country. Charles's uncle claimed that the Moluccas rightly belonged to Portugal, and that the proposed Spanish expedition was 'a thing unheard of among cavaliers, and was accounted both ill-judged and ill-seeming'. King Charles brushed this aside: he was a proud Habsburg, too, had taken a strong fancy to the scarred, limping Portuguese who had promised such a prize. King Manoel then resorted to underhand methods, instructing his agents to disrupt

Charles V when young. By Bernardo Strigel

Magellan's preparations. He also laid plans to intercept and destroy the armada in Portuguese waters after it sailed.

Even more serious and delaying were the conspiracies that developed among the most powerful and influencial figures in Spain. Rich and devious sinecurists, bankers and brokers, shippers and merchants, recognised the threat of their long-established monopolies and cartels. At every level of the far-flung trading machinery of Europe there was some measure of unease, from those who had for years dreamed of their share of the Moluccas's riches to some small-time merchant in Cadiz with a cosy corner in cinnamon.

Fear and jealousy together spawned a conspiring cabal, so Machiavellian that we need trouble ourselves only with its general shape. The Barbosas and Magellan had presented the case for their enterprise so successfully to King Charles, and stood to gain so much from it, that Spanish interests which had agreed to back it financially began to have second thoughts. Why should expatriate Portuguese grow rich and powerful from a Spanish expedition backed by Spanish money? The leading conspirator was the Bishop of Burgos, Juan Rodriguez de Fonseca, head of India House and one of the most powerful men in Spain. He had a bastard son, Juan de Cartagena, a foolish fop of a fellow with little seagoing experience, who was to captain one of the ships and succeed to the command of the armada if Magellan died. Two more of the five-ship armada were to be captained by Spaniards, and both of them were in the conspiracy, too. The early assassination of Magellan after the armada sailed was the cabal's first object. Yet they would be helpless without a good pilot to guide them to the *paso*, and thence to the Moluccas; and a good pilot meant a Portuguese pilot.

Discreet enquiries about their loyalty to Magellan were made among the pilots he had brought with him. There was one, Estevan Gomes, who was jealous and—so it proved—corruptible. Gomes agreed, for a fat share of the profit, to take over the armada's navigation after Magellan's death.

Unaware of the forces working against him, Magellan continued with the preparations of his armada, strongly supported at every stage by the Barbosas. For good measure he married Diogo Barbosa's niece, Beatriz, an heiress to a fortune. The five ships of the armada were the *San Antonio*, 120 tons, *Trinidad*, 110 tons, *Concepción*, 90 tons, *Victoria*, 85 tons, and the shallow-draft *Santiago* of only 75 tons; all two- or three-masted vessels, heavy of aspect, wide in the beam, with prominent castles—the *obras muertas*—over the bows and stern. These *naos* (merchantmen) were in poor condition and required a complete refit. The Spaniards were as far behind the Portuguese in their marine architecture as they were in navigation. The Portuguese in their numerous expeditions to the East had learned how to guard against the effects of storm stress on the structure of their ships and to protect them from the worst ravages of the *teredo navalis*, which could eat through the bottom of a ship in a few months.

Besides the arming, renovating and fitting out of his ships, the provisioning for a two-years' voyage was a monumental responsibility, which Magellan insisted on supervising personally. 508 butts of wine from Jerez, 984 cheeses, 16 quarter casks of figs, one hundredweight of mustard and 200 arrobas of vinegar, all figured in a long list of stores; while the 'hardware' included a forge, bellows and anvil, 89 lanterns, 100 mess bowls and $9\frac{1}{2}$ pounds of wax candles for the consecration of the ships. They were to take five drums and 20 tambourines 'given to the people of the fleet to serve for their pastime', and 35 padlocks, with iron handcuffs to deal with malcontents; and a dozen skins of parchment for the making of charts. For native barter they were to carry no fewer than 20,000 small bells of different kinds, 2,000 brass bracelets, 30 pieces of 'valuable coloured cloth', and 10,000 fish hooks, For more serious trade the armada carried copper bars and flasks of quicksilver, highly prized by the more affluent native chieftains and Oriental rulers for their coinage mints.

They were well-equipped for trouble, too: 120 javelins, 200 pikes, a thousand lances, 95 dozen darts and 360 dozen arrows; while for longer-range destruction they carried 62 culverins, ten falcons, ten bombards, and 5,600 pounds of powder.

The efforts of the Portuguese agents to sabotage the preparations by pilfering and bribing the dockyard men at Seville to work slowly continued throughout the summer of 1519. In spite of this, all seemed ready by the middle of August. King Charles, now elected Holy Roman Emperor, decreed that the armada must sail by 10 August.

The Blessing and Departure

The usual High Mass of farewell was organised to bless the expedition and keep it safe from danger. The church was packed with local notables and with the entire complement of the armada, numbering some two hundred and seventy, a motley collection of

Portuguese and Spaniards and Basques, a few French and Flemings and Germans, one or two Greeks and Neapolitans, a single Englishman from Bristol (master-gunner of the flagship *Trinidad*), and Magellan's personal manservant, Enrique, whom he had purchased many years before in Malaya as a slave — and, incidentally, was destined to become the first ever circumnavigator. After the benediction, Magellan stepped forward and knelt at the feet of the Corregidor of Seville, swearing that he would carry out the instructions of His Royal Highness King Charles, Caesar Augustus Romanorum, and received in solemn ceremony the great silk standard bearing the arms of the kingdoms of Leon, Aragon and Castille. Magellan then arose, and with the banner in one hand, prepared to receive the oath of allegiance 'promising to follow the course offered by him and to obey him in everything. Alas for man's sincerity and honour! Many of those who knelt before the altar were at that moment pledged to join in open mutiny against their leader directly the fitting opportunity should arrive.'

Contemporary accounts confirm that the impressiveness of the departure from Seville matched the momentousness of the occasion. The quayside was packed with wailing women, many with children in their arms. Among them was Beatriz, with Magellan's six-month-old son Rodrigo, now residuary legatee to the fortune he might one day inherit. She was heavy with child again. Beside her was her uncle, Diogo, come to bid farewell both to his son Duarte, and Magellan himself, due to embark together in the *Trinidad*. One by one the five ships drifted from their berths. Oarsmen in the waist rowed them out into the river and then shipped their sweeps, 'and firing all the artillery' wrote one eyewitness, 'we made sail only on the foremast, and came to the end of a river . . . called Guadalcavir.'

It was a passage of some thirty-five miles to the estuary, 'passing by many little villages lying along the said river', to the impressive castle of the Duke of Medina Sidonia, grandfather of the Captain-General of another and greater armada that was to sail north to disaster at the hands of Queen Elizabeth I's fleets sixty-one years hence. Here at the little port of San Lucar, Magellan was forced to put in to repair some of the omissions he had already discovered among their provisions and to receive from Seville other goods forgotten in the rush of embarkation. Magellan fretted at the delay, which must lower the morale of the men, and also help the Portuguese to complete their offensive dispositions at sea. It was altogether an anticlimactic occasion after the solemn celebrations up-river, and was considered by many to be a bad omen.

At last, on 20 September 1519, the five vessels weighed and put to sea without further ceremony and with sails filling out, set their helms on a south-westerly course.

Among the curious assortment of the armada's company was a Venetian patrician, Ser Antonio Francesco Pigafetta, an observant, cultured and amiable young fellow who was one among a number of semi-official emissaries despatched from Venice to try to retrieve the republic's economic fortunes. These had declined to a disastrous level since the Portuguese had opened up a direct route by sea to the East. The Venetians had offered their distribution and marketing experience to Portugal; and had been brusquely rebuffed. Now, with the prospect of Spain breaking in to the spice trade as a serious competitor, it was decided in Venice to investigate this new market and learn, at first hand if possible, the likelihood of a dramatic switch in economic power from Portugal to its neighbour and chief rival. Pigafetta knew all about the spice business, was an experienced traveller and of an enterprising and bold nature. In the company of the Pope's ambassador, he arrived at King Charles's court, and was received in audience. The King evidently took to the young man and sent him with a note of credential to Magellan in Seville. Magellan liked him, too, and when Pigafetta suggested that he should join the expedition as supernumerary, observer and diarist, and to see 'the very great and awful things of the ocean', the Captain-General agreed.

It was a blessed decision. Without it there would have been only sparse and formal records and logs kept by several of the pilots, and we should have had none of the detailed observations and spritely comments of this Venetian scribe; although honest Pigafetta, ever loyal to his Captain-General, suffered from the prevailing weakness for exaggeration of most mariners. And who can blame them, so far from home, so unlikely to return; such wondrous sights, such credulous audiences?

On the six-day voyage to Tenerife in the Canaries, a Spanish possession and their first port of call, Magellan concerned himself mainly with the fighting efficiency of his fleet. Back in Seville and San Lucar the rumours of threatened attack on the armada, by Moorish war galleys and a Portuguese squadron which was known to have left Lisbon, were too strong to be based only on rumour. Evolutions and simulated attacks by one vessel against another were carried out daily, and the crews and ships went through the age-old practice of 'shaking down'. The ordinances, which Magellan had issued to his captains for successful navigation and 'so that during the storms at sea, which often come on by night and day, his ships should not go away and separate from one another', were rehearsed. Pigafetta was fascinated by these, and recorded them in detail: how 'the Captain-General willed that the vessel in which he himself was should go before the other vessels, and that the others should follow it; therefore he carried by night on the poop of his ship a torch or faggot of burning wood . . . so that the ships should not lose sight of him', how Magellan, when he 'wished the other ships to lower the sail he had four lights shown', or 'when he discovered any land, or shoal, that is to say, a rock at sea, he made several lights to be shown or had a bombard fired off '.

It was a trouble-free voyage to Tenerife, without evidence of Moors or Portuguese, or of insubordination among the Spanish captains. Juan de Cartagena kept the *San Antonio* in correct station astern of the *Trinidad*. There was a special air of elegance about the ship of the second-in-command, the dandy aristocrat who would automatically succeed Magellan if he should die. The flag of Santiago fluttering at the masthead appeared to possess a special sheen, and on the poop deck Cartagena himself, elegant, colourful and clearly recognisable from afar, surrounded by his retinue (he had ten personal servants, Magellan had one body-guard), made his humble *naos* look like some royal barge. But wait for the first real storm. And would the untravelled Cartagena look such a *dandi* after three months of searching the Brazilian coastline for the strait?

The Warning

On the morning of 26 September the five ships sailed in line ahead between the cliffs guarding the harbour of Santa Cruz to collect some cheeses and kindling. Twenty-four hours later, a little caravel hove into sight and dropped anchor close to the *Trinidad*, and a messenger was rowed to the flagship. He carried a letter from Diogo Barbosa. Be warned, the old man had written after the armada had left Spain, I have certain evidence that there is a plan afoot to oust you from your command and kill you or hand you over to the Portuguese. Then he named Cartagena as the ringleader. It seemed that tongues had loosened in the taverns, that rumours rife on the Seville waterfront before they left had now harded into certainty, and that Diogo had been

sufficiently alarmed to commission a fast ship to intercept the
armada before it finally left Spanish territory.

Magellan was already fully on his guard. The news 'did not
dishearten him one whit. He sent back answer to Barbosa that,
were they good men or evil, he would do his works as a servant of
the Emperor, and to this end, he added, he had offered his life'.
When Barbosa received this reply he was, it seems, reassured, and
'greatly lauded the stout heart of Magellan'.

The stoutness of Magellan's heart was never in doubt. More
questionable was his ability to counter Machiavellian cunning.
But the rugged mariner had learned much of the finer arts of
plotting and counter plotting since he had crossed the frontier
into Spain and witnessed at first hand the complex manipulations
of political machinery and the ways of the Spanish court. He did
not put it past that sly old Bishop of Burgos to have come to an
agreement with King Manoel—perhaps Magellan dead or alive
for half the Moluccas? When the stakes were high, Magellan now
knew, there was no limit to cupidity.

A meeting of the captains and pilots on board the *Trinidad*
supported Magellan's suspicion that some sort of deal had been
made with the Portuguese. Magellan announced his decision to
follow a course far to the south, hugging the African coastline,
before steering for South America, in the hope of throwing off the
scent the Portuguese squadron ordered to intercept them. At this
meeting Cartagena vehemently—too vehemently?—protested at
this change of plan and was hotly supported by the Spanish
captains, Gaspar Quesada of the *Concepción* and Luis de Mendoza
of the *Victoria*, as well as Gomes and several of the other pilots.
Calmly Magellan bowed to the majority opinion. If the noble son
of the Bishop of Burgos desired it, then they would follow the
customary and predictable course for the coast of Brazil. Cartagena
expressed his satisfaction and the meeting broke up.

The armada sailed from Tenerife at midnight 3 October and
picked up the sweet sirocco which took them on a south-westerly
course at a steady four knots. The *Trinidad* retained its station in
the van, and Cartagena and the other captains followed obedient-
ly, conforming to the regulation 'each evening you will give your
salutes' by running alongside the flagship in turn, hailing the
Captain-General, 'God save you, Sir Captain-General and Master
and good Ship's company.' If there was a Portuguese trap, the
armada was heading straight into it, at least until the *Trinidad*
was seen to be altering course to the south and instructing her

consorts to follow her. For some time the course now varied between south and south by west, and Cartagena especially became increasingly alarmed. He ordered the *San Antonio* to run under the stern of the flagship, and when within hailing distance demanded of Gomes the course on which they were now heading. 'South by west', came back the answer. 'Why has our course been changed without consultation and against the agreed decision at Tenerife?'

The Captain-General, standing alongside his pilot on the poop deck of the *Trinidad*, broke into these exchanges. '*Que le siguissen y no le pidiessen mas cuenta!*' he peremptorily ordered—cease your questions and follow me.

Cartagena responded to this public rebuke by engaging over the days that followed in a series of petty acts of insubordination, hauling out of line from time to time, and with Mendoza's *Victoria* following, steering a more westerly course. The two errant vessels would be hull down on the horizon before they altered course back to rejoin the flag. They had made their petulant gesture.

Three weeks of calm, and almost a month of storm, put insurrection out of the minds of all but the principal plotters. The doldrums, normally avoided by experienced navigators and selected by Magellan for this reason to evade his Portuguese searchers, were acutely demoralising: twenty days of wallowing in oily rollers, sails slack, airless alike on the burning decks and in the fetid quarters below. During this calm Magellan witnessed a sinister traffic between the three Spanish-commanded ships, the captains being rowed in turn from one to the other as if to fill their time with more plotting. One of the priests carried by the fleet also had himself taken from ship to ship, too. He was Father Pedro Sanchez de Reina, a young and Rabelaisian protégé of Cartagena's, full of wine and bawdy music, who broke off his cheering songs and salty tales to talk quietly to groups of men.

The period of storm that followed was more immediately alarming. At one time 'we were in tears', reported Pigafetta, 'only expecting the hour of perishing'. Incessant rain in the neighbour-hood of the Equator completed the demoralisation of many of the crews, and they emerged from the ordeal, now on reduced rations, ripe for insurrection. Cartagena decided to reopen his campaign of provocation. He began by reducing the title by which Magellan was nightly saluted to that of plain Captain and ordering his boatswain to deliver it. This brought forth the expected protest

from Magellan, who demanded the presence of Cartagena on
deck. What was the reason for this insubordination? In future he
was to be correctly addressed by the captain himself. Cartagena
replied pertly that he had 'sent the best man in the ship to salute
you, and another day, if you so wish, I will salute you through one
of my pages'.

The Ringleader Seized

It was impossible to continue like this, with the most dangerous
part of their journey still ahead. An opportunity to strike back
occurred a few days later. Two of Mendoza's men had committed
the capital offence of sodomy, which required trial by court
martial. It was customary for courts martial to sit in the flagship,
and for all captains to attend and pass judgement. In turn
Mendoza, Quesada, Cartagena and John Serrano, Magellan's
one loyal captain, came on board the *Trinidad* with their staffs.

After the court martial ('Guilty' was the verdict, the hanging to
take place in Brazil) Cartagena 'emboldened by Magellan's
quiescence and the success of his former insults', again demanded
to know why they had not followed the agreed course across the
Atlantic. He was told sharply that it was his business to obey
orders, not to question them. Cartagena persisted, voices in the
cabin rose. There is no detailed record of what was said and what
followed, for Pigafetta was not present, and indeed judiciously
avoided controversial events. But certainly weapons flashed, there
was a scuffle, and at one point Magellan was seen with one hand
clutching a raised dagger, the other Cartagena's fancy jerkin,
calling out 'You are my prisoner!'

The brief mutiny was over, Magellan's authority completely
reasserted. Cartagena was led away in irons, and placed on
parole on board the *Victoria* in the charge of Mendoza, who was
required to swear on oath that he would be faithful to his trust.
It was a shrewd move for, in the reports of the incident, it would
reduce the apparent divisiveness existing in the armada; and in
any case the little *Victoria*, with few stores on board, was helpless
without the support of the other vessels.

The men were in great need of fresh water and meat and fruit
when the look-outs in the mast-heads sighted land on 29th
November. They had struck the Brazilian coast close to the site
of present-day Pernambuco, but there was not yet to be any
shore leave. Magellan had decided to be circumspect. They were
still deep in the Portuguese zone, and it was known that there

were several Portuguese trading stations along this coastline. It was possible that the squadron which had missed them south of the Canaries had now crossed the Atlantic ahead of them and was lying in wait on this side. So for two more weeks the armada continued on its southerly course, the land in sight only to the look-outs, until they rounded Cape Frio.

Beyond this cape was a magnificent bay and natural harbour with great sandy semi-circular beaches fringed with rich vegetation, and a mountain shaped like the ceremonial hat of the Bishop of Burgos towered up into the azure sky. They would have to land soon anyway, and the temptations of this place were irresistible. So with guns run out and manned, they sailed slowly into the still waters. For the first time for more than two months the men walked steady decks, and a refreshing rain was falling. There were natives along the shoreline, too, dark, stark naked, running through the trees and evidently intent on offering a friendly reception.

Rest and Refreshment

Magellan named this place the Bay of Santa Lucia, after the saint on whose day they entered it. For all those who were to die on this expedition the land on which the city of Rio de Janeiro was one day to be built offered them their last days of pleasure and contentment. For these white men in their great ships brought with them not only blessed rain and an end to the drought which had dried up their streams (sufficient magic in itself), but an abundance of other miracles, too: scissors and combs and mirrors, knives for cutting, hooks for catching fish and little brass cylinders which emitted intriguing tinkling notes. 'For a bell they gave a full basket of the fruit named battate,' Pigafetta recorded, 'and in order to have a knife, or a hook for catching fish, five or six fowls, and for a comb they gave two geese, and for a small mirror, or a pair of scissors, they gave so much fish that ten men could have eaten of it.' Young maidens were no more expensive. At first it was a formalised business, with the younger warriors trading their sisters for weapons, but when these girls returned from the ships loaded with more gifts, others joined the queue as volunteers, and supply began to outrun demand.

Magellan knew from long experience that a measure of licence must be allowed to his officers and men, and that one of the qualities that good leadership demanded was judgement of the permitted degree. Unfortunately, his old friend and patron gave a bad example. There was work to be done here—refitting and revictualling of the ships—as well as womanising, but Duarte Barbosa disappeared ashore for days at a time to his private harem. In the end Magellan had reluctantly to order a party of marines to bring him back on board forcibly. Duarte was quite unrepentant. This was very disappointing because Magellan above all needed reliable supporters, not amiable womanisers. There was more trouble with Cartagena, too. He was released against orders and attempted to foment a new uprising. But Cartagena was a rotten mutineer: he always got his timing wrong, for one thing. At the Bay of Santa Lucia everybody was happy and Cartagena was soon back in irons.

Duty demanded that the customary conversion to Christianity should be carried out. These natives were ready converts for had not the white men brought much bounty and joy? So when Mass was said on shore—twice every day—there were increasing numbers of natives 'who remained on their knees, and their hands joined in great reverence during the Mass, so that it was a pleasure and a subject of compassion to see them'.

The natives also from gratitude built a house for the white men, believing that they had permanent guests. But the expedition was already far behind its timetable, midsummer would soon be past and the Cape of Saint Mary, and the *paso*, were still far to the south. On Christmas Day the shore was searched for missing sailors, the ships were combed for hidden women, and on 26 December 1519 the armada left its paradisaical anchorage for the open sea.

Now that they were leaving the Portuguese zone, Magellan felt safe enough to hug and chart the coastline, searching every inlet and estuary in case earlier explorers had missed a more northerly *paso* than Cape Saint Mary, anchoring close inshore by night and sailing only in daylight. For this reason the armada logged scarcely fifty miles a day, in spite of favourable winds, and it was not until 10 January 1520 that the three hills were sighted and that Francisco Alvo, one of the pilots, logged 'I took the sun in 75°; it had a declination of 20°, and our latitude came to 35°. We were to the right of the Cape of Sta. Maria. Thenceforward the coast runs East and West, and the land is sandy . . .' They could see the great cape projecting southwards, surely marking the end of the land mass of America, as the Cape of Good Hope on approximately the same latitude was the African continent's turning point. Beyond, across the water south of the cape, was the

unknown land of *Terra Australis*: at least that was what the most
learned and up-to-date geographers believed. Besides confirming
the existence of the *paso*, Magellan determined, while he was here,
to explore the extreme northern coastline of this great southern
continent.

The First Disillusionment

From a safe anchorage inside the cape, Magellan despatched
Serrano with the light draught *Santiago* on a westerly course to
report on the *paso*, while he sailed south to search for *Terra
Australis*, and become the first European ever to land on the
unexplored continent. The strait, he discovered, was quite narrow,
and the landscape and topography were remarkably similar to
that of America—a sandy shore, semi-tropical trees, a scrubby
undulating hinterland. He worked his ship north-west up this
coast, noting that the strait narrowed, recrossed it, and saw a fine
mountain ('Monte video!' he is reputed to have cried).

Back at the anchorage, he was surprised to see that Serrano had
already returned. The old man came aboard with grave news.
There was no strait. He had sailed far to the west, taking soundings
and drawing up water in barrels. The depth had decreased to a
mere three fathoms, the salt content of the water had diminished
until it was scarcely brackish; and they had noted that the ebb
tide remained strong while the flood tide had grown steadily more
feeble. There was no doubt, reported Serrano, that they were at
the mouth of a massive river: the River Plate as it was later to be
named.

Magellan at first refused to believe this shattering news that the
secret charts he had seen in Lisbon were a fabrication or a hoax.
His confidence that a passage at this parallel led through to the
Mar del Sur was widely known throughout the armada, and he
knew how dangerous a loss of confidence in his leadership could
become. Even at Santa Lucia insurrection had been simmering; a
setback like this, serious privations, a prolonged storm or two, the
onset of winter—any of these could enflame the men to violence.
No, the strait *must* be somewhere up these wide waters, and they
would find it.

Tenacity and the gambling spirit are characteristics of all the
great mariners and explorers. Either might have impelled Magellan to continue the search and to waste three precious weeks of the
declining summer. This time the longboats were ordered out, and
the men rowed up and down the banks of the estuary of one of

the world's greatest rivers exploring brackish creeks for a channel
—no matter how narrow or how shallow—that might lead them
to the ocean beyond. These journeyings brought only tired backs
and increasing dissidence. Still the Captain-General would not
give up. Perhaps there was only a minor inaccuracy in the charts.
A conviction that had been lived with for so long and on which
his reputation, his fortune, and even his life depended could not
be shattered so quickly. They would sail south. The *paso* could
not be so distant.

The Long Passage South

Their progress was slow and halting and heartrending. The
weather worsened, winds carrying the first chill of the Antarctic
drove them back on their course, yet every night when they
could they anchored offshore so that no inlet or bay might be
missed in the hours of darkness. Once 'they lost sight of land for a
matter of two or three days', wrote a Genoese pilot of the armada,
'when they again made for the land, and they came to a bay,
which they entered, and ran within it the whole day, thinking
that there was an outlet for Maluco, and when night came they
found that it was quite closed up, and in the same night they
again stood out by the way which they had come in.' First the
Victoria ran ashore and scraped off at high tide; then the flagship,
caught without searoom, was almost smashed on some rocks.

America seemed to stretch south for ever and to grow more
barren and dangerous and impregnable. The land became flat
and grey and hopeless, the seas more turbulent, the winds more
icy. There were days on end when no fires could be lit to warm
the food, when the men were ceaselessly ordered up and down
the rigging, their fingers stiff with cold. The spray froze on their
beards and frozen clothing chaffed their skin. As in the progress
of Bunyan's Christian, they left behind them a charted record of
their sufferings. Of a promising inlet where their hopes were again
shattered it was recorded that 'at last it pleased God that they
should leave that bay—and they named it Bay of Toil'.

The *paso* was near. Magellan's conviction never wavered
through all these storms and sufferings. But seven weeks out from
the great estuary, he at last recognised that winter was too far
advanced for them to continue the search any longer. They had
lost too much time, and now they must await the spring. Yet to
turn back would be fatal. After a mellow winter of self-indulgence
in Brazil, he could never hope to bring his armada down to these

hellish seas again. Somehow they must stick it out in some sheltered anchorage. It would be a winter of thin rations and certain mutiny.

On 31 March there appeared another break in the shoreline. Taking careful soundings, Magellan brought the *Trinidad* close inshore, through a half-mile-wide channel, over a bar and into a land-locked bay, shaped like an hourglass running north-south parallel with the coastline. He named it Puerto San Julian. If they

A View of Port St Julian up the River, Here we landed with our Boats, in order to take in Salt, of which are several Ponds two and three Miles from ye River-side, where we observed ye Tide to Ebb and Flow with ye Tide in ye River, so that at high Water ye Salt was cover'd in many places, and ye Mudd very soft, but at low water it became hard all over, The Salt is but thinly crusted in ye Ponds, not much exceeding a quarter of an Inch, This is an open desart Country, a dry and gravel

had to endure a winter in these dreary latitudes, then they were unlikely to find a better place than this, with plenty of trees for firewood and for repairing the ships, fresh water and game and fish. There were even several shelving islands which, with the exceptional 37-foot tide, would make careening a simple business: although the resulting current at full tide would have to be watched and the vessels triple anchored.

The Mutiny

Magellan was busy with plans even before the flagship's anchors splashed. They would build huts ashore, pile up great fires, organise hunting parties for seal and for those strange beasts which they had already observed ashore from their ships. (These were guanaco, which Pigafetta describes as having the 'head and ears of the size of a mule, and the neck and body of the fashion of a camel, the legs of a deer, and the tail like that of a horse, and it neighs like a horse.') Their skins would make fine winter clothing. The wine and biscuit rations would again have to be cut, but fresh fish would supplement their diet. There was even a little mountain (Monte Cristo they named it) on which to erect a cross and to give thanks to God for preserving them on this long voyage, and they would erect an altar on one of the islands, too. The prospect was not so bad after all.

Sir Francis Drake: 'the little captain'.

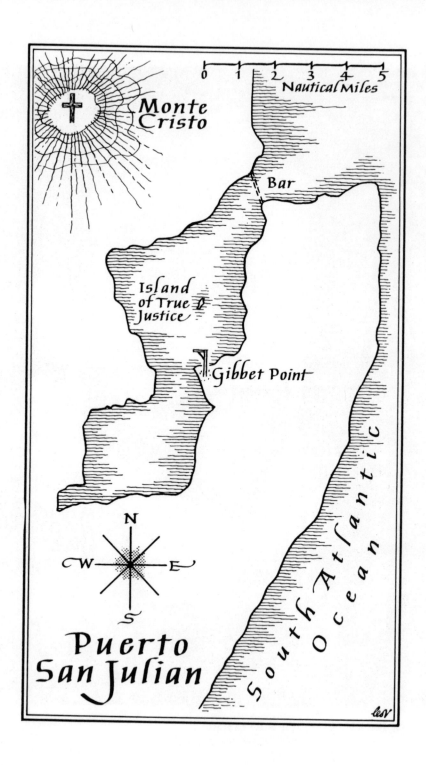

But the mutineers struck sooner than Magellan and his supporters expected. Skiffs with their complements of intriguers were bustling from ship to ship before nightfall, and the word was soon spreading that they were to remain here for a long semi-Antarctic winter on short rations, for had not the Captain-General deliberately failed to find for them the magic Moluccas? He was in the secret pay of King Manoel to seal the doom of the enterprise. This was the story doing the rounds.

Cold such as they had never before experienced, long forced continence, the memory of dangers endured to no purpose, all stirred up old divisions, Basque against Sevillian, Spaniard against Portuguese, and above all the leading elements of the Fonseca cabal against the man who had duped their young King Emperor. Around the confined Cartagena the cabal numbered besides Quesada and Mendoza, the pilots Gomes and Carvalho, Antonio de Coca, Juan Sebastian del Cano, Geronimo Guerra and the priest de Reina. And the first object of the mutineers was the capture of the *San Antonio*, largest of the vessels, carrying most of their supplies, and now captained by Magellan's weak cousin, Alvaro de Mesquita.

Easter was a sullen feast day in this lonely anchorage, farther to the south than any mariners had ever before penetrated, and rumours of threatening violence passed from the *Concepción* to the *San Antonio* and *Victoria*, anchored deep inside the harbour, and thence to the loyal *Santiago* and at length to the cabin of the Captain-General. Magellan sent a message to his cousin ordering him to keep a strong watch, and told his own marines to arm themselves. It was clear that an Easter uprising was imminent.

Easter Mass was to be held before the island altar. Magellan issued a general order for all to attend, and invited his captains to breakfast in the flagship afterwards. Magellan was rowed ashore with a strong bodyguard, recognizing from long experience the scent of danger in the air. The service passed off peacefully, the men dispersed to their vessels, though neither Mendoza nor Quesada turned up for breakfast. The night of Easter Sunday was also uneventful. It was not until early on the Monday morning that Magellan learned that there had been a major insurrection during the night and that he was already heavily outnumbered by more than three to two.

The *Trinidad*'s longboat went off on a routine watering duty, collecting shore party members from each ship. On approaching the *San Antonio* the crew 'were hailed and told to keep off, and informed that the ship was under the orders of Gaspar Quesada, and not Magellan. Hearing the news, and at once suspecting the serious nature of the affair with which he had to deal, the Captain-General ordered the boat to go round to the ships and ask for whom they declared. Quesada's reply was, 'For the King and for myself', and like answers were given from all except the *Santiago*. The leading mutineers had already donned armour and helmets, the guns had been run out and the decks cleared for action. Below decks, Mesquita was in irons, his loyal ship's master mortally wounded.

Thirty armed men, led by del Cano, Quesada and Cartagena, released from confinement, had boarded the big ship from the *Concepción* and forced their way into Mesquita's cabin. When the Basque master intervened and ordered Quesada off the ship, Quesada, exclaiming, 'We cannot be foiled in our work by this fool', sprang at him and stabbed him repeatedly with a dagger. Mendoza was in the plot, of course, so the capture of the *San Antonio* meant that three of the five ships were now for Cartagena.

The situation was delicate and dangerous for both sides. Neither wanted an open clash of arms. All their strength was required either to survive the winter and sail on south, or to return to Spain. The armada's security was in numbers, in the stores in each ship and the skilled manpower to sail them. For Magellan, the destruction of the *San Antonio* would be fatal to his plans. Equally the loss of the flagship would be a serious handicap to Cartagena on his way home. Magellan also wanted the *San Antonio* intact and Cartagena alive. Wits rather than brawn were to count in this situation; and Magellan had the better brain.

Cartagena began by sending a message, conciliatory in tone, asking Magellan to come on board the *San Antonio* for a conference. He would not be harmed, he was assured, and he would remain in command of his own ship, indeed he could be senior captain if he liked; all he would have to do was to bow to majority opinion about their future plans. Magellan sent back a fierce reply, ignoring Cartagena and ordering Quesada and Mendoza to report instantly to the flagship.

The *impasse* was broken later in the day by a tragi-comic incident caused by typical Cartagena ineptitude. He wanted the powerful *San Antonio* to be manned only by out-and-out mutineers in preparation for possible battle. So, forgetting to check the state of the tide, he ordered some neutral elements among the crew to row to the *Concepción* in a longboat. As soon as it touched the water, the boat was swept away with its alarmed and frantically rowing complement, past all three mutinous ships and towards the *Trinidad* and *Santiago*, the foaming bar at the entrance to the bay, and the turbulent open sea beyond. It was a nasty situation, and the men cried for help as they raced towards the flagship. Magellan ordered a rope to be thrown to them, it was caught by the petty officer in charge, and after a good deal of difficulty, the longboat was hauled alongside.

The men were grateful for their salvation, and also for the generous ration of wine the Captain-General gave them. They soon told all they knew. They were even prepared to yield up without protest 'such clothing as was distinctive'. Magellan then ordered fifteen of his stoutest marines to don this clothing, conceal beneath it their weapons, and, when the tide had abated, climb into the longboat as if they were the original occupants. Duarte Barbosa, a reformed character now and never lacking courage, headed this party, while another loyal and stalwart officer, one Gonzalo Gomes de Espinosa, took five more marines in a skiff towards the *Victoria*, to deliver a message to Captain Mendoza. Espinosa and his party were allowed on board—what harm could six men do?—and approached the captain with the letter. It demanded his presence on board the flagship. 'Mendoza smiled at its contents—as though he would say, *"no me tomara alla"*—"I am not to be caught thus" . . . As he shook his head Espinosa drew his dagger and stabbed him in the throat, and at the same instant he was cut down by another of Magellan's men.'

On the signal from Espinosa that the deed had been done, Barbosa altered the course of the longboat and rowed rapidly to give support. The marines scrambled aboard and took the ship without a fight. Hands manned the capstan, the anchors were raised, and before Cartagena understood what was happening, the *Victoria* was being rowed with her long sweeps towards the flagship and the *Santiago*. Now three ships blocked the harbour entrance to Cartagena.

Puerto San Julian's violent tide ended Cartagena's mutiny as neatly as it had swept the *San Antonio*'s longboat into Magellan's hands. At midnight Quesada, intent now only on escape from the Captain-General's wrath, ordered two of his ship's three anchors to be cut ready to sail secretly past the flagship before dawn for the open sea, abandoning the *Concepción* to her fate. But the strength of the tide was too much for the last rope (or perhaps it was severed by some unknown loyalist) and the big ship began to drift straight towards the *Trinidad*'s guns. Magellan's marines, alert and ready for action, hurled grappling irons at the *San Antonio* in the darkness and the marines leaped aboard. It was all over within a few minutes, without a casualty on either side, and the cowed *Concepción* surrendered at dawn.

Trial and Execution

All the formalities were observed at the trial, even to the presence in the dock of Mendoza's propped-up bloody corpse, and a record of the proceedings was retained for presentation to the King on their return. Forty of the seamen were found guilty, but Magellan knew that he could not afford the loss of their numbers and they were given hard labour in chains and on short rations. All the other ringleaders were found guilty, too—Cartagena, Quesada, del Cano, de Coca, the priest Reina, and the rest. Magellan wanted no bloodbath, just an example made; besides, it would hardly be politic to kill the son of the Bishop of Burgos, even if he was a bastard, and a mutinous one at that. So Cartagena's life was spared. Instead he was ordered to be marooned, along with his padre crony Reina, when they left. This was a common sentence for the lighter misdemeanour at that time. In the end only Quesada was executed, by his personal servant in exchange for a pardon, and his remains, along with those of the unfortunate Mendoza, were drawn and quartered and hung from gibbets erected on a prominent position ashore.

Serrano's Reconnaisance

The men were given no time to brood over these events. They were set to work on the ships, careening, caulking, painting. For these tasks, the holds had to be emptied and storehouses set up ashore, every item checked and double-checked and entered in the inventory. Magellan was a master of this task; there was no more miserly and minutely accurate storekeeper. But now, with increasing anxiety as the lists came in, he was forced to recognise that even his tireless supervision at Seville had not prevented the light-fingered and the corrupt among the dockers (with King Manoel's agents inciting them on?) from swindling the armada. For, with mid-winter approaching, six months' sailing from home, and without hope of succour, they were short of every commodity, as well as their basic stores of biscuits and flour and dried beans. They had just enough to see them through the winter and get them back to Spain, but no more, and none to cover emergencies and delays. Their failure to find the *paso* at Cape Saint Mary, now that the winter had caught them, could now be recognised in all its seriousness. There would be no food to spare to continue the search in the spring. What was the use of suffering all the miseries and dangers of this frightful place, only to have to return home defeated?

More than the most restless of his men, Magellan abhorred inaction, and he knew its dangers. In a place like Santa Lucia leisure bred corruption of the body and at Puerto San Julian corruption of the mind. Moreover, his mariner's instinct, which could give warning of a storm, judge the friendliness or hostility of a distant vessel, and alert him to the danger of an unseen reef, continued to repeat the message he anxiously needed to believe: the *paso* was near, only a few days' sailing away. It was still not too late to find it, now, even with the icy winds from the Andes sweeping across the plains and the first snow flurries drifting against the gunwales. They must reconnoitre south again, before it was too late.

The shallow-draught *Santiago* had completed her refit and was ready for sea. Magellan ordered old John Serrano to the flagship and gave him his instructions. Search every bay and inlet and estuary, he was told. Do not hazard your ship. Report back promptly. So the little *Santiago*, with thirty-seven men aboard her, hoisted sail and ran out across the bar and dug her stubby bows into the heaving slate-grey seas. She remained in sight a long time, bucking and rolling under a small spread of canvas. It was as well that Serrano was the most experienced captain in the armada.

While he was away Magellan ordered hunting parties ashore to hunt guanaco and rhea, the grey, flightless, ostrich-like creatures they sometimes saw flitting on fast-moving legs between the trees. Their bay was to be combed for fish, too, for salting and casking away. Who could tell how wide the *Mar del Sur* might be, how many weeks and months they might have to sail before they reached the Moluccas?

The Giants

The guanaco proved an elusive prey, which made it all the more exasperating when natives, evidently alerted by the fruitless musket shots, appeared on the shore for the first time, leading guanaco 'with a cord in the manner of dogs coupled together'. Their hunting methods were odd but effective. 'When these

people wish to catch these animals with which they clothe themselves, they fasten one of the young ones to a bush, and after the
large ones come to play with the little one, and the giants are hid
behind some hedge, and by shooting their arrows they kill the
large one,' Pigafetta observed. The hunters were giants indeed,
'so tall that the tallest of us only came up to his waist', and clothed
in a guanaco skin 'very skilfully sewed'. With hair painted white,
eyes circled in yellow, faces in red, and with two hearts painted
on their cheeks, they made a colourful sight on the shoreline as
they sang and leaped and pointed their fingers to the sky. Such
abandonment in such a bleak spot!

Magellan was captivated by these tall lively creatures, offered
them food and drink, bells, a comb and beads. One, shown a
mirror 'saw his likeness in it' and was 'greatly terrified, leaping
backwards, and made three or four of our men fall down'.
Magellan named them Patagonians for their big feet, and
determined to utilise their strength and skill; so 'our men brought
eighteen of these giants, both men and women, whom they placed
in two divisions, half on one side of the port, and the other half at
the other, to hunt the said animals'.

Relations between these wintering sailors and the savage
nomadic tribesmen, each curious about the other, were never
settled on any firm basis, and were one moment friendly, the next
hostile. Magellan had no idea how to manage them. He took a
special fancy to one, an especially energetic dancer and leaper;
so he was baptised and named John and taught to pronounce
'the name of Jesus, the Pater noster, Ave Maria, and his name as
clearly as we did: but he had a terribly strong and loud voice'.
But two others were tricked into irons to take back to Spain, one
each in the *Trinidad* and *San Antonio*, and this created a terrible
uproar and resulted in an exchange of musket shots and poisoned
arrows and the instant death of one of the sailors from a mere
graze. After that they had to do their own guanaco hunting.

Magellan waited impatiently and anxiously for the return of
the *Santiago*. Some four weeks passed before he learned of the
disaster which had overcome his cousin and their useful little ship.
Two starved seamen were sighted by the guards crawling along
the seashore. For eleven days they had been struggling overland,
living on roots and shellfish and drinking melted snow. They told
how Serrano had discovered a sheltered river estuary, rich in fish,
how the *Santiago* had been caught in a sudden squall and thrown
up on the shore and wrecked, and how all had escaped except

Serrano's Ethiopian slave.

Magellan despatched a relief party overland. The castaways were discovered, emaciated and suffering from exposure, and helped back to the ships.

Puerto San Julian had brought them nothing but misfortune. It was a mournful and hostile place, sombre with the memories of failure and sudden death. Magellan determined to leave it for ever, in spite of the mid-winter weather, and the disaster which had so soon overcome the experienced Serrano when he had taken to the open sea. Once in the *paso* they would be secure from these fearsome storms, reckoned Magellan, and beyond lay the *Mar del Sur*, the ocean Balboa had once described as 'that glorious sight which we have so much desired'.

With the loyal Mesquita commanding the *San Antonio*, Barbosa the *Victoria*, and Serrano the newly appointed captain of the *Concepción*, there was for the time being no risk of active opposition to Magellan's decision to explore farther south again. The last rite performed at Puerto San Julian cruelly underlined the Captain-General's total authority. There were risks enough in these storm-wracked southern latitudes, where the *Santiago* had been battered to pieces within minutes of striking: there was certainly no room for subversiveness aboard the surviving vessels. Before anchors were raised, Cartagena and the once-bawdy priest Reina, 'with an abundance of bread and wine', were rowed ashore and left on the beach, 'judged to be worse off, considering the country in which they were left, than the others who were drawn and quartered'. Their pitiful cries were heard by every man as the ships of the armada one by one hoisted sail and ran slowly out, past the gibbets, past the cross-crowned hill, over the bar and out into the South Atlantic.

The Cape of the Eleven Thousand Virgins

Of the next weeks, Pigafetta was to write that 'God, in his favour, aided us'. But the torments to which they were subjected were nevertheless frightful. A storm struck them as soon as they had left their anchorage, and battered them for two days and nights, until Magellan was forced to seek shelter in the river estuary of the Santa Cruz, which Serrano had recently discovered. Further progress appeared impossible, and the four ships were forced to hole up in this unappetising spot—later mildly described by Charles Darwin as 'extremely uninteresting . . . stunted and dwarf plants'—during the worst of the mid-winter weather.

Survival from the cold, the gales and the driving sleet was their first consideration. But during brief less savage intervals parties made their way up the coast to salvage what they could from the wreck of the *Santiago*, and more fish were caught, dried, salted and stored away in the holds.

A longer mellow period was enough to set Magellan on the move again. It was not yet full spring, but the worst of the winter was surely past. On 18 October 1520 they steered out of that ugly, barren estuary. For two more days it seemed that the elements fought a last tenacious battle to withhold the secret of the *paso*. Contrary winds drove them back and the armada rolled and heaved under bare masts just off the grey-brown featureless shoreline. All hope was dead, except in the eyes and mind of one man. A year of bleakness and hazard, of discomfort, hunger and labour (with only those few days with the sun and the fruit and native women of San Lucar as a remote happy memory) had dulled their palates for adventure and driven out the last remnant of expectation. The winds were against them, the nature of the shore had not changed in months, the rationed wine was stale, the meat and fish as unvarying as the decks and quarters and the faces about them.

Late on 19 October the wind suddenly veered through 180 degrees, freshened and drove them fast on their southerly course. The sky lightened, great skuas and black-and-white gulls shadowed them from astern and dropped for the smallest morsel, and higher hills far inland presaged a change in the topography, if nothing more.

'And then we had a fair wind,' prosaically noted the pilot Alvo, 'and went to the S.S.W. for two days, and in that time we took the sun in 50 2/3°, and it was on the 20th.'

It was just twenty-four hours later when Alvo entered the reference 'we saw an opening like unto a bay' in his log.

A Southern Paradise

The *Trinidad* led the way through the first narrows with the full thrust of the tide under her keel on 27 October. For Magellan it was a day of vindication. All the omens had become favourable, too. The weather had mellowed, the gales had turned to gentle and favourable winds, and as they entered farther into the *paso* the landscape was suddenly transformed from the arid and featureless plains of Patagonia into rolling wooded hills. Close to the shoreline they could make out grassy areas as rich in flowers

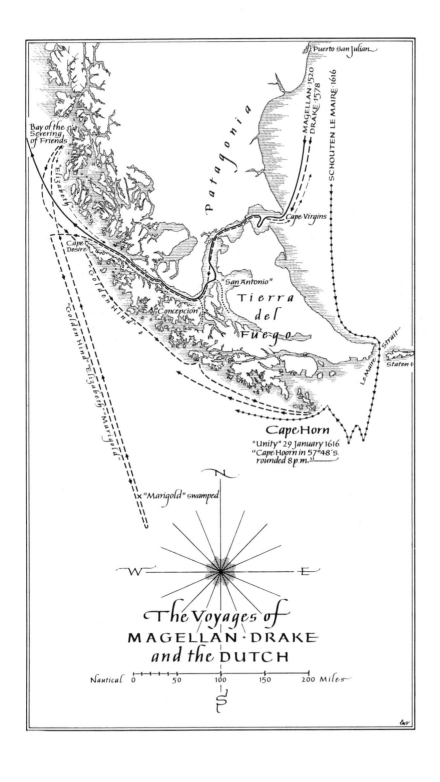

Puerto San Julian

MAGELLAN 1520
DRAKE 1578

SCHOUTEN LE MAIRE 1616

Patagonia

Bay of the
Severing
of Friends

"Elizabeth"

Cape
Desire

"Golden Hind"

"Golden Hind" "Elizabeth" "Marigold"

Cape Virgins

"San Antonio"

"Concepcion"

Tierra
del
Fuego

Le Maire Strait

Staten I

Cape Horn

"Unity" 29 January 1616
"Cape Hoorn in 57°48′S.
rounded 8 p.m."

x "Marigold" swamped

N

W ——— E

The Voyages of
MAGELLAN · DRAKE
and the DUTCH

Nautical   0   50   100   150   200 Miles

S

Magellan in the *paso*

as any riverside meadow back in Spain. Streams tumbled down
from the hills, offering them all the fresh water they could need,
and the forests promised game and berries. Far to the west and the
south they could make out higher hills rising to a spectacular
white mountainous silhouette. 'I think that there is not in the
world a more beautiful country, or better strait than this one',
wrote Pigafetta joyously. In the lee of an island (Elizabeth Island)
past the second narrows where they hove to 'there were many
sea wolves and large birds'—sea lions and penguins—and the
waters were rich in fish.

Magellan did not allow the success and happiness of this
moment to hazard his judgement. Not only was their discovery
an event worth placing on record but he recognised that this was
the right time to convene a meeting of his captains and pilots for
a decision on their future plans. Of course these were unalterable;
of course they would go on, probing through the channels until
they broke out into the *Mar del Sur*. No power on earth could turn
back the Captain-General now. But here, at the apex point of
their travels, the decision, unanimously and democratically

reached, that they should continue west, must be noted as evidence for the time when they returned home. It was a better place than Puerto San Julian for policy decisions.

But there was, after all, a dissident voice at this council in the *Trinidad*. It came from Estevan Gomes, who was now pilot of the *San Antonio* and had remained discreetly in the background during the mutiny. 'Now that we have apparently found the strait,' he said, 'it is better to go back to Spain and return with another armada. For the way that lies before us is no small matter, and, if we encounter any lengthened period either of calms or storms, it is probable that all will perish.' Magellan replied as those who knew him expected him to reply '*Con semblante muy compuesto*'— 'That if they had to eat the leather on the ships' yards he would still go on, and discover what he had promised to the Emperor, and that he trusted that God would aid them and give them good fortune.'

It is curious that Gomes, still harbouring mutinous thoughts, should have spoken out against the majority decision, thus re-arousing Magellan's suspicions. It is equally curious that Magellan did not act on these suspicions. Perhaps he could not bring himself to believe that a fellow countryman would ever betray him. And yet he knew that the rumblings of discontent had not been silenced by the discovery of the *paso*, and felt it necessary to issue a general order that, under pain of death, there must be an end to all grumbling and speculation about the adequacy of their supplies.

The Land of Fire, and Death

From Elizabeth Island there was only one way to go. The wide channel took them due south towards the snow clad peaks. The starboard or western shore, the last of America's mainland, appeared lifeless and still. Nothing moved among the scrubby shrubs or the woods of evergreen beach or patches of green flanking the little rivers. If there was any life in this strange and haunting land, it was on the island they were passing on the port quarter. Once they thought they had located a village of crude huts, and a party went ashore to investigate. It was an uneasy experience for the sailors. As they neared the beach they were met by an overwhelming stench of rotting fish. It came from the corpse of a stranded whale, the first whale, alive or dead, they had ever seen, tangible evidence of the truth of all the super-stitious tales they had ever heard of sea monsters. A cloud of scavenging birds arose from the corpse, revealing its vastness and putrescence.

The supposed village was equally macabre. It was no more than a graveyard, suggestive of black tribal rites. More than two hundred corpses, smoked and mummified in sewn shrouds of albatross skins, had been placed in rows of thatched barrows raised above the ground. Many had been laid out with their weapons beside them—wooden spears and knives and clubs studded with sharks' teeth—and with their feathered war head-dresses on their skulls. There was no sound nor sign of life any-where; it was as if the whole tribal population had by some black magic simultaneously been laid to rest.

Only later that day, after the exploring party had returned thankfully to their vessels, was evidence seen of some activity, if not of life, on that island. Columns of smoke were seen to rise from the forests inland. There were many of them, and as soon as one disappeared another arose elsewhere as if some darting tireless firebrand was at work. It was truly a land of fire, and so Magellan named it—Tierra del Fuego.

It was also a perplexing place. The end of America was geographically confusing as well as mysterious. Tierra del Fuego soon began to break up into a multitude of smaller islands fringed with snaking kelp strands, low rocky cliffs rising to the green of moss and tussock and the unvarying beeches, to outcrops and bluffs of bare tertiary granite, then to the undulating snow mantle that covered all but the sharpest rocky peaks above. It was a nightmare prospect for any cartographer or navigator. This maze of channels, with its unpredictable currents and winds, might have been sliced out of the tip of the continent as a final wicked joke to break the spirit of men who had already suffered so much to get here. Perhaps there were many ways that led to the ocean lying beyond; there might be only one. But for the four ships to explore all of them in company would take many weeks.

The Armada Divides

As they neared the mountains ahead, dense crowds of sea birds crying and howling about them, Magellan made the decision to split his armada and arrange a rendezvous some distance up the most westerly channel, which the flagship and the *Victoria* would explore in company, placing an identifying cross on some promi-nent landmark. The other most promising outlets tended to the south, one (Canal Whiteside) much broader but hinting at a later more easterly turn; the other narrower, more tortuous and with a more precipitous shoreline. The second would call for high navigational skill, and towards it Magellan despatched the experienced Serrano with the *Concepción*. Mesquita, the least skilful captain but with the more skilful pilot, Gomes, was ordered to follow the broader of the two arms in the *San Antonio*.

The big *San Antonio* was soon gone and for half a day the remaining three ships kept company on the south-south-westerly course. With every half league the channel narrowed and the scenery became more spectacular. Due south a great twin-peaked mountain, snowclad from summit to shoreline, rose high above the broad bases of its glaciers, dominating all the others, Here, at this second dividing of the ways, some thought that they could feel through the timbers of their ships the throbbing pulse, the distant heartbeat, of a great ocean. Its direction was impossible to judge. But they were near, of that they were certain.

The *Concepción* set course due south, cautiously feeling her way between high capes and bluffs, rocks and islets, convoyed by a thousand sea birds—great skuas, terns and gulls and a dozen smaller breeds—wheeling above her masts and her high stern. The flagship turned west, steering in close to a high dark cliff (Cape Froward), the end of mainland America and (though Magellan did not yet know it) the turning point for any ship navigating between the two great oceans through the Magellan Strait. The prospect was not hopeful. The channel narrowed, but 'in it we found at every half league a good port and place for anchoring, good waters, wood all of cedar [antarctic beech], and fish like sardines, missiglioni, and a very sweet herb named appio [wild celery]'.

The two ships dropped anchor in one of these bays, which they named the Bay of Sardines, and went ashore for water and wood, and launched boats for fishing. One of the longboats, more suitable than a *naos* for these narrow waters, made off on reconnaissance in a north-westerly direction up the channel under its single sail, threading carefully between the islands.

For three days the Captain-General awaited the return of his scattered vessels. All might well fail. On every point of the compass winding strips of water, any of which might lead to the open sea, became lost among the snow crags.

The Traitorous Pilot

But at the end of the third day Magellan's craving for news was

The *Concepción* passes Mount Sarmiento

Cape Froward from the west—the southernmost tip of the South American continent

suddenly satisfied. The longboat was the first to reappear, the crew in an evident state of excitement. 'They told us', Pigafetta noted, 'that they had found the cape and the sea great and wide. At the joy which the Captain-General had at this he began to cry, and he gave the name of Cape of Desire to this cape, as a thing which had been much desired for a long time.'

Now more than ever impatient to be away, Magellan returned eastwards in search of his other two ships. The *Concepción* soon hove into sight. Serrano had nothing to report, only that he had pierced treacherous channels, passed beneath the great twin-peaked mountain and the entrance to numerous creeks, inlets, passages and canals, and that he had seen nothing of the *San Antonio*.

More days were wasted searching the channel into which their biggest and most valuable ship had sailed. Their predicament was now desperate. The *San Antonio* had in her holds the greater part of their supplies. Even if they could find her wreck they might salvage some part of these. But though they sailed to the limit of the channel (Admiralty Sound) and up many of the inlets scattered along its southern shores, they found only a monotonously similar shoreline of rock and beech forest empty of all life, soundless except for the cries from the sea birds and the crashing of the waterfalls that fell from the snowline to the channel edge.

Fearing that the *San Antonio* had been driven north and east again by some sudden squall, Magellan sent the *Victoria* alone through the narrows. She was to leave a cross prominently in view at two points *en route* and messages in upturned jars at their base. Many days later Barbosa reported back to the flagship, having completed his mission. He had sailed as far as the Cape of the Eleven Thousand Virgins, he told Magellan, and still had not sighted the missing ship.

Magellan dared not waste more time. The ships of his depleted armada had supplies for a month, perhaps two months. Their crews, and certainly their officers, appeared loyal. They had solved America's greatest mystery and discovered the *paso*. Now they must be gone. On about 25 November 1520 the *Trinidad*, the *Victoria* and the *Concepción* weighed and, hoisting sail and with a rare fair wind astern, sailed for the second time down the narrow strait that was to carry for all time the name of its discoverer: three old *naos*, hulls encrusted and storm-battered, short on supplies, manned by a mixed complement of European Christian races and one disconsolate Patagonian giant who would not make the sign of the cross for fear 'it would enter into my stomach and make me die'.

Cape Desire and the rocky archipelago to the north presented themselves just as the members of the reconnaissance party had described them: a worthy proscenium to the blue stage of the world's greatest ocean, which was calm and serene when Magellan first set eyes upon it.

In the Mar del Sur

The Captain-General had a proper sense of the occasion. As the keel of the *Trinidad* drove into these waters, touched for the first time by the timbers of a European vessel, his ships closed and the surviving priest in full vestments raised his crucifix from the poop deck of the *Trinidad* and every man knelt in prayer. He appealed for the favour of St. Andrew the Apostle, whose day it was, and bestowed a benediction both on this new ocean and on those who were about to sail across it. To the sound of the discharge of cannon, Magellan held aloft the great silk banner of his command which he had so long ago received from the hands of Emperor Charles, and prayed that the waters might always be as peaceful as they were that morning. In the hope that they might be, he pronounced that 'I shall name this sea the *Mar Pacifico*.'

Their prayers for pacific seas were answered and the winds and the currents remained favourable. But their worst sufferings still lay ahead. It was the vast distance they had to sail before reaching land that killed so many of them and crippled almost all with the scurvy. Contemporary cartographers always underestimated distances. According to the crude and speculative charts carried by Magellan, the west coast of America joined with the eastern extension of the Asian mainland at about 35 degrees south of the Equator. Magellan therefore steered north up the coast of Chile expecting soon to reach Asia, and a warmer climate for his men, before he gave up and changed course to the north-west. This only added further to the thousands of leagues he had to sail, and to their privations. 'We remained three months and twenty days without taking in provisions or other refreshments', recorded Pigafetta, 'and we only ate old biscuit reduced to powder, and full of grubs, and stinking from the dirt which the rats had made on it . . . and we drank water that was yellow and stinking.' Just as Magellan had feared. 'We also ate the ox hides which were under the main-yard . . .' first softening them in the ocean for several days.

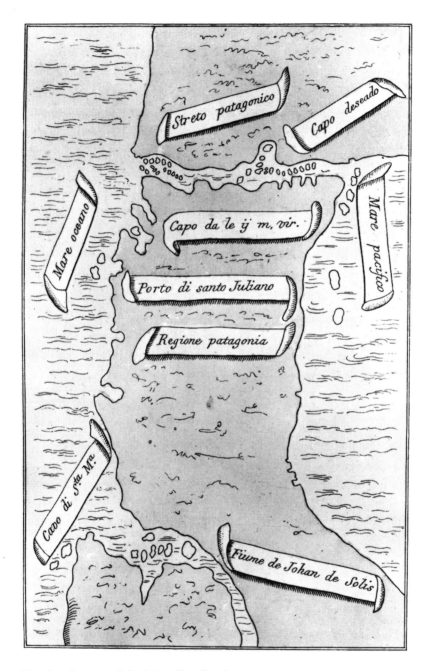

Pigafetta's map of the Magellan Strait

The swellings and pains of the scurvy spread rapidly. One of the first to succumb was their Patagonian giant, now christened Paul, who in the last extremity took the cross and kissed it. The weakened survivors had tossed the corpses of nineteen of their shipmates overboard before at last they sighted the Marianas. But here and among the Philippines, Magellan showed himself too eager to convert the natives to the Catholic faith and bring them under the flag of Castille, and too unforgiving of their robust behaviour and pilfering. As at Puerto San Julian, there was violence and bloodshed; and in one scuffle on the little island of Mactan in the Philippines, the Captain-General and his party on an ill-judged punitive expedition, found themselves greatly outnumbered by a ferocious enemy, and 'the Indians threw themselves upon him, and ran him through with lances and scimitars . . . so that they deprived of life our mirror, light, comfort and true guide'.

And so Magellan died, waist deep in the surf of an island, on a hopeless mission to quell some petty affront: a distressing end to a noble career of courageous ventures.

He had foiled the Portuguese, subjugated his enemies, navigated with sublime skill, discovered the *paso*, and the Moluccas were so close that he could almost reach out for the prize. The rock-like obstinacy and remorselessness which had made possible these achievements at last proved fatal when a measure of restraint and understanding would have saved him.

Only the *Victoria* and the *Trinidad*, after many combats with *praus* and junks, native tribes and Chinese traders, at length reached the Moluccas, where it was learned that Francisco Serrano and his king had been poisoned at about the time Magellan had been killed. And only the *Victoria* was fit to load her holds with the treasured spices and sail back to Spain. The *Concepción*, riddled with *teredo navalis*, had been burned. The *Trinidad*, unable to tackle the long journey round Africa, set course for Mexico but was cast ashore on Ternate and broke up.

The Circumnavigators

Pigafetta, who had survived that terrible Pacific crossing without scurvy, and the wounds he had suffered in the fight on Mactan, was among the eighteen of the *Victoria*'s company still alive when the Spanish coastline was sighted almost three years after the armada's hopeful and ceremonious departure. 'We cast anchor near the mole of Seville', he concluded his narrative, '. . . and we all went in shirts and barefoot, with a taper in our hands to visit the shrine of St. Maria of Victory, and of St. Maria de Antigua'.

One irony is not touched on by this stalwart Genoese. The *Victoria*'s commander, the man who was feted as the first circumnavigator and made rich for life by the spices he brought back from the Moluccas, had been one of the ringleaders of the Puerto San Julian mutiny. Sebastian del Cano had been driven south to discover the end of America only by the dogged will and the strength of the man he had wished to destroy. Now he was honoured by the Emperor with a coat of arms and a generous pension, and today his statue stands in Guipozoa.

Alvaro de la Mesquita, late captain of the *San Antonio*, was among those most pleased to learn of the *Victoria*'s belated return, for he had been in irons or in prison for nearly two years. The big supply ship had not after all been wrecked among the Fuegian islands. Somewhere in Admiralty Sound, no one knows where, Gomes had whipped up a mutiny. Mesquita was stabbed and incarcerated, and under cover of darkness the *San Antonio* sailed

The first ship to circumnavigate the globe

Juan Sebastian del Cano

back into the *paso*, through the narrows for Spain, anchoring in Puerto San Julian to search fruitlessly for the castaways, Cartagena and the rebellious priest. Little is known of this voyage; only that the *San Antonio*'s unfortunate Patagonian died at sea like his fellow captive in the *Trinidad*, that water and provisions were picked up on the coast of Guinea, and that she docked at Seville on 6 May 1521. Gomes and his cronies had plenty of time to concoct a cover story and to extract, under torture, a confession from Mesquita. Magellan had been brutal as well as incompetent. And Mesquita had sided with him against the common will. That was their version of the story.

But the authorities of India House were not so gullible as Gomes had expected. They were used to mariners' yarns. If there had been dirty work down in the sub-Antarctic it was best, they decided, to await the return of the rest of the armada and the tales of more independent witnesses. So Gomes, too, was thrown into jail; though he was released, along with Mesquita, the man he had stabbed and tortured, when the *Victoria* returned.

Nor did Diogo Barbosa gain anything from the voyage, losing many kinsmen, his son-in-law, and Duarte, who had been struck down by natives soon after Magellan. For him it had been a total financial and personal disaster.

Pigafetta returned jauntily to Italy, 'where I established for ever my abode'. He does not record any enquiry into the welfare of the widow of his late 'noble captain'. But poor Beatriz suffered as sadly as any of the armada's company who endured the agonies of scurvy at the Equator, thirst in the African tropics or the cold and tedium of a winter in Patagonia. On the return of the *San Antonio* she was watched day and night 'in order that she should not escape to Portugal until the facts are better understood'. Her second child died at birth, Magellan's son died soon after, and Beatriz succumbed to sickness and grief when she learned that her man would never return.

2

'I was the only man that might do this exploit'

Francis Drake, quoting Queen Elizabeth I

THE first penetration of the uttermost south had exacted a heavy toll of lives, the armada's Captain-General in combat, his second-in-command by stranding, pilots and masters and many of the seamen by the executioner's axe, assassination, starvation or disease—all these had either died there or succumbed afterwards to the special influences which were to make this place an object of fear and superstition for more than three centuries. Only one of the five ships had fulfilled its mission.

By any hasty calculation, the armada had been a catastrophic failure. And yet, by the reckoning of the accountants and the geographers alike, the late Captain-General, for all the handicaps and mischances under which he had suffered and the misjudgments he had committed, had shown the way and made a handsome profit—the contents of the little *Victoria*'s hold had seen to that. The Moluccas had justified their reputation. Those forty thousand square miles of Ternate, Tidore, Motil, Maquian, and the other islands and islets about them were indeed the most precious and highly productive in the world.

The armada's one great failure was not to secure this golden land for the Spanish crown. At so great a distance and with such fallible charting, the demarcation line between the empires of Portugal and Spain bent to the successes and failures of conquest. And with the return of the *Victoria* it became evident to King Charles that the Portuguese had got there first—tentatively and hazardously, by shaky treaties with kings and chieftains made under duress. But they were at the Moluccas, with a few scattered, undermanned trading posts.

Now that the secret of the short-cut *paso* was his and the first fruit of the Moluccas, brought home for the first time in a Spanish bottom, was safely there in the Seville warehouses, the officials of India House, spurred on by King Charles, determined to emulate the *Victoria*'s success, confident that there could be a steady build-up of traffic to the East by the short western route. There was good reason for their confidence. They could argue that Magellan brought about his own disasters: poor planning, bad timing, inadequate provisioning, and divisiveness among the crews. (It had been a mistake to appoint a Portuguese as Captain-General and they would not make that mistake again.) The *paso* itself had not been troublesome. The winds had been fair down in Tierra del Fuego, the fish, fresh water and timber plentiful.

The Spanish expeditions which followed Magellan discovered the real dangers and the real character of this land: its serene sunny calms and sudden bursts of violence, its deceptions of climate and topography, its unpredictability. These later voyagers learnt how the winds could tear through those harsh white peaks in the south and west, whipping up the waters of the strait and its channels, snapping any anchor hawser and tossing the ship on shore; how horizontal mid-summer sleet could blind a man who opened his eyes towards it; and how the next minute the wind died to a balmy breeze, the clouds were whisked away, the sun steamed dry wooden decks and the kelp-strewn rocks ashore, and seabirds clustered to give sudden praise.

The climate itself changed rapidly from one area to another. Near the Cape of the Eleven Thousand Virgins the land was stark and arid; within a few miles along the strait, Patagonian scrub turned to mellower forest and pasture land, well washed by streams and rivers. Farther west Magellan had found himself in almost continuous rain; farther south, paradoxically, Barbosa in the *Concepción* had experienced a mellower climate. The only consistent feature was changeability, and the changes were sudden. The islands of Tierra del Fuego had let all these first ships pass through and did not claim a single life. It was an invitation to others to follow.

The Emulators

The armadas that followed Magellan's all met disastrous ends. Some never reached the Cape of the Eleven Thousand Virgins. Many of the ships that penetrated the *paso* were wrecked, others were punched back into the Atlantic by wind and tide or deserted

Part of a map of the world on the mercator projection contained in
some copies of the first edition of Hakluyt's *Principles of Navigation*, 1589

and sailed back to Brazil or Spain to report impossible seas and winds. The death rate by shipwreck, starvation, scurvy and even mutiny was dreadfully high. Spain would have given up this short, but savage, western route earlier but for the establishment of new Spanish colonies. Although she had failed to gain the Moluccas, the Philippines were now Spain's. Then Francisco Pizzaro conspired and fought his way into the heart of the Inca kingdoms of Peru and unearthed riches on a scale that made Spanish failure in the Moluccas seem a trivial loss. The establishment of Spanish viceroyalties on the western coast of South America increased still further the importance of the Magellan Strait as a link between New Spain and Old Spain, and the Pacific possessions.

In 1540 Don Alonso de Carmargo completed the voyage from Seville to Peru for the first time. But the price he paid was penal. His flagship was sunk, his second ship was driven far to the south and he never saw it again. It did, however, succeed in returning to Spain, and the report of her (unnamed) captain revealed more of the nature of the land south of the *paso*, though Cape Horn still kept its secret.

This unidentified little caravel was thrust farther south than any ship before her, clear down the western coast of the main island of Tierra del Fuego. 'In the night,' wrote her captain in his journal, 'such a wind sprang up that we could show no sail. Next day, in the afternoon, we saw a point of land, and as it seemed that if we could double it there would be no more to the south, we got round it with much trouble.'

Historians agree that this vessel had probably doubled Cape San Diego and entered a strait that was in later years to become notorious for its foul weather and dangerous currents, Le Maire Strait. The caravel's company was looking for the first time on one of the most inhospitable and spectacular islands in the world, the Isla de los Estados, or Staten Island, whose steeple-like peaks rising three thousand feet straight from the foam-slashed rocks, stand like a guard to America's eastern approaches. Illuminated by a shaft of summer sunshine (as the author first saw this island) it is like a glinting strip of a huge cross-cut saw blade. There is nothing to compare with it, even in the Fuegian archipelago, and whether seen through a storm or in a patch of clear weather, every early voyager was struck by its awful appearance. 'I cannot but remark that though Tierra del Fuego had an aspect extremely barren and desolate', wrote one, 'yet this island . . . far surpasses it in the wildness and horror of its appearance; it seeming to be

entirely composed of inaccessible rocks, without the least mixture
of earth or mould between them. These rocks terminate in a vast
number of ragged points, which spire up to a prodigious height,
and are all of them covered with everlasting snow; the points
themselves being surrounded on every side with frightful preci-
pices, and often overhang in an astonishing manner. Nothing
can be imagined more savage and gloomy than the whole aspect
of this coast.' Another officer said that the island 'makes the most
horrid appearance of anything I ever saw', calling it 'a proper
nursery for desperation'. To the east, the nearest land mass is
Africa.

After twenty years, from 1520 to 1540, the Spaniards at last
acknowledged defeat, and for a further forty years no white man
was seen in the Magellan Strait or among the islands of Tierra del
Fuego. In spite of the discovery of Staten Island, the geographers
still believed that the continent of America continued from
Newfoundland to *Terra Australis* and the South Pole, broken
only by Magellan's *paso*: and this was now considered so dangerous
that it could be discounted as a feasible route. The only boats seen
on these waters were canoes slipping from island to island and
sometimes crossing the strait about their business, which was
mostly fishing but also battle, for desultory but vicious inter-tribal
warfare was carried on, as if life was not difficult enough to
sustain without spearing and clubbing. By the 1570s Spain had
almost forgotten about the place. Only a few old men remembered
the excitement and high expectations that accompanied the
departure of that first expedition back in King Charles's day, and
the logs and records brought back by Del Cano in the *Victoria*
remained unread in the vaults of India House.

This long period of neglect of the uttermost south coincided
with the birth, a century after the first harvest of Portuguese and
Spanish reconnaissance and conquest, of new maritime ambitions
in northern Europe. The French, the Dutch and the English were
all beginning to sail far, and in strength. As Henry the Navigator
had inspired the Portuguese discoverers of the 15th century and
acted as a charge to the explosive growth of Iberian conquest, so
Henry Tudor brought into being England's first real navy; what
is more, within a few years this enthusiastic navalist had the most
advanced ships and the best fighting seamen in the world. You
needed good ships to reach the other side of the world, and for the
first time, the English now had them. The spirit of enterprise and
self-confidence and the new progressiveness and inventiveness

extended to the nation's shipyards. Shipbuilders like Matthew Baker worked with the enthusiastic co-operation of experienced sea captains, like the Hawkins family, to produce the fleetest and most seaworthy men-of-war in the world, with fine hull lines and much reduced castles fore and aft, by contrast with the topheavy Iberian galleons.

This new naval power came of age in 1545, when it drove off an attempted French invasion by 60,000 men in over two hundred vessels—as powerful and as relatively superior a force as Spain was to send against the island forty-three years later. This year marked the discovery of the Potosí silver mines in Peru, and probably also the date of birth of the greatest of all Tudor seamen, a man who was to break the spell of the strait and ransack the riches of those same mines.

'*The Little Captain*'

There is a close similarity between Ferdinand Magellan and Francis Drake and the circumstances of their voyages and the manner in which they drew the eyes of the maritime-conscious world to the southern tip of the American continent. Both men were short in stature, and were already hard-bitten warriors carrying the wounds of past campaigns when they left on their circumnavigations. Both were troubled by a sense of social inferiority and were embarrassed *en route* by their social superiors who reckoned they should have been Captain-General. Drake was quite the equal of Magellan as a navigator, was equally dogged and tough, and fretful with human problems. Of the two, Drake was cooler and more decisive in a crisis, and it was this quality that brought him safely, and richly, home, by contrast with Magellan's miserable end in a fit of pique when the worst was over. Nothing can ever detract from Magellan's triumph in being the first to find and the first to navigate the *paso*, and the first to thrust the keel of his vessel into the Pacific. The memorials to his greatness are everywhere, from the great statue in the square of Punta Arenas, halfway along his strait, to his own name on the strait and the name he gave to his ocean in every atlas in every language. He deserves it all. He found the way through, and changed the map of the world as radically as his fellow-country-men, Dias and da Gama, had done sailing east twenty years earlier, even if few were to follow Magellan.

Drake's accomplishment was at once complementary and confirmatory and a denial of the importance of Magellan's

discovery. Magellan discovered nothing of what lay to the south
as he made his way through his strait, at times within a quarter
mile of either shore. He saw only fire-studded islands and noted
that below the *paso* and these broken islands the land mass of
America continued, as everyone had assumed, to become *Terra
Australis*. Drake exploded all this by proving that Magellan's
strait was only one, rather dangerous, way into the Pacific.

But a comparative assessment of these two men's achievements
is less interesting than the similarity of their voyages, and this will
become clearer after Drake sails out of Plymouth Sound on his
way south, farther south than any man before him, to become the
first true Cape Horner and the first Englishman to sail the Pacific.

This is what he had determined to do five years earlier: 'After
our Captain had ascended to this bower [in a tree above Panama]
and having, as it pleased God, at this time by reason of a breeze
a very fair day, had seen that sea of which he had heard such
golden reports, he besought Almighty God of his goodness to give
him life and leave to sail once in an English ship in that sea.' At
this time Francis Drake was about twenty-eight years old, already
a feared corsair on the Spanish Main, busily building up a
reputation for singeing the king of Spain's beard and engaging in
semi-piratical activities which were to put pace and colour into
the history lessons of many generations of English schoolboys.

In the social scale of the time Drake ranked lower in England
than Magellan in Portugal. He was of yeoman farmer stock,
which in the West Country often also meant that you had strong
connections with the sea. The Drakes had for long been farmers
near Tavistock. As a younger son, Francis's father Edmund went
to sea as a boy and returned to the land with enough money to
settle down and start a family, with Francis as the first child, in
1544. Now, besides being part-sailor, part-farmer, Edmund Drake
had 'something in him of what was called in the slang of the day
"a hot-gospeller" . . . with a taste for preaching and hot for the
new opinions'. Anyone born at this time—above all in the West
country—must be aware of the growing English revolt against
Rome, and this tide of the Reformation flowed with the new zeal
for maritime enterprise.

Almost nothing is known of Francis Drake as a boy. But it is
certain that he was infected with his father's deep sense of religion
and his fanatical hatred of Rome. Throughout all his voyages as
corsair and explorer it is 'God's Almighty providence' which saves
him from shipwreck, brings him wind when becalmed and

provisions when starving, and victory with sword and culverin against the Spaniards. At this time, as his biographer Julian Corbett puts it, 'We can see the making of the man in whose hatred of Spaniard and Papist there was always a sweetening of the love of God, in whose most high-handed and least defensible exploits there sounds a note of piety that rings sincere, and with those moods of most reckless daring was always mixed some sober calculation and something of a child-like faith that Heaven was answering his prayers.' It was the same 'child-like faith' possessed in full measure by Magellan. Never mind whether it stemmed from the Church of England or the Church of Rome, anyone who went to sea without it in the 16th century was impossibly handicapped.

For all his life Drake's religious faiths and beliefs were as unwavering as those of Magellan. Drake's were also touched with the reality of witchcraft and sorcery, a more or less accepted canon of 16th century Protestant faith. It was this dark side of his religious beliefs which was to play such an important part in the most critical period of his circumnavigation, in the uttermost south.

Drake's Protestant upbringing was simple and clear. But beyond the boundaries of the Devonshire farm passionate and violent disturbances were taking place. In the West Country especially, the counter-Reformation forces, led by dissident priests, were daily gathering strength as the enclosing of common land pressed more heavily on the peasantry. Drake was probably only four or five when the new Prayer Book, from which 'the idolatrous rite of the Mass' was omitted, was ordered to be used from Whit Sunday 1549. In the bloody insurrection which at once exploded in Devonshire, the supporters of the Reformation were forced to flee. Edmund Drake and his family got safely away, probably with no more than a few of their possessions, and the father was lucky enough to get a job as preacher to the seamen at the new naval establishment at Gillingham Reach on the Thames estuary: a sort of hot-gospeller to the Reformation navy.

The family lived on board an old hulk, thus most of the Drake boys—and there were twelve in all—were born in the element in which most were to die. But even in this muddy backwater, the Drakes could not escape from the turbulent religious conflicts which continued to rake the country after the death of Edward VI and the accession to the throne of Catholic Mary. Wyatt's uprising against the counter-Reformation, his successful fight with the

Queen's troops, his subsequent defeat, the public hanging of
many of his supporters, all took place almost within sound and
sight of Gillingham Reach. In the wave of persecution against all
reforming elements in the country, Edmund Drake then lost his
precarious job.

Thus one more steel thread was woven into the pattern of
Francis's fierce hatred against the Catholic faith. Francis was
lucky enough to be apprenticed to the skipper of a lowly channel
coaster, and while the tide of Catholic counter-Reformation ebbed
and flowed at home, the boy learned the elements of seamanship
and navigation in the hardest and lowest school of all.

He was still only about thirteen years old when Elizabeth
became Queen. He was to become the most spectacular star in the
dazzling firmament of her naval commanders, be knighted by her
for his Pacific corsair activities, steal the limelight in the Channel
harrassment of the Spanish Armada, and to die in her service.
Meanwhile, Edmund Drake was relieved from his condition of
fear and penury, and by the time Francis had completed his
apprenticeship, had taken holy orders and was earning a reasonable stipend as the vicar of Upchurch on the River Medway.

In 1577, at the age of thirty-two, Drake was a well-established
and well-recognised sea captain with a successful record in the
rough-and-ready school of trade-cum-piracy which was proving
so highly profitable. He was a short and stumpy figure, already
known as 'the little captain', and walked with a quick rolling gait,
typical of his type and his time, induced partly by heaving decks
and partly by a strutting well-merited conceit—after all, he was
self-improved yeoman stock with God and the Queen on his side
and gold in his pockets. He had high colour on his high cheekbones,
short curly red hair and small beady grey eyes below high arched
eyebrows, and—always carefully tended—a red goatee beard and
red curly handlebar moustache. He was known to like his comforts, such as you could expect in a tossing carrack. In his tiny
cabin he had a page standing always behind him at his solitary
meals, to replenish his silver goblet and serve his food on silver
plate. Ashore he was foppish and particular in his dress.

Drake was a deep-dyed 16th century democrat, with many of
the confused prejudices of a man who has made good from the
lower ranks in an unjust world. He favoured the lower deck, and
was loved by them in return. You can say he probably had the
lowest mutiny-risk of any of his contemporaries. But you also have
to admit that he was terribly bigoted about the upper classes, and

regarded the court set as effete and unreliable. Nor was he, any more than Magellan, a match for the professional court conspirators when it came to a showdown, as we shall see.

Since he had left that Channel coaster, things had worked out well for him. He had been lucky, and as a born opportunist had taken every advantage of every piece of good fortune. He had also shown himself brave and shrewd. His greatest bit of luck was to have as a godfather Francis Russell, the eldest son of Lord Russell, Edmund Drake's old landlord. In the complex structure of the

Tudor hierarchy, this start offered Drake an *entrée* into far higher social and political strata than his lowly birth would otherwise have allowed. Of almost equal value was his family's relationship with the Hawkins's, a worthy and respected family of Plymouth, with many successful maritime enterprises behind them. While the name of Russell was a passport to the Court, Hawkins was synonymous with West Country trading enterprise to the New World. Old William Hawkins' sons, John and William, were contemporaries of Drake and called him cousin, though the relationship was probably not as close as that. What is more important is that the Hawkins's were to Drake in his early days what the Barbosa family had been to Magellan. The Hawkins brothers were among the first to attempt to break the Portuguese and Spanish slave trade monopoly from Africa to Hispaniola, and they cheerfully brought their young cousin, when he was about twenty, into the risky but highly profitable business.

Sailing with John Hawkins among the dangerous waters of the West Indies and the Spanish Main, Drake learned to refine his instinctive talent for navigation, and to exercise his seamanship and fighting prowess under the worst conditions. With every violent reaction to their activities, a new degree of fanaticism was added to his hatred of all things Spanish. At the same time, he was able to witness at first hand the prodigious riches of the new Spanish empire, and to recognise the bitter truth of the Catholic carve-up of the world and the need to wrest forcibly some of it if England was to have any sort of a share. A glimpse of the Spanish gold fleet homeward bound out of Nombre de Dios, a glimpse of the Pacific from that tree-top, were all that Drake had needed to inflame his resolve and settle his plans: the Caribbean, thick with French and English corsairs and counter-attacking Spanish men-of-war, was becoming too hot a place for either slave-trading or piracy. So why not fit out a powerful fleet and strike at the undefended end of the Spanish route from Peru, in the Pacific, before it reached the Isthmus?

Piracy, with Royal Authority

All through the year 1576 and the early months of 1577 Drake was ashore seeking to further his plans to lead an expedition through Magellan's old strait and up the Chilean, Peruvian and Mexican coasts in search of plunder. He knew that to succeed it must have the official blessing of the crown, and also for political reasons that this could not be overtly given. The situation was further complicated by Queen Elizabeth's ever-vacillating foreign policy—a really feminine foreign policy, blowing hot and cold by turn on the Netherlands, France and Spain. She was, in 1576, doing her usual precarious tight-rope act, leaning so far in all directions in turn that only a balancing genius could have recovered, as she always did.

Behind this theatre work were the two parties, playing their own opposing policies, the hawks as we call them today, led by the Earl of Leicester and the new Secretary of State, Francis Walsingham; and the doves of peace, who were not so high-minded as all that: they believed that there would in the end be more profit in expanding trade with Spain and the Netherlands than in going to war, at least until England was stronger in allies and ships. The party for peace—or at least for not deliberately provoking Spanish retaliation—was led by Lord Burghley, the Lord High Treasurer.

Oversimplification is necessary to discern Drake's tortuous route through the corridors of power, which he was obliged to follow in order to acquire the ships and the men and the authority. It is, in any case, doubtful if at the time anyone could claim an objective enough view to judge what was going on in the maze of intrigue at court. And all we have are fragments of highly prejudiced records. Again, Drake's task was not so very different from Magellan's at the court of King Charles fifty years earlier.

The key figure, the man who claimed to have persuaded the Queen that it was good policy to let Drake loose on the soft, undefended side of Spain's American empire, was Thomas Doughty, a gentleman at court and the servant of the Queen's current favourite, Sir Christopher Hatton. Doughty was an avid conspirator, 'a man of high education, a scholar in Greek and Hebrew, a lawyer of the Temple, and of, apparently, high religious convictions, but one to whom intrigue was as the breath of his nostrils'. Doughty, who was to bring about the most critical and sinister crisis in Drake's career, is as shadowy a figure as most of his contemporaries. But he was certainly a man of great power and charm; and Drake needed the first and was highly susceptible to the second quality.

Doughty seems at least to have played a large part in bringing about the Queen's audience with Drake, during which she spoke of her 'divers injuries of the King of Spain, for which she desired to have some revenge'. Drake, recalling the occasion later, claimed that Her Majesty 'said further that I was the only man that might do this exploit and withal craved my advice therein', but that 'Her

Majesty did swear by her Crown that if any within her realm did
give the King of Spain to understand hereof (as she suspected too
well) they should lose their heads therefor'. Finally, Drake swore,
'Her Majesty gave me special commandment that of all men my
Lord Treasurer should not know of it.'

So Drake could go with the Queen's blessing and supported by
a thousand guineas of her money, but it was not an official blessing
and it was not to be made publicly, or even privately, known. It
was to be done behind the back of the Queen's most trusted and
powerful minister. The story put about was that Drake was going
to Alexandria in search of currents. Even the crews were to be told
that was their destination. But there was small likelihood that
either Burghley, or the Spanish authorities for that matter, would
believe it. The best guess would be that he was off to the Spanish
Main once more. Spain would not suspect that Drake was bound
for the *paso*, for Magellan's strait had been left out of all Spanish
reckonings for decades, and more or less forgotten.

Doughty is Suspected

He had five ships — the same number as Magellan — and being a
vain man 'neither had he omitted to make provision also for
ornament and delight' (as Francis Fletcher, 'Preacher in his
employment' and official narrator of the voyage wrote) 'carrying
for this purpose with him, expert musicians, rich furniture (all the
vessels for his table, yea, many belonging even to the Cook-room
being of pure silver), and divers shows of all sorts of curious
workmanship, whereby the civility and magnificence of his native
country might, among all nations withersoever he should come,
be the more admired'.

Like Magellan, he had his troubles from the departure on
15 November 1577, and they stemmed from the same cause, a
cabal which disputed his leadership and was intent on disruption.
Drake's Cartagena was Thomas Doughty himself, his brother
John, and a group of adventurous gentlemen volunteers and
friends who despised the Captain-General for his low birth.
Similarly, Drake was restrained from taking action against them
(although he probably had suspicions of trouble before they
embarked) because of the powerful influence Doughty wielded.

The squadron prospered during the early part of the voyage
south, replenishing supplies from captured Spanish and Portuguese ships and retaining one of them, together with its Portuguese
pilot, Nuño de Silva, whose skill and experience later proved

The *Golden Hind*

priceless. Nor was there any evidence of trouble between Drake and Doughty. This began only later, when Doughty was appointed to command the Portuguese prize and Drake's suspicions were aroused that he was pilfering the valuable cargo. When he was angrily accused of this crime, Doughty pointed to Drake's own younger brother Thomas, who was serving as an officer in the vessel. Drake promptly relieved Doughty of the command, and replaced him as captain with his brother, ordering Doughty in disgrace back to the flagship.

Drake's suspicions of Doughty's behaviour grew stronger as the squadron sailed on the long and arduous journey across the South Atlantic. Was he spreading disaffection among the men? Did he intend to seize one of the vessels and desert, as the *San Antonio* had deserted with the greater part of Magellan's stores? Or was he intending to drive the whole squadron to mutiny, then sail it back

in order to curry favour with Burghley? Suspicion fermented
rapidly in the baking heat of the tropics, with provisions running
low, and long periods of inactivity when for weeks on end the
sultry dawn revealed only the same familiar silhouettes of the
ships dipping and heaving in the rollers. The yeast of the process
was already present, in the bitter taste of class inferiority of a
Captain-General who had come up the hard way by his own
energies, by his prowess with sword and astrolabe, who had the
loyalty of the common seaman, and was not now going to see this
undermined by a sweet-talking gentleman-courtier and his
cronies.

We now reach the most curious and little-recorded period of
Drake's voyage. In the sequence of events there is an almost
uncanny similarity with Magellan's experiences. Their contrasting
reactions to them underline the gulf between the creeds of the
Catholic Portuguese mariner and the Protestant Englishman from
the north. Both expeditions suffered the inevitable increasing
hostility of the sea as they neared the strait, and the two leaders
were one another's equals in their fierce determination to defeat
their human and elemental enemies and break through into the
Pacific. The courage of both men was sublime. But where the
Catholic Magellan regarded the storms and the cold, the starvation
and disease, and the risk of shipwreck, as sent by the will of God,
to be endured in God's name and with his divine help survived,
Drake's equally firm belief, inherited from countless generations
of superstitious northern mariners, was that these sufferings were
the product of a sorcerer's magic. While the 16th century Catholic
navigator in some fearful crisis would promise great gifts to the
church if they could only be spared and called 'on God our Lord,
on his most blessed Mother, and on the Saints, that they would
intercede for us with our Lord Jesus Christ, so that he might have
mercy upon us', Drake's generation of Protestant seamen, God-
fearing though they might be, was in the grip of many of the same
dark superstitions believed by the Saxons and Vikings centuries
earlier.

'A Seditious Fellow'

Even before they struck the Brazilian coast Drake was convinced
that someone was practising the black art in order to drive them
back. The finger pointed clearly at Thomas Doughty, with his
brother John as assistant sorcerer. The events after landfall was
made confirmed all Drake's suspicions. The land was deceptively

promising, 'very pleasant, a fair bay, and a sandy ground, fit for our purpose', and they were 'very joyful'. But it disappeared with frightening suddenness, 'with such a haziness as if it had been a most deadly fog, with the palpable darkness of Egypt, that never a ship could see another', and there at once followed a storm which drove them out to sea again and scattered the ships.

Drake had no doubt who was behind all this. The natives, it was said, built great fires and then cast upon them heaps of sand, as a sacrifice to the devils. They had been stirred up by Doughty. The fury of these spirits was aroused again and again as they bore south, sometimes scattered, sometimes together, sometimes becalmed, at others concealed from one another in dense fogs, or tossed about under bare masts for days on end. They were victims of hostile supernatural powers.

Nothing was normal in this black corner of the world, neither the sea nor the land, nor the natives and wild life when they went ashore—the Patagonians were giants, the ostriches on which they fed had legs bigger than the greatest legs of mutton, and the attractive-seeming herbs which they gathered were on 'one side green and full of white specks as the belly of a toad' and turned out to be the source of poison for the arrows of the natives. Even the birds had nightmarish characteristics. At one island on which they landed, in search of water and eggs, 'every third bird could not find any room, in so much that they sought to settle themselves upon our heads and shoulders, arms, and all parts of our body they could in most strange manner, without any fear; yea they were so speedy to place themselves upon us, that one of us was glad to help another, and when no beating with poles, cudgels, swords, and daggers would keep them off from our bodies, we were driven with our hands to pull them away from another, till with pulling and killing we fainted.' To be driven from an island by the weight and agressive nature of the birds, to witness such weird sights and suffer such uncanny extremities, was enough to confirm to the most sceptical mariner that necromantic powers commanded the land and sea alike.

Drake, needing no such convincing, now had confirmation of the origin of their troubles. Doughty's brother John was reported to be boasting to the men 'that he and his brother could conjure as well as any men and that they could raise the devil and make him to meet any man in the likeness of a bear, a lion, or a man in harness'. Another officer reported that Drake 'never ceased to inveigh against him [Doughty], terming him a conjuror and a witch, and at any time when we had any foul weather he would say that Thomas Doughty was the occasioner thereof'.

These reports may have been false, and Doughty quite innocent. Or he may have been playing on the fears of the men to persuade them to turn against their Captain-General. Whether he was a power of darkness, a foolish conspirator who underrated Drake's strength and the loyalty of his men, or a victim of Drake's own fear, Thomas Doughty was risking the fate of any unfortunate found guilty of witchcraft back in some English village.

Far down the Patagonian coast, with the weather daily becoming more foul, Drake decided to get the two brothers off his flagship, the *Pelican*. It is reasonable to suppose that he wished to be separated from their black influences, and that he was fearful for the loyalty of his crew. Somebody else could have them for a time. Drake's continuing reluctance to rid himself entirely of the Doughtys is a measure of the respect he held for their power. Like Magellan with Cartagena, Drake was prepared to concede doubtful points in their favour; yet the score mounted with every gale and every report of mutinous mutterings that came to his ears.

The *Elizabeth* would have these conspirators for a while. But before he had the brothers trans-shipped, 'Master Drake himself came aboard the *Elizabeth*, and calling all the company together told them he was going to send thither a very bad couple of men, the which he did not know how to carry along with him this voyage and go through therewithal, "as namely", quote he, "Thomas Doughty who is", quote he, "a conjuror a seditious fellow, and a very bad lewd fellow . . . and his brother the younger Doughty a witch, a poisoner, and such a one as the world can judge of. I cannot tell you from whence he came, but from the devil I think".' No one was to talk to them, Drake warned. And so with these devils out of the way they could continue in greater safety, and he would 'fill the ships with gold and make the meanest boy in the fleet a gentleman'.

A Grisly Monument

It was now mid-winter and the weather was frightful. As anxious about the condition of his ships, the morale of his men, and their provisions as Magellan had been at this same place and in this season, when he sighted the narrow break in the coastline which marked the entrance to Puerto San Julian, Drake sailed over the bar and entered the long hour-glass anchorage. Every officer knew of the crisis which Magellan had faced in Puerto San Julian, and there on a promontory on the eastern shore of the bay was the sombre reminder of how it had been resolved—the stump of a fir post, with bones at its base, all that was left of the gibbet from which the quartered remains of Gaspar Quesada and Luis de Mendoza had once hung. The eerie and forbidding nature of this place, which had at length driven out Magellan in search of a more congenial harbour, was at once evident to Drake and his men. The omens could hardly be worse for a squadron already in a dangerous state of restless unease, although they tried to make light of their discovery by getting the cooper to carve memorial drinking tankards from the gibbet's old wood.

Drake went ashore to reconnoitre and establish contact with the natives. He had done this whenever he landed in Patagonia, and though the giants had at first filled them with awe, they had always found them friendly enough. And so they seemed here at first. They showed pleasure at the gifts, and wonder at the range of the English arrows when one soldier stretched his bow. But when this same soldier tried to repeat the demonstration and the string broke, other newly arrived natives took advantage of the situation and attacked. The English attempted to reply with their firearms, which were only fouling pieces for shooting game, and damp at that because it was raining. It was a nasty moment. One of the soldiers was shot through the heart, another mortally wounded, before Drake—as cool as ever in close action—managed to reprime and fire one of the guns, striking the leading Patagonian 'in the panch with hale shott, and sent his guts abroad'. His wild bellows of pain were so frightening that his fellow warriors scattered.

The Trial of Doughty

The incident was trivial in itself, but it served to confirm in Drake's superstitious mind that the squadron could expect nothing but misfortune while the baleful influence of Thomas Doughty brooded over their affairs. For nearly three months, since they had made landfall in Brazil, they had been almost continuously dogged by trouble, danger and fear. Doughty must go.

Drake began his proceedings against the elder Doughty with two obstacles to overcome, though they do not appear to have given him much trouble. Firstly, there was nothing in his commission granting him power over life and death in his squadron. Secondly, so thin was his material evidence that it was hard to know under what terms an indictment might be drawn up. In the end it was a loose one, capable of almost any interpretation: in essence, he was accused of forming a conspiracy to prevent the completion of their voyage.

The proceedings opened on 30 June, in a setting as bizarre as the occasion. Doughty's real supposed crime was one of practising witchcraft, and Drake, rather than risk infecting with Doughty's sorcery the decks of his ships, had chosen the bleakest islet in this godforsaken stretch of water for the trial. Here a tent was set up, a jury including some of Doughty's closest friends was impanelled, with Drake's second-in-command Captain John Winter as foreman, and Drake himself took the chair as judge, with another of his captains, John Thomas, as assessor.

Doughty was led in and the curious court martial began with the reading of the charge that he had discredited Drake and sought by various means to 'overthrow this voyage'. How will you be tried? Doughty was asked.

Doughty: Why, good General, let me live to come to my country. I will there be tried by Her Majesty's laws.

Drake: Nay, Thomas Doughty, I will here impanel a jury.

Doughty: Why General, I hope you will see your commission is good.

Drake: I warrant you, my commission is good enough.

Doughty: Why then, General, produce it.

Drake: My masters, this fellow is full of prating. Bind me his arms, for I will be safe of my life.

For this man—this mutinous wizard-conspirator—who had made life such a miserable anxiety for so long, to question his authority was more than Drake could tolerate, and with the

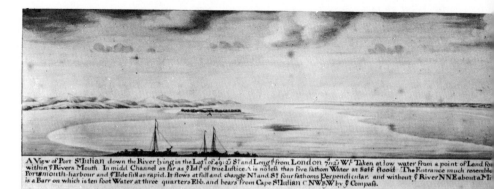

A View of Port S! Iulian down the River lying in the Lat! of 49:27 S! and Long! from London 7½:27 W! Taken at low water from a point of Land for within ɤ Rivers Mouth In midd! Channel as far as ɤ Is! ! of true Iustice. \ is no less than five fathom Water at half flood The Entrance much resemble Portsmouth-harbour and ɤ Tide full as rapid. It flows at full and change N! and S! four fathoms perpendicular. and without ɤ River N NE about a M! is a Barr on which is ten foot Water at three quarters Ebb. and bears from Cape S! Iulian C NWB.W by ɤ Compass.

prisoner bound before him, he poured forth a stream of accusation, abuse and invective. When the flow had at last ceased, Captain Thomas, in strong contrast with the tone of his superior officer, soberly read out the list of alleged crimes.

Doughty was by now reconciled to his fate. He had made his one protest and could not expect even a hearing, let alone justice according to English civil law—in this tent, on this islet, in this bitter windswept corner of a hostile land, facing the implacably hostile face of this fierce little man. He made no attempt to deny the charges. What was the use? No matter what he said, he would soon die on the block. To act with dignity and bravery was his last and only obligation.

And yet Drake still remained uneasy about executing a court favourite of such power and influence on the charges which had been made. The evidence would sound unspecific and fragmentary, and often uncorroborated, in the record he would have to present when he returned to England. Something more specific was wanted. It was provided by an officer witness, Edward Bright, who stood up and gave evidence that Doughty had said to him, in the garden of Drake's Plymouth house before they sailed, 'that the Queen Majesty and Council would be corrupted' by the massive bribe Drake had offered in exchange for the official authority to sail into Spanish Pacific waters and commit piracy. At this the accused broke in.

Doughty: What has made you lie to me, Ned Bright? You know that such familiarity has never existed between us. I may have said that if we brought home gold we should be the better welcomed, but more than that I do not remember. [There were further unrecorded exchanges before he continued]. My Lord Treasurer had a plot of the voyage.

Drake: No, that he has not.

Doughty: General, he has.

Drake: How has he?

Doughty: He had it from me.

Drake: Lo, my masters! What this fellow has done, God will know of this treachery, for her Majesty gave me special command that of all men my Lord Treasurer should not know. But now his own mouth has betrayed him.

What Drake said was all too true. It seems almost as if Doughty was anxious to accelerate the proclamation of his guilt, to have the affair over and done with, So Burghley had known all along! There was collusion between my Lord Treasurer and this mutinous fellow, this court conspirator! The reason behind Doughty's sustained campaign, through witchcraft or mutiny, to turn back the squadron before it reached the strait, was now revealed in all its stark clarity. As only a man who has been simultaneously wronged, endangered and fooled can display his wrath, so Drake released a renewed torrent of abuse and contempt. He had him now. The proceedings of this court martial would make interesting reading to the Queen. Moreover, they instantly justified the execution of the prisoner. Now the jury could safely be asked for their verdict.

The verdict was unanimous, and as soon as Drake heard the cry of 'Guilty!' from Captain John Winter, he closed the court, and leaving behind only the prisoner and his guard, called all the ships' companies down to the shore of the islet and there addressed them. It was an occasion when Drake's close understanding with the lower deck and his powers of exhortation were again to prove their value.

Drake Appeals to His Men

Consider for a moment the state of mind of these West Country seamen. They had left their families and homes in the belief that they would return rich (this had been the promise) within the year, encouraged to face the discomforts and hazards by the matchless reputation of their Captain-General. But instead of the Mediterranean, they had found themselves crossing the South Atlantic on a bearing that would take them to the hostile Brazils, and at length to the land of fire and the strait with the most evil reputation of any in the world. League by league as the squadron worked south, their fears and superstitions had been substantiated with every whispered incitement to mutiny, with every storm and becalming, with the sight on land and on sea of every weird and unfamiliar man and beast, giant whale and flying fish and vast bird. And now they knew for sure (for had not their Captain-General confirmed it?) that they had been sailing with men who were in communion with the devil. So here they were in mid-winter, as remote from the promised prizes as ever, in an uncharted area where freezing winds, squalls and snowstorms swept the bleak shore, helpless witnesses to a division in the expedition's leadership. The whole voyage seemed too ill-fated to be worth the risk of continuing.

Drake began by producing a bundle of papers brought from his cabin, holding them up for all to see, and reading from some. (He had forgotten to bring from his cabin the promised commission, he told the men, as he shuffled through the papers.) Doughty had boasted again and again on the voyage that, but for his influence, Drake would never have been granted authority to leave with his squadron. Drake appeared to demolish this claim and further discredit Doughty by reading from letters which refuted absolutely the prisoner's claim. Thus Thomas Doughty was a vain and lying knave as well as a mutineer and a witch who had conspired to prevent them from ever reaching the strait.

The little captain, who had appealed to suffering and dissident crews for support in the past, in places as dangerous and almost as remote as this anchorage, used all his powers of oratory and persuasion to bring these men unanimously behind him.

'My masters [he began] you may see whether this fellow has sought me discredit or no, and what should hereby be meant but the very overthrow of the voyage, as first by taking away of my good name, and altogether discrediting me, and then my life. So then what would you have done? You would not have found your way to your country without me. And now, my masters, consider what a great voyage we are going to make, the like of which was never made out of England, for as a result the worst of you shall become a gentleman. And if this voyage does not go forward, which I cannot see as possible while this man still lives, what a reproach it would be, not only to your country but especially to us all.'

He had said all that there was to say, with all the passion he could muster. He recognised that the next moments were decisive, that his success and with it his fortune and his fame depended on the verdict of these men. For the jury's verdict was not enough. There must be no single voice raised against him. Without their complete support, he could never bring them through the trials that he knew lay ahead in the strait. And with Doughty alive, Drake's canny, suspicious instinct told him that they would all be doomed. This was indeed the culminating critical moment in his life.

'Therefore, my masters', he concluded, 'they that think this man worthy to die let them with me hold up their hands, and they that think him not worthy to die hold down their hands.'

All joined their Captain-General in settling the fate of Thomas Doughty—or if any abstained there is no record of their name. Drake returned triumphantly to the tent and 'pronounced the

child of death'. Now, and only now, could he afford to show
magnanimity. Once more he addressed the company. 'If any man',
he said, 'could between now and the next day devise a way that
might save Doughty's life he would gladly listen to it.'

Doughty was the first with a suggestion, and who could blame
him? 'I pray you, General, seeing that it has come to this pass and
you will do away with me, take me instead to Peru and there
set me ashore.'

There is no doubt that Drake's mind had been made up since
the popular vote in his favour. But it cost him nothing to say, no,
he would not agree to transport him to Peru, but if anyone else
will be prepared to have you as his passenger and 'will warrant
me to be safe from your hands and will undertake to keep you',
then we shall see.

Doughty turned to the squadron's second-in-command. Perhaps
salvation lay there? 'Will you be so good as to undertake this for
me, Master Winter?'

Winter agreed. Yes, he would have him.

The Captain-General's response was savagely and unnecessarily
cruel by any standards at any time. All right, then, he said, this
we will do. We must nail him close under the hatches and return
home to England without completing our voyage. If this is what
you want, then so be it.

This proposition was received with a howl of dismay by a
section of the seamen. 'God forbid, good general!' they cried—
'which voice', noted Drake's detractor, John Cooke, 'was no less
attentively heard, for there needed no spur to a willing horse.'

Doughty himself recognised that there was to be no mercy, if
any had ever been considered by his angry leader, and that further
pleas were useless. From this moment, and this is beyond all
dispute, Thomas Doughty determined to act with the dignified
grace and fearlessness his upbringing as a gentleman had instilled
in him. He was given two nights and a day to set his affairs in
order and for prayer. And as a gentleman he chose as the manner
of his death to 'lose his head'.

The Execution

Doughty's comportment during his last hours was beyond all
praise, and even at the time, when chivalry and heroism were
taken as a matter of course among gentleman-adventurers, it was
noted with respect by all those who were with him. 'It was not
seen that of all this day before his death', wrote Cooke, 'that ever

he altered one jot his countenance, but kept it as staid and firm as if he had had some message to deliver to some nobleman.' And the official narrative, strongly prejudiced in Drake's favour, praised his worthy manner, which 'fully blotted out whatever stain his fault might seem to bring upon him'.

Shortly before the end, 'with a more cheerful countenance than ever he had in all his life', Doughty begged to be allowed to receive the sacrament. Drake's manner now matched that of his victim, and the last formalities were performed side by side with appropriate ceremony and courtesy, Doughty always referring to Drake as 'my good captain'. They went together to the table to receive the sacrament, and then to another table, set with a blanket for a cloth and with cutlery and silver goblets for two where they sat and took a last meal together. They dined, it seems, 'as cheerfully in sobriety as ever in their lives they had done aforetime, each cheering up the other and taking their leave by drinking to each other, as if some journey only had been in hand'.

'I am ready when it pleases you', said Doughty at the end of the meal. 'But please may I first have a few words with you in private?'

Drake assented and the two stood apart from those who had assembled about them, talking for seven or eight minutes. Drake never revealed what was said.

Then Doughty allowed himself to be led to the place of execution by the provost marshal, where he addressed the company, asking them to forgive him and pray for his soul. No other man, he continued addressing his good captain, had practised any treachery towards him, but if there were any who had caused him displeasure—and he named Thomas Cuttle, Hugh Smith and others —then he hoped that they, too, would be forgiven.

For the last time he addressed Drake, asking to embrace him. 'Farewell, good captain', he was heard to say, before he knelt with his head upon the block. The blow was struck, and at once Drake stepped forward and, raising the severed head, held it high before the company, crying 'Lo, this is the end of traitors!'

Now they could continue their voyage in good heart, with all talk of insurrection silenced and with all black powers exorcised. Whether or not Drake had the judicial powers to take life, the law had been upheld and Doughty buried. For Drake at least this islet was the Island of True Justice and Judgement, and so he named it.

In the life of Francis Drake and his most famous voyage, the

symbolic element in Thomas Doughty's death is inescapable, for
the execution at once marked the turning point in his career and
the fortunes of his squadron, which in its turn was soon to go
forward in good heart to the turning point of the American
continent—there to make a discovery as pregnant as Magellan's.
The events that followed appear to justify Drake's ruthlessness
and his judgement that Doughty's malevolent influence was a
fatal obstacle to the voyage's fortunes and progress. Almost from
the moment he triumphantly raised the severed head from the
block the expedition enjoyed mainly favourable winds. Even the
evil spirits of the strait itself seemed to be appeased by the
sacrifice.

Everyone noticed the change in the Captain-General. There was
a new hardness and seriousness in his demeanour, a tenseness in
his manner which those who had seen him in those happy-go-lucky
piratical days on the Spanish Main had never witnessed. In the
past he had had to deal with occasional unrest, but never mutiny
on the scale which had threatened. It is as if at Puerto San Julian
he awoke to the awareness of his responsibilities, for the first time
Captain-General of a powerful squadron, for the first time playing
the leading role in a devious and dangerous game of international
politics. He was no longer the joyous amateur. He was a serious
instrument in the policy of a Protestant nation against a greater,
a deeply hated, Catholic nation. Here, at Puerto San Julian, his
resolve to succeed sharpened with this new consciousness.

A Blessed Passage to the Pacific

August was a bleak and bitter month at Puerto San Julian, as
Magellan had discovered, and now that they were rested and
watered and trimmed, and, like Magellan, purged of traitorous
elements, Drake decided to press on in spite of the winter weather;
for they were now, in the words of Fletcher, 'in great hope of a
happy issue to our enterprise'. Their Portuguese prize was burned,
as she was leaky, and her crew shared out among the other three
vessels, which would need a full complement for the critical
passage of the strait. The surviving ships were the flagship *Pelican*,
120 tons, the *Elizabeth*, (John Winter), 80 tons, both carracks, and
the little 30-ton barque *Marigold*, whose master, under the
captaincy of John Thomas, was the newly-promoted Edward
Bright. On 17 August this reduced squadron departed thankfully
from this evil bay where (like Magellan) three of their company
had met violent ends.

The days that followed were in startling contrast with their benighted passage down the Brazilian and Patagonian coasts, as if they were under the spell of some magical blessing. A gentle wind carried them in three days to (the now abbreviated) Cape Virgins, and so benign was their welcome to the mouth of the strait that Drake was able to perform a celebratory ceremony at sea. Topsails were struck on the bunt in homage to Her Majesty and as a token of obedience to their sovereign and a formal gesture that she had full right to their discovery. In the flagship, Fletcher preached a sermon, and all knelt to give prayers of thanks for God's blessing—as well they might, for they were enjoying an almost unprecedented spell of mellow winter weather. Drake, of course, was gratified, but with his busy practical mind he also recognised that this was the ripe moment, for the all-important record on his return, to do honour to Doughty's patron, the rich and powerful Sir Christopher Hatton. In case the record of the trial and execution of his friend proved inadequate to appease Hatton, Drake shrewdly ordered his flagship's name to be changed from *Pelican* to *Golden Hind* in honour of Hatton, whose crest was a 'hind trippant or'.

The weather continued marvellously fair, and they had little difficulty in penetrating the narrows and out into the broad waters beyond. Thankfulness and curiosity, rather than fear of the bizarre nature of their discoveries is discernable in the narrative recording their easy passage. Off Elizabeth Island, where Pigafetta had noted the 'many sea wolves and large birds' and Magellan had held his momentous council meeting, the squadron hove to and they went ashore for the 'strange birds, which could not fly, nor yet run so fast as that they could escape us with their lives'. Their first penguins were a delightful surprise, 'a very good and wholesome victual', and they killed three thousand in one day for salting down.

Later, as they stood off to the south again and doubled Cape Froward, they met their first natives among the islands. Not one of their number had seen savages as curious as these Fuegian canoe natives; yet by contrast with the Patagonians of Puerto San Julian, they found them 'comely and harmless' people and Fletcher enjoyed making notes of their appearance and their nomadic life. Their fires were remarked on with detachment, the great jagged peaks of the mountains, even the glaciers (the first that any had seen) were observed without any hint of fear of the supernatural. In their contented frame of mind they found the foothills 'very fruitful, the grass green and natural . . . the soil agreeing to any grain which we have growing in our country'.

It must, indeed, have been a balmy Fuegian winter if their reports are to be believed. The narrows up the second arm of the strait gave them a little trouble, it is true, the unpredictable winds and currents exercising their navigational skill. But the whole length of the strait was traversed, with easy stops for water, wood, provisions and some peaceful offerings of trinkets and cloth to the natives, in seventeen days; and on 6 September 1578, Drake caught sight, above the *Golden Hind*'s unsteady bowsprit, of the Pacific Ocean. It was almost nine years since he had stood up in that tree on the Darien Cordilleras and been shown a blue fragment of the *Mar del Sur*, and had made his vow.

'*The Most Mad Seas*'

Drake had wanted to go ashore on Desolation Island, have Fletcher deliver a sermon on the tip of Cape Desire and leave there a monument, 'ingrained in metal, for a perpetual remembrance' which he had prepared. But suddenly the wind got up, increasing quickly to a gale, and there was no possibility of anchoring. Without warning, as Fletcher put it, *Mare pacificum* had become *Mare furiosum*. Had the ghost of Thomas Doughty after all returned to wreak his vengeance? Or was it only that God (as their preacher believed) 'seemed to set himself against us . . . as if he had pronounced a sentence, not to stay his hand, nor to withdraw his judgement, till he had buried our bodies, and ships also, in the bottomless depth of the raging sea?'

The helpless little vessels, stripped of all canvas but somehow remaining together, were hurled south-west by a storm which in length and intensity seems to have been outside the previous experience even of these hardened mariners. Cooke describes it as 'an extreme tempest', and Fletcher in the official narrative tells of the 'intolerable tempest' they endured. It lasted from 7 September until the end of the month, with screaming winds and snow squalls. On one night the clouds opened to reveal the moon, and the Pacific rollers suddenly flaunted their contours in its yellow light; then this light dimmed as the shadow of the earth cut across the moon's face. By a strange chance it was an eclipse they were witnessing—at a time when their sufferings were at their worst and their situation the most hazardous. The symbolic message of doom seemed all too clear, and was spelled out some terrible nights later, on 30 September, when the *Marigold* was at last swamped by a huge sea and began to go down. In the *Golden Hind* those on deck, helpless to give aid, heard the mournful cries of the barque's crew before they were all drowned.

Everyone remembered, with renewed fears, that the *Marigold*'s master had been Doughty's chief accuser; nor had the vessel's captain, John Thomas, raised a voice in protest against the execution. The powers of darkness had not been exorcised at Puerto San Julian. They had, indeed, returned with a new and terrible vigour, destroying in one great wave 'many of our dear friends'. There seemed at this time little hope for those who remained.

They were as far south as the 57th parallel before the storms died and the wind swung through 180 degrees, driving them back on a reverse course until, on 7 October, they regained the western mouth of the strait and were able to seek shelter among the islands to the north. The respite lasted for only a few hours. A squall struck the two carracks, the *Golden Hind* lost her anchor, and both were forced out into the open sea, where they separated and never saw one another again. Drake, who had already witnessed the end of his other captain, named this place The Bay of the Severing of Friends. John Winter was an old and trusty companion, and he greatly missed him. Now he was alone, with just one ship, the *Golden Hind*, to complete the great task that lay before him. The *Golden Hind*, Fletcher noted wryly in his narrative, 'if she had retained her old name . . . might now indeed be said to be a pelican alone in the wilderness'.

The squall that had separated the last two ships of the squadron turned into a new gale which again swept Drake to the south, this time on a south-easterly course parallel with the splintered coastline of Tierra del Fuego. He would have caught glimpses of the cliffs of the Grafton, Agnes, Magill and Camden groups of rocky islands that form an undisciplined outer defence line to the larger Fuegian islands beyond, and sailed close to the western shore of Santa Inés Island, which is still marked 'Inexplorado' on modern charts. Drake's seamanship was masterly; as well, it seemed to all who went through these appalling winter days with him that a divine hand guided him along the most lethal coastline in the world.

Again, they were given a brief respite, just long enough to anchor close inshore, dry out the ship, land for water and collect some herbs (probably wild celery), which 'afforded great help and refreshing to our wearied and sickly bodies'. Their records show that they were on the 55th parallel or thereabouts, and may well have been in the Canal O'Brien, a sheltered channel sometimes used today by small ships anxious to avoid doubling the Horn. The weather broke about them again two days later. It was the last storm in their Fuegian ordeal, and as if the elements were making one final effort to destroy this surviving vessel and complete the holocaust, the tempest when it struck was worse even than the one which had overwhelmed the little *Marigold*.

Drake's chaplain watched in awe, and reported it as if he was now a convert to some of the primitive pagan beliefs of his reduced flock. At one time all hope disappeared, and 'we were rather looking for immediate death than hope for any delivery . . . The winds were such as if the bowels of the earth had set all at liberty, or as if all the clouds under heaven had been called together to lay their force upon that one place. The seas . . . were rolled up from the depths, even from the base of the rocks, as if they had been a scroll of parchment . . . The impossibility of anchoring or spreading any sail, the most mad seas, the lee shores, the dangerous rocks, the contrary and most intolerable winds . . . and the inevitable perils on every side, all offered us such small likelihood of escaping destruction, that if the special providence of God himself had not supported us, we could never have endured this woeful state: as being surrounded by all the most fearful and terrible judgments. For truly it was more likely that the mountains should have been rent asunder from the top to the bottom, and cast headlong into the sea by these unnatural winds than that any of us would survive.'

This final storm had brought the *Golden Hind* almost as far south as before, and by a chance as strange as the occurrence of that eclipse, led them to a momentous discovery. For when the skies cleared and the wind died they found that they had reached the end of America. They could see through the mist and scudding clouds how the Fuegian archipelago thinned as it reached farther towards the south-east, how the many-shaped rocky islands and islets became fewer and more widely spread out, until they sighted 'the uttermost cape or headland of all these Islands'.

Ashore at Cape Horn?

Fletcher himself, a remarkably accurate observer, claimed to have gone ashore on this island to see for himself that nothing lay to the south. He was very explicit. 'Myself having landed', he wrote, 'did, with my bag, travel to the southernmost point of the

A heavy gale off Cape Horn

island, to the sea on that side where I found that island to be more southerly three parts of a degree than any of the rest of the islands. Where, having set up on end a stone of some bigness, and with such tools as I had brought with me, engraved Her Majesty's name, her kingdom, the year of Christ, and the day of the month, I returned again in reasonable time to our company.'

Drake, too, claimed to have landed on this island. After he returned home he told Sir Richard Hawkins how he had gone ashore, making his way up the cliff and to the south where he 'cast himself down upon the uttermost point, grovelling and so reached out his body over it'. When he returned to the *Golden Hind* he was able to make the claim that he had been farther south than any of them, 'yea, or as any man yet known'. It was a typical Drake boast and gesture, such as his men loved.

The storms they had suffered, and the loss of so many of their friends, seem in no way to have diminished their enthusiastic glee at their discovery of this place where 'the Atlantic Ocean and the South Sea meet in a large and free scope'. Fletcher especially, after his little patriotic ceremony, was delighted that they had got one up on the Spaniards, who had told the world, after they had found a way through the American continent, that to the south lay the land mass of *Terra Australis*. Ever since that first circumnavigation the map of the world had shown below the strait the continent of America continuing south to the pole and west across the Pacific to the coast of New Guinea in one great land mass. Now they knew the falsity of the Spanish claim, and that Magellan's strait was only the most northerly passage among many through the islands that splintered off the tip of the continent, and that 'the seas in 55 degrees and under are both one'. Magellan, in effect, had been wasting his time in those dangerous narrow waters that boasted his name.

It is pleasant to share Fletcher's and Drake's satisfaction, after all that they had endured. They had proved wrong one of the most revered Catholic navigators. For more than a hundred years reconnaissance and conquest had been a virtual Spanish and Portuguese monopoly. Now this limitless channel offered a less hazardous and less vulnerable route to the Pacific and to Spanish gold and eastern spices. For his part, Drake, as a professional corsair, recognised at once the strategic value of this easy way into the Pacific as well as the absolute necessity of keeping this knowledge from the Spanish authorities.

Whether the *Golden Hind* really anchored off the uttermost island, and it was over the dizzy headland of Cape Horn that Drake leaned on that fine day at the end of October 1578, has been disputed for nearly four hundred years. The arguments are as tortuous as the channels between those islands and the truth will never be known. After weeks of frightful weather, da Silva's navigational prowess had lost its fine edge, and even on the best days visibility is poor and the pattern of the islands confusing. Years later, the findings of the most diligent Spanish enquiry was that the *Golden Hind* had been cast east of the Horn, and even as far north as the entrance to the Beagle Channel, and then beaten her way back. The various narratives differ. That of da Silva suggests that they found islands at 57 degrees south, where none exist, which has led to theories of volcanic groups of islands that have since fallen back into the sea. On the other hand, the accounts of Fletcher in his authorised narrative, John Drake (the Captain-General's nephew and page) who was later captured by the Spaniards and closely interrogated, and Francis Drake himself, all agree that this uttermost island was 'near in 56 degrees', Cape Horn's position, and that nothing lay to its south.

It does not much matter. What was important then was that they had found that the American continent ended and that you could sail a thousand English carracks line abreast from the Atlantic to the Pacific, and thus amputate Peru and Chile from the Spanish empire. The satisfaction of this strategical and geographical discovery was enough compensation for all their sufferings and losses. Moreover, for these survivors of the Fuegian storms, there was the additional satisfaction that they, at least, had defeated the forces of darkness. Now they would sail on, with new heart and new confidence, to face a more tangible foe.

The Rewards

With her last secret now disclosed, the south treated Drake and his men leniently, releasing them with the same benign demeanour as this land of islands had welcomed them two months earlier. There were to be no more surprise ordeals by storm or tempest, nor more lee shore terrors, nor alarums from weird natives nor fabulous beasts. Naming the archipelagic tip they had discovered the *Elizabethides*, the *Golden Hind* made sail and shaped course with a fair wind back along the route down which they had been so furiously driven. On the following day they hove to off two small islands—probably the Ildefonsos, noted today for their profusion of albatross, magellanic and rockhopper penguins— where they replenished their supplies with eggs and penguin meat. Then on 1 November they shaped course north-west, for the treasure houses of Chile and Peru, still many weeks' sailing away.

Every expectation was realised, surprise was complete, their haul so great that there was scarcely room in their hold for the plundered Spanish treasure. The innocent settlers at Valparaiso gave them the traditional welcome to friends, with beating drums and proffered barrels of wine. Lying in the harbour was the ship of a great navigator, one Pedro Sarmiento de Gamboa. In her holds were 'fine Valdivia gold to the value of about 37,000 ducats' (say £600,000 in modern money); and ashore—the astonished inhabitants were by now running for the foothills—there was more food and wine than they could store, as well as the chapel plate, the first target of any raid against a Catholic port. Some Potosí silver was later taken, ships found at sea captured with their cargoes of gold, and the exciting intelligence gained from a prisoner that the richest prize in the Pacific was not far to the north, loaded with bullion for Panama, and only lightly armed. Her capture was Drake's greatest *coup* of all, and a bloodless one at that: the reality of every corsair's dream—hundreds of thousands of *pesos*-worth of gold and silver, jewels and plate—and enough, it was said, to pay for the fleet that was to break the back of the Invincible Armada eight years later.

The viceroyalties of Peru and Chile were thrown into a state of pandemonium, and the well-oiled communications system, by land and by sea, from the source of the King of Spain's wealth to Panama, was disrupted for months. Coastal towns were evacuated, and soldiers and guns which had been busily engaged in dealing with the tiresomely obstinate natives—especially the Aztecs— had to be brought back from the hinterland in mid-campaign, and deployed to defend the coast from the English invasion—for no one believed that there could be only one pirate ship at work.

As far away as Mexico the inhabitants were given arms and cities prepared themselves for siege. The Bishop of Guatemala, in an excess of war fever, offered the bells of his cathedral for melting down into guns.

The Spanish-American empire was at the very climax point of its nervous breakdown when Drake stood out to sea from the Californian coast for the last time, to complete his circumnavigation.

The Severed Friend

There is one last footnote to the story of Francis Drake at America's 'uttermost southerly point'. And it serves to underline, once again, the similarity of his experiences with those of Magellan —as if Protestant Drake was impelled, step by step, to follow the Catholic pioneer; at least until that terrible tempest had shown Drake the narrow limit of his predecessor's discovery.

Captain John Winter—Drake's old friend and sturdy companion—had not succumbed in that storm after all, any more than Mesquita and the treacherous Gomes had gone down in the *San Antonio*. From the Bay of the Severing of Friends (an unapt name, if ever there was), Winter made for the shelter of the strait, and there paused to pay lip service to a subordinate's loyalty by lighting fires to attract the attention of the Captain-General. But Winter had really had enough of it, and despaired of ever breaking clear of this evil coast into the Pacific. He decided, therefore, to go home, against the wishes of his seamen (according to one of them, who cannot be considered an unprejudiced witness), and had as comfortable a journey back in the *Elizabeth* as Gomes in the *San Antonio*: 'for it pleased God to bring us safe into our own native country, to enjoy the presence of our dear friends and kinsfolk; to whom be praise, honour, and glory, for ever and ever, *Amen*'.

John Winter, like others before and after him, had sampled the dangers and noted the nature of Tierra del Fuego; had weighed

Queen Elizabeth knighting Sir Francis Drake on board the *Golden Hind*

in the balance the chances of survival against the supposed riches of the *Mar del Sur,* and made his own quick judgement. And who can blame him, when he was so weary and cold and frightened? For history was to show that only the most ferociously brave and tenacious captains broke through from one side to the other of this continent's pivotal point.

3

Pedro Sarmiento: he left them 'to dye like dogges in their houses'

Among those sent to search for 'Francisco Draquez . . . who has entered into this sea and committed robberies and injuries' was Pedro Sarmiento de Gambóa, whose ship Drake had just taken. He was a highly successful scientific navigator in the service of King Philip of Spain. He was born 42 years earlier in Pontevedra in Galicia, the exposed north-west corner of Spain, which bred many of Iberia's hardiest mariners. Sarmiento had led a turbulent and warlike life since he had joined the army at eighteen, serving first in Europe, and from 1555 in the New World. In the following years he carried out successfully a number of exploratory voyages into the Pacific. He acquired the reputation for being a fine navigator; and also for being an awkward fellow, volatile, hasty and impetuous, and utterly unscrupulous and heartless. He got into political difficulties on a number of occasions, became involved in petty feuds and controversies, and was up before the local Inquisition several times. His surviving records also reveal a strong strain of self-righteousness in his character. In 1571 the last of the Incas—he was no more than a boy—was brought to Cuzco and publicly executed. Liberal elements in Peru considered this a cruel and injudicious act. Pedro Sarmiento had personally captured the boy and brought him to the city. For his part in the crime, many of his contemporaries said that Sarmiento would now carry the curse of ill-luck for the rest of his days. He later came to be called 'Sarmiento the unlucky': and he remains one of those rare figures in history who deserved even worse luck than they got.

The Inca curse (if such it was) struck its worst blow of all in the Magellan Strait, and among the islands of Tierra del Fuego. By the time Drake sailed through the strait the Spanish colonists of Peru and Chile had almost forgotten its existence. In the years since Camargo had made the passage, it had become increasingly difficult to persuade any captain or crew to sail south from Peru. It was said that as soon as you neared the *paso* gales sprang up that carried you under bare masts far to the south, into a land of perpetual ice, and threw every vessel onto a frozen shore. There was no escape from it. On the other hand it was also believed that the strait had only been imagined; or, again, that if it had once existed, it had since been mysteriously closed by some natural convulsion. The speculations and superstitions were even rendered into verse.

> For lack of a sure pilot, or mayhap
> For other reasons, far beyond our ken,
> The secret of this Passage, once discovered.
> For ever after hidden has remained:
> Perchance a thunderbolt from Heaven hurled,
> Perchance some island lifted from its base
> And driven by the furious wind and waves
> Blocks that mysterious entrance evermore.

The few sailors who had once beaten their way through that strait as young men were now old, and were listened to by a new generation as if they were veterans of some mythical military campaign.

Instead, the less satisfactory northern land-sea route was perfected: by sea in Pacific-built galleons and carracks from Valparaiso and Callao to Panama, and to Nombre de Dios or Puerto Bello by paved road and jungle track—'the thirty miles of misery and curses' where horses and native slaves shared their sufferings and died in tens of thousands. It was clumsy and costly, but it worked.

The arrival of Francis Drake off Valparaiso was a salutory reminder that the *paso* still existed, and that English seamen were skilled and courageous navigators as well as pirates. It was also a terrible affront, the worse for being inflicted at a time when the pride and self-esteem of the conquistadors was at its highest. Who could tell when a dozen more corsairs might follow Drake's route and end for ever the stately progression of the deep-laden carracks and caravels from Callao to Panama?

The Viceroy Prepares His Defences

On 15 February 1579 Drake cleared Callao and was lost

forever by his pursuers. Sarmiento returned to Lima. The city was already buzzing with alarming rumours of new piratical raids. There was good reason for them. As soon as the phenomenal success of Drake's raid became known—and news like this seemed to travel faster than the swiftest vessel—many more pirates must follow in the wake of the *Golden Hind*. The Viceroy decided that three measures, each of great hazard and daring, would have to be taken at once to stem this imminent onrush of further piracy. Ignorant of Drake's discovery that Atlantic and Pacific Oceans were linked by a great sea south of the American continent's end, the Viceroy decreed that, not only should Magellan's dreaded strait be braved again; it should, no less, be colonised and fortified, to prohibit the passage of pirates and enemy fleets alike.

For Spain these were days of enterprises on a scale with the most extravagant legends, of forced marches through impossible terrain and conquests against odds of a hundred to one, of great ocean voyages, and the exploitation within a few years of incalculable riches. Nothing seemed to daunt the conquistador spirit, not even the prospect of colonising an unexplored sub-Antarctic region scattered with the rotting wreckage of old ships, where life subsisted—if at all—at the most primitive level, and even high summer could bring snowstorms and shrieking gales. Again one sees the clear-cut picture forming in the minds of a dauntless and imaginative people: castellated stone forts dominating both sides of the strait, brass culverins pointing out to sea. Sheltering behind a ditch and palisade is the town, straight roads flanked by the living quarters of the soldiers, the happy colonists and their families, the church, the store houses. Beyond are the well-tilled, well-watered fields, grazing goats and sheep, lines of maturing beans and vines. It is a solid, well-found settlement, in the established tradition of Spanish colonisation.

Early in October 1579 Pedro Sarmiento was instructed to carry out a reconnaissance of the strait from east to west, as the first stage towards the realisation of this vision. He was appointed Captain-General of an expedition comprising two vessels, the *Nuestra Senora de Esperanza* and *San Francisco*, the object being, in Sarmiento's words, 'to dispel this [general dread of the navigation] once for all, and that the Strait might be explored and properly surveyed and examined throughout to ascertain the best plan for closing it and so guarding those kingdoms against an enemy . . .' The two ships, selected by the Viceroy were prepared for sea with all dispatch (too quickly as it turned out), and

Sarmiento began to search for crews. 'This was a very troublesome business', he reported, 'for as the enterprise was one of great danger and little profit, no one wished to embark on it, and many ran away and hid themselves.' Eventually, by means he does not describe, a sufficient number was found, 112 in all, half of them sailors and half soldiers.

On 10 October the Viceroy was taken from Lima to the docks at Callao and went on board the *Esperanza* to bid the expedition farewell and read aloud the instructions to the officers and men. The preamble to the instructions is worth quoting in full because in its style it is typical of the time and circumstances and the formality and solemnity of these departures, with the leading dignitaries and the senior officers in gowns and uniforms drawn up facing one another on the poop deck beneath the great silk flag, the crews massed in the well of the vessel below. There will be prayers and anointings, psalms will be sung, and the bishop will be much in evidence with his elaborately sculptured cross—and here, in Peru, it will be of silver or gold and studded with diamonds, a symbol of the wealth of the church and the King which this expedition is to safeguard. It is a solemn and splendidly colourful moment, calculated to instil reverential importance to the occasion and courage and respect in the hearts of the unwilling crews.

'For the honour and glory of God', began the Viceroy, 'and of the Virgin Mary His Mother and our Lady, whom you Captain Pedro Sarmiento are to take for Advocate and Patron of the ships and crews under your orders, for this discovery and enterprise in the Strait of Magellan, with which you have been entrusted by reason of the experience which you have acquired in your own person in undertakings and operations of war both by sea and land during the ten years that I have been in this kingdom; and that you may, by your labours and diligence, further the service of His Majesty the King our Lord and safeguard these realms so that they may not be occupied by the enemies of our Holy Catholic Faith as they would desire, thus placing in peril what has been gained . . .'

The instructions that followed were precise and detailed, calling on the expedition to take note and to chart the channels and islands, with special attention to the entrances at both ends, 'for it will be of little use to discover one if another is left for the pirates'. There were some chilling passages too, as the Viceroy read out page after page. 'I am given to understand that the weather is often bad along the coast of the Strait', he remarked ominously at one point; and continued to detail what steps should be taken when one of the two ships is shipwrecked. Then, too, if they met 'any English or other piratical ships' they were to do what they thought most appropriate without hazarding the main purpose of the expedition. 'But,' added the Viceroy, certainly with great emphasis, 'if you should encounter or receive news of the ship in which Francisco Draquez, the English Pirate, sails, who has entered into this sea and coast of the South, and committed the robberies and injuries that are known to you, you are to endeavour to take, kill or destroy him, fighting at whatever risk.'

In short, on this journey they needed every blessing and benediction the bishop could offer them from the temporary altar erected high above them on the after part of the *Esperanza*.

Sarmiento Continues Alone

In spite of all the prayers and exhortations, the first days of Sarmiento's voyage could not have been more inauspicious. The flagship began to leak right from the start; 'the haste in despatching the expedition did not give time for the overseers to see to everything', that was Sarmiento's own explanation. A week later they limped into the port of Pisco to affect repairs.

Then there was trouble of a different nature with the *San Francisco*. Sarmiento had been particularly careful to brief her captain, Juan de Villalobos, instructing him to enforce 'strict Christian and military discipline'. But Villalobos was as reluctant to face the mysteries and dangers of the *paso* as the common mariners. As early as 23 October Villalobos was showing the first signs of restlessness, and according to Sarmiento 'had clearly begun to show a desire to part company.' Only by ordering him not to lose sight of the *Esperanza* by day or night, on pain of death, was Sarmiento able to keep his second-in-command with him. Villalobos eventually made his get-away some three months later in a storm which hit them just north of the entrance to the strait. One later report told how he managed to entice some island natives on board his ship, which he sold profitably to mineowners back at Lima. Like many of the commanders who flinched away at the last moment from the terrors of Tierra del Fuego, Villalobos did rather well for himself.

But perhaps one should not be too severe on Villalobos. By the time of his desertion, they had all suffered hardships—near starvation, freezing temperatures and other dangers and privations by then associated with exploration in these southern climes—and even Sarmiento was despairing of finding the eastern entrance to the *paso* among the multitudinous channels of the Chilean archipelago. He had plenty of trouble in his own ship, too, and formal pleas to return made by his pilots nearly turned into a nasty outbreak of mutiny.

After a series of hair-raising experiences at anchorages just inside the stormy western entrance of the strait, south-east of Cape Desire, conditions improved for the flagship and her crew. From early February 1580 until they emerged, still alone, from the eastern entrance three weeks later, Sarmiento and his men experienced favourable weather and suffered few discomforts. It was as if treacherous Tierra del Fuego had laid on a special bland one-month programme of blue skies and warm breezes to deceive Pedro Sarmiento about the real character of the place and lead him to believe that this was in truth a mellow, misjudged land.

Only some of the natives were seriously hostile during the *Esperanza*'s cruise, and who can blame them? The treatment of the Fuegian and Patagonian natives by the Spaniards is beyond our comprehension today. Even if they had been only passing through the country, it would have been sensible to cultivate good relations in case they were shipwrecked. It would have cost them nothing—some patience and tolerance and a few trinkets. But Sarmiento was planning to colonise the place. Any strangers coming here for the first time would have difficulty enough to stay alive, without being harrassed by hostile locals. But, treated in a friendly fashion, the natives could offer all sorts of survival tips. The Spaniards were now experienced colonists; they were also a very practical people. It is curious indeed that they never learned how to get the best out of the natives, in Mexico, Peru, the Philippines, or in Tierra del Fuego.

Not that Spanish intentions were altogether bad. Sarmiento had been bidden to treat them well and to offer them 'scissors, combs, knives, fishhooks, coloured buttons, mirrors, bells, glass beads and other articles of that kind'. But he had also been ordered 'to take some Indians for interpreters from that place to any other which seems most convenient'. This was asking for trouble.

Sarmiento's Captives

Sarmiento met his first natives early during his passage through the strait, when he landed on Desolation Island. They were primitive canoe Indians of the Alakaluf tribe, shy, small, dirty,

'his first natives'

naked and grease-coated against the cold. They were a very debased breed, with low brows, a flat nose, full lips, small black eyes set wide apart, and a loose wrinkled skin. They survived on fish and crustaceans, and by their knowledge of fire. Without fire, made by rubbing 'stone against stone, streaked and coloured with ores of silver and gold' and with feathers as kindling, they would soon have died. Once alight, they carried their fires in crucible-like rocks wherever they went, and even into their canoes from which they fished. Here at last was the explanation of Magellan's columns of smoke, moving mysteriously like will o' the wisps through the forests and along the shores. It was a comfort to have disposed of that superstition.

But it was not these natives' first meeting with white men. When Sarmiento's party went ashore with gifts to greet them, they fled, and one sailor had to go forward alone before contact could be made. The natives at length emerged from shelter and were seen to be carrying little pennants on staves, like flags of truce, the least expected objects to be found in their hands. The material was of three kinds, blanket, Anjou cloth and coarse linen.

This was their first chilling, confirming clue that the English pirates had passed this way, and by sign language the natives indicated that 'two ships with bearded people like us, armed and dressed as we were', had sailed up the strait from the south-east. Two ships, and now the *Esperanza* was alone, armed with only two cannon and the 40 arquebuses of the soldiers! This was no place for a battle with a ruthless and well-armed enemy, but before hurrying on Sarmiento determined at least to go through the formality (as he had been ordered) of taking possession of the area, even if the English had already claimed it. So he went ashore in the afternoon, and a very flowery ceremony it was, too, with speeches by Sarmiento and the royal notary they had brought with them specially for these occasions, all properly witnessed by the ship's priest. A large wooden cross was then set up in a prominent position, just to show any who passed by that all this belonged to 'the most Catholic and very powerful Lord Don Philip II, King of Spain and the Indies and their dependencies, our Lord and natural King, whom God preserve for many years'.

One further and less glorious act has still to be played. They have not yet succeeded in catching their 'interpreters'. It is a bizarre scene to behold. The *Esperanza* is anchored close inshore in a bay now called Tuesday Bay (that was the day of the week it was later charted by John Narborough, the English geographer, on 15 November 1670), an indescribably bleak inlet fifteen miles up the strait from its entrance at Cape Desire. Behind there is a frantic landscape of jagged peaks, snow-capped in mid-summer, cut almost through, time and again, by precipitous inlets that become ravines, and then inlets again, now battered by the waves of the Pacific only a mile or two beyond. Desolation Island is nothing more than a giant breakwater chipped by age and the elements. Across the strait, the scene is no less fearsome: inlets and creeks, channels leading far up towards the tail end of the Andes, while others are cut short within a few hundred yards by cliffs; flat little islets not worth naming, perpendicular rocks thrusting out of the water, bigger islets, islands of every shape and size, the first hundred of tens of thousands of them that continue north in a navigator's nightmare for six hundred miles. The wind is blowing hard from the west, the sky is dead grey, and it is hailing.

From the *Esperanza* a skiff is rowed through seas that are choppy, although no better shelter can be found than this almost enclosed bay. Six men are rowing, under the command of the ship's pilot, Hernando Alonso, and an ensign. They bring with them the usual trinkets, and also their arms.

The natives are there, on a rocky outcrop, but they retreat suspiciously as the boat draws close inshore. The soldiers spring from the boat onto the rocks and hold up their bright trinkets as a lure. The natives are not to be tempted and retreat farther, now seriously alarmed. Dropping their combs and beads and strips of bright cloth, the six soldiers race off in pursuit. It is a hard chase, for these savages have lived all their lives on this terrain, but they are undernourished, stunted specimens, with short thin bandy legs. Two of them are soon caught, two soldiers seizing a single native. They fight furiously, giving the soldiers many blows, and they are difficult to hold because of the thick coating of seal oil on their dark naked bodies. It is like securing a struggling seal, and the smell is much worse, and there are many cries and incoherent curses. But they are dragged safely to the boat, which is quickly cast off and rowed back to the *Esperanza*.

Communications are haphazard among these western islands of Tierra del Fuego. But in a surprisingly short time the word spread that these bearded white men who come in their great boat are hostile and savage and treacherous. There is little hope of aid for any who follow Sarmiento and meet trouble in this strait. Like the Yaghans of the south and east of Tierra del Fuego, with whom

Yaghan Indians of Tierra del Fuego (about 1880)

the Alakalufs shared many characteristics, their lives were dominated by their fear of the great men of the north—the Onas of the main island of Tierra del Fuego, and the Patagonian Tehuelches who inhabited the land north of the strait.

Francisco and Juan (as Sarmiento's men merrily named their captives) were quick to point out the dangers from these giants when fires were sighted on the north shore soon after they were taken on board. They wept and indicated that the men were 'great men who fought much, and had arrows', and suggested that their captors should go ashore that night and kill them. Sarmiento did not do so at once, but a few days later, he sent another boat ashore after more live human game. The 'giants' were as cautious as the Alakalufs had been, and were altogether more formidable in their arms as well as in their appearance. The boat's crew saw them hiding in the woods with their women and their bows and arrows, and let off a few shots from their arquebuses in their direction, ceasing fire only when they heard the sound of the women lamenting. No capture was made.

It was not until they reached the entrance to the second narrows that Sarmiento added a Patagonian 'giant' to his collection. He

Mount Sarmiento seen from the north in rare mid-summer sunshine, with its cap of vapour.

saw a crowd of them on the beach and quickly landed a well-armed shore party. Again the friendly overtures with displayed trinkets were abortive, and this time there was a real fight with injuries on both sides, before the Spaniards succeeded in holding one of the natives and retreating with him amidst a hail of arrows. 'Although we offered things to the captive (which he willingly took)', wrote Sarmiento, 'he could not be re-assured. He would eat nothing all that day and night.' Later they christened him Felipe.

'A Good and Pleasant Land'

But only the natives were hostile during Sarmiento's passage of the strait. Otherwise the omens for the proposed colonisation appeared favourable. The weather remained fine and warm, and especially in an area half way along the northern shore of the *paso*, the land looked inviting enough for any successful settlement. By 12 February they had rounded Cape Froward, the turning point between the two arms of the strait, and had sailed north to a wide hospitable bay and a river which they named San Juan. 'It looks a good land and pleasant to the sight,' reported Sarmiento, and 'there were large glades and spaces of very good pasture for sheep.' Even the natives here were friendly. Timber, fresh water, rich grazing, a kindly climate—what more could they ask for?

It now seemed appropriate to discard the name of Magellan for this strait, with its disastrous connotations, and to rename it The Strait of the Mother of God. One night they had seen 'a circular, red, meteor-like flame, in the shape of a dagger, which rose and ascended in the heavens. Over a high mountain it became prolonged and appeared like a lance, turning to a crescent shape, between red and white'. To superstitious mariners, it seemed like one more sign that the notoriety of the strait, if it had ever been deserved, had now, like Sarmiento's own reputation for ill-luck, been cast away for ever.

They re-embarked, sailed out of their bay, round a rocky promontory which they named Santa Ana, and back into the strait. With favourable winds they were past Cape Virgins by 24 February. After all the terrors and sufferings of their voyage south from Callao, culminating in the treachery of the *San Francisco*, the passage through the *paso* had been a comfortable and reassuring episode. 'Praise be God our Lord, and his blessed Mother St. Mary,' wrote Sarmiento thankfully, 'who guided and directed, and suffered us to go forward without delivering our souls to the wiles of the Devil who sought our destruction, that this voyage might not have a good end.'

For good King Philip, Pedro Sarmiento had (besides one large and two small natives) a full and favourable report on the Strait of the Mother of God as a new colony of his Most Catholic Majesty, and the site of great forts to prohibit the *Mar del Sur* to the English pirates.

A Well=Defended and Prosperous Settlement

The return to Spain of Pedro Sarmiento occurred within a few weeks of the completion of Drake's circumnavigation loaded with the riches of his Callao raid. The rumours of the fitting out of new English expeditions to sail for the strait and Peru were becoming more specific. The King and the authorities of India House reacted with commendable speed. Sarmiento arrived at Badajoz to kiss the royal hand late in September 1580. Within a few weeks the decision had been made to prepare a great armada of twenty-three ships to carry colonists and their families, soldiers to man the forts, and the weapons and supplies they would need, to the strait.

Here was a logistical nightmare which must stretch the resources and experience of India House to the limit. The finding and collection of sufficient sound vessels was bad enough—and to survive an ocean passage to the stormiest seas in the world demanded complete soundness. They would have to take every-thing, absolutely everything, with them: their weapons and ammunition, their armour and uniform, provisions for the voyage and for their first months in the strait—everything from fishing tackle to spears, barrelled wine to dried figs. But this was not just a military operation. Besides the ten blacksmiths and twenty carpenters, the twenty-one masons and six stone-cutters and four trumpeters and the four hundred soldiers to man the two forts, the armada was to ship out to this new colony a contingent of friars, 43 married men and their wives, their 87 children, and 173 single men, all of whom would have to be housed and fed and provided with the agricultural equipment, the seeds and vines and plants to farm that promising land. (Felipe the Patagonian and the Fuegians Francisco and Juan would be returned to their tribes, full of talk about their presentation to King Philip and their colourful life at court.)

These frenzied and complicated preparations were favoured by the buoyant enthusiasm and single-minded certainty of the authorities and the participants that this was a desirable enterprise. Only one wise, anxious voice spoke against it, that of the Duke of Alba. 'They would be overloaded if they only took on board enough cables and anchors to weather the storms in those parts of the world,' he warned. But nobody took any notice of this ageing warrior's opinion: unlike Sarmiento, he had never even been to the strait.

The armada was also favoured by the fact that Spain and Portugal were now one nation. Not only could the expedition draw on the matchless Portuguese pilots for guidance. It could sail at will through once-hostile waters and call at any ports *en route*. This vastly simplified all the arrangements.

In all the total complement of this southern armada was over three thousand men, women and children. Not all were destined for the King's new colony. Some were to continue the journey through the strait with the new Viceroy of Chile, Don Alonso de Sotomayor, another contingent was to return to Brazil to reinforce the colonists there after the forts in the narrows had been established. The overall command was in the hands of one Diego Flores de Valdes; Pedro Sarmiento was to act as Governor and Commander-in-Chief at the strait colony, but until they arrived there he had no formal authority.

An Aristocrat Is Given Command

No one has ever satisfactorily explained why, time and again, the Spaniards—so enterprising, so undaunted and skilful in reconnaissance and empire-building—selected for the leading commands of their expeditions men who were inevitably going to quarrel. It was too much to hope that there would be no disputes between the captains and their Captain-General on long and arduous journeys, especially when things began to go wrong and scurvy and storm began to take their toll. But most of these Spanish senior officers fell out even before they embarked. Goodness knows, the Dutch and the French and the English had their difficulties (like Drake's at Puerto San Julian). But no nation could match Spain for mutinous disruption on so many maritime enterprises.

Part of the answer can be found in the lunatic tendency of Spanish authority to allow—and even encourage—political considerations to sway them in their selection of commanders.

Captains-General acquired increased status as well as riches. In France and the Netherlands and in England, court conspirators and ambitious political aspirants tended to be fat and self-indulgent stay-at-homes. The English especially relied more on good clean piratical skill, and this professionalism survived until Trafalgar. In Spain, the conquistador spirit of adventure burned in the breast of the most aged nobleman, no matter how inexperienced a mariner or soldier he might be. Seven years after the southern colonising expedition sailed for the *paso*, the Duke of Medina Sidonia, whose chief adviser on the flagship was none other than Diego Flores, was to demonstrate more publicly to the world how another incompetently led armada, the Invincible Armada, could come to rapid grief.

Diego Flores's appointment as Captain-General was a strictly political one. He was a middle-aged soldier, rather flashy, one imagines, with no maritime experience, an Asturian Knight of the Order of Santiago, and totally incompetent to handle either a stormy petrel, full of self-righteousness and conceit, like Pedro Sarmiento, or an armada of twenty-three vessels and three thousand souls destined for the uttermost south.

Pedro Sarmiento, ever more irascible and impatient as the date for the departure neared, had good reason to be dissatisfied with the preparations and the quality of the leadership. His position was anomalous. Here he was, one of the most famed and experienced navigators in the Spanish service, who had sailed the north and south Pacific, the north and south Atlantic, had charted more accurately than anyone before him the Strait of the Mother of God, and broken its dreaded spell, and now destined to govern and defend this new imperial acquisition. Yet he was fated to sail there in a capacity subordinate to an incapable novice. It was a bitter pill, and Sarmiento did not swallow it with good grace. He grumbled and complained continuously to the King throughout the hectic period of preparation. Of the ships that he inspected he found (and we may be sure with good reason) 'that many are weak and old'. Even the drawing of the charts was unsatisfactory: the rumb lines were badly ruled, and there was such a dearth of skilled draughtsmen, that as Sarmiento later wrote, 'I had to take sole charge myself, working incessantly because the time was so short.'

Yet somehow, in spite of the ineptitudes and crises, in spite of the conflict in high places, with Diego Flores conceiving 'such hatred of Sarmiento that he showed it both in words and deeds, speaking against him in public, and trying to thwart him in all his business', this ragged mixed armada with its complement of women and children, stonemasons and priests, government officials and soldiers (none of whom had been to sea in their lives and all packed below decks), embarked at San Lucar on 15 September 1581.

The timing could not have been more ill-judged. The equi-noctial period was imminent; they would arrive in Brazil too late to catch the summer season in the strait. They raised anchors and ran out of San Lucar for Cadiz nonetheless, a motley collection of vessels, mostly ill-found, hustled away, against the advice of every experienced pilot, by the officious Duke of Medina Sidonia, who liked to have a hand in everything.

Behind the sardonic, world-weary words of Pedro Sarmiento himself, the true horror of what followed can be imagined—the fear and helplessness of landsmen and their children still in a state of stunned wonderment at this new element, the struggles of pilots and helmsmen to avoid the inevitable impact against spume-lashed rocks, the cries and shrieks as vessel after vessel was torn asunder.

'Three days had not passed [ran Sarmiento's report] before . . . a furious wind sprang up from South and S.W when the fleet was between two capes, without power to navigate either to north or south. Thus it was that all began to drift towards the shore, without hope of being saved. Diego Flores ordered the cargo and anchors to be thrown overboard. Pedro Sarmiento prevented this from being done, and caused the poop of the ship to be strengthened, for great seas were coming over it, and pouring on the deck where the soldiers were stationed in much anxiety of mind, believing that they would perish . . .

'Eighteen ships reached Cadiz with much difficulty, but the *Gallega* was swallowed up, and foundered with all hands at the entrance of the bay, and in the midst of the other ships, with one blow of the sea. Four others were lost off Rota, on the Pacacho, and on the Arenas-gordas, with 800 men who were on board . . .'

Sarmiento found much of his time at Cadiz taken up with 'keeping watch in person, and through his people and servants, to prevent the crews from deserting'. Captain-General Diego Flores, already 'in a state of dismay and perturbation', was as reluctant to carry on as Cartagena or John Winter had been, and required encouragement and the offer of great rewards from King Philip before he would again venture to re-embark his repaired armada.

They sailed on 9 December 1581, calling at the Cape Verde islands, and heading thence for Rio de Janeiro. The seas were calm, the winds favourable, the weather warm. It seemed for a time as if this expedition might after all be blessed by good fortune. Then disease broke out in one packed vessel after another, the bodies of some one hundred and fifty men, women and children being cast overboard before they made landfall off the Brazilian coast and dropped anchor in Rio de Janeiro harbour on 24 March 1582, where they were to winter. Here the mysterious disease spread more rapidly than ever, many hundreds being struck down and another one hundred and fifty dying. 'It is easy to cure by those who understand it,' noted Sarmiento in deep distress, 'but if it is not understood or not cured within two or three days, there is no remedy and it becomes incurable, killing by excessive vomiting.'

For those who avoided this plague, there was not much to do in this new Portuguese colonial settlement, where sixty years earlier Magellan's men had enjoyed themselves so liberally with the native girls. What was needed to sustain the morale of the survivors was a disciplined regime with a lot of physical activity. It was not applied. Apart from the construction of a wooden prefabricated storehouse for their settlement in the strait, the men were left very much to their own devices, and that meant selling off to the locals many of the irreplaceable stores, for hard cash. Diego Flores was not unduly worried; Sarmiento became more and more exasperated but was without the authority to do anything about it.

The Calamities Multiply

Meanwhile the *teredo navalis*, which flourished in these waters, busied themselves with the hulls of the anchored vessels, all but the King's own ships which were lead-sheathed. Many of the others, including the great 500-ton *Arriola*, were in an unseaworthy condition when the armada proceeded out of Rio de Janeiro bay and headed south again. A small brigantine and its launch went down in the first high wind, and the *Arriola* began to take in water. She, too, was soon at the bottom, and not a soul was saved of the 350 on board.

A second large ship was lost before they made the little port of Don Rodrigo, where they hoped to find respite and security for a few days. But there was no hope of either. In this anchorage was a shipload of Franciscan friars, on their way to the River Plate, where they intended to convert the local natives living around the new colony to the Catholic faith. These friars had recently had a very unpleasant experience. When they first arrived at Don Rodrigo there were three ships already at anchor. They had at first been reassured to find protective company for the last leg of their journey. Instead these ships turned out to belong to English pirates, who robbed them of everything they had, then hoisted sail and disappeared from sight. Their destination, the friars reported, was the strait.

So they were already too late! If Drake's single man o'war could create such havoc and carry off such riches in one Peruvian raid, the possible depredations these three unknown ships, working together, could commit were too terrible to contemplate.

Diego Flores wanted to go back to Spain as quickly as possible. What was the use of remaining on this inhospitable coast any longer? They had, it seemed, lost the race to the strait—and you never could tell where these English pirates might be lurking. Besides, they had already lost or consumed most of their best stores. Other officers were for pressing on and completing their duties. Among them, of course, and the most vocal, was Pedro Sarmiento. The arguments went on for many days, with much to-ing and fro-ing between the vessels, and much pleading and recrimination. This divisiveness extended even to the friars. Some decided that they would prefer to remain where they were, and when threatened got ashore and disappeared into the jungle. The ever-busy Sarmiento went after them. 'His object was to entreat them, for the love of God, to return to the ships and comply with the obligations and rules of their order.' Some of them fled farther into the jungle, others he induced to return.

A compromise was eventually reached. Diego Flores decided to divide his armada, leaving at the island of Santa Catalina, for later collection, some of his best ships, three hundred soldiers, and a good part of their stores. The rest would sail south, the Captain-General in a different ship, 'a swifter and stauncher frigate', noted Sarmiento sourly, 'so as to be in greater safety, and be able to take to flight more readily if the English should be encountered'. The strength of the armada was further reduced when they reached the River Plate. Don Alonso de Sotomayor, Chile's new governor, either decided that he was weary of this bickering and could get to his destination better by his own devices, or that he did not fancy the idea of meeting the English pirates in battle, or that he had had enough of the sea. Anyway, he made his own decision to go ashore here and try to march overland, across the Pampas, over the Andes, to Chile. (He made it, but that is another, and remarkable, story of endurance.)

The armada of twenty-three vessels which had left San Lucar was now reduced to two galleons and three frigates, carrying the surviving settlers, a few soldiers, and a mere remnant of their provisions, stores and arms. With favourable winds, they made Cape Virgins by early January, mid-summer. Here at the mouth of the strait they were given the usual inhospitable reception. Both tide and wind turned against them driving them back out to sea. Twice they attempted the entry to the strait, and once succeeded in anchoring in the shelter of the cape. None of this was a surprise to Sarmiento, or any experienced navigator for that matter. Since Magellan's experiences here more than sixty years earlier it was known that the waters of the eastern end of the *paso* acted almost with the power of a piston driving in a cylinder, according to the swift predictable tides and fierce unpredictable winds.

But Diego Flores had already had enough, and on the next tide rode out of this hated place, never to return. Sarmiento followed in swift pursuit to remonstrate. Flores's reply was emphatic. 'I am going to Brazil', he answered. 'He who pleases can follow me. I shall not remain here.' Sarmiento then tried to plead to his better nature, calling on his duty to God and the King. 'Your worship has not even seen a flower in the sea,' he cried out to the flagship, 'nor passed into the South Sea; whither it may seem impossible to go. God helps the weak and resolute, when we make discoveries and pass on with His grace, to whom be many thanks. Some arrive here in one small vessel to the honour and glory of our Lord God, not being more immortal than your worship, for the more of a knight, the greater the obligation to show constancy in an arduous service.'

Diego Flores ignored this moral homily, shouted from ship to ship across the waves of a hostile ocean, and drove on northward. Sarmiento was helpless. Even the officers of his own ship favoured the retreat, however disorderly it might be. And it was a chaotic business. The vessels were scattered, rejoined and were scattered again by another gale, taking four months in all to reach Rio de Janeiro.

Diego Flores Goes Home

It was now May 1582, and the expedition was in a condition of total shambles. Of the vessels earlier left behind, one had been sunk by the English pirates who were still roaming the Brazilian coast, and the survivors had suffered terribly. Indiscipline and corruption were rife, the remaining stores were bartered for food and clothing with the local colonists, the friars and priests being as enthusiastic black marketeers as anyone. Diego Flores seemed unwilling or unable to do anything to control the tide of nihilism, and at length fled out to sea with the best ships, the pleas and imprecations of Sarmiento ringing in his ears.

Now whatever may be thought of Pedro Sarmiento, it is difficult not to be sorry for him at this time, nor to admire his doggedness. Of the many persevering and resilient navigator-colonists of this age of reconnaissance and conquest, none can surpass Sarmiento for these qualities. He must by now have recognised that he was the victim of a curse of bad luck. Yet there is no evidence, certainly in any of his writings, that he hesitated for one moment in his determination to complete his tasks; and he liked this to be recognised by his sovereign, and the world at large. 'So long as he had a plank on which to go,' he once wrote of himself in the third person, 'no one could induce him to fail in his duty to your Majesty.' And all through that terrible second winter in Brazil, after Diego Flores had sailed away back to Spain, Sarmiento struggled to bring some order out of the chaos, making shift to re-clothe those who had bartered away their clothing, applying discipline to the colonists, rationing the food and wine, and collecting together some of the scattered stores, caulking and refitting the remaining ships.

The new, revived mini-armada got away from Rio de Janeiro on 2 December 1583, well supplied with provisions for the journey and to last them for eight months after their arrival at the strait. By the end of that time it had been hoped that farming would have got under way and reinforcements would have arrived. They took on board vegetables and seeds, livestock including sheep and goats and calves, young fruit trees and vines.

Their only serious lack was of friars. According to Sarmiento, it appears that the contingent of Franciscan friars had proved troublesome from the beginning. We have already seen that they were prone to disappearing the moment shore leave was granted, no

matter how inhospitable the hinterland might be. The expedition
had lost a lot of them by the time of the final embarkation
from Rio de Janeiro. Even when Diego Flores was Captain-
General many had disappeared, some to become colonists, others
to be eaten by cannibals, and still more went back to Spain with
the Captain-General. On the way south from Rio de Janeiro,
Sarmiento had constant trouble with the remainder. They
managed to get ashore on the smallest pretext, and then it was
very difficult to round them up again. Nor was their behaviour
exemplary. One, Friar Bartolomé, was found selling 'many pieces
of cloth that had been brought for habits, as well as damask for
chausibles', ornaments, complete altars and silver chalices. Others
committed acts which 'for the honour of the habit of the blessed
and seraphic St. Francis it is not decent to mention in public'.
In the end their numbers were reduced to two friars, named
Antonio Rodriguez and Geronimo Portugues, quite insufficient
for the three small and two larger vessels which comprised the
armada and their five hundred or so souls, for the taking of
confessions and the saying of mass and the numerous other
religious duties.

Sailing with fair winds and fine weather, Sarmiento sighted the
low white cliff of Cape Virgins on 1 February 1584. It was the
fourth time that he had rounded this cape in four years. It held no
terrors for him, nor did the strait beyond. Granted that they had
been blown out to sea last time with the faint-hearted Diego
Flores, but Sarmiento knew that they could have gained entry
then if they had only been more resolute. Now he believed that
he had loyal officers, and he had the equipment and the men to
set up the colony and the forts, belatedly and on a much smaller
scale than had been planned, but they would be established
nonetheless.

The strait was in a puckish humour, deceiving them first with
fine weather and favourable tides and winds, so that the five vessels
were drawn easily through the first narrows, and were well towards
the second narrows before the tide turned and they hove to and
anchored. Then in turn the strait demonstrated all the evil sides
of its character. The wind began to rise with the turning of the
tide, and a large boat which one of the frigates had been towing
was smashed against its counter before it could be brought on
board, and was broken to pieces within a few seconds. 'Then the
wind came down from the snowy mountains with great force,'
wrote Sarmiento of this sudden change in their fortunes, and one

by one the cables parted as the ships were thrown about. Already, on their first day here, the Duke of Alba's prophecy that they would have room on board for only cables and anchors, and still they would not be enough, was coming true. In another two days there was hardly a cable left to each ship.

This strait seemed to be able to eject with disdainful ease any number of ships at a time, tossing them out like cannon shot from the barrel into the ocean beyond the muzzle mouth. For those who had never been to these parts before, it seemed that Tierra del Fuego was reasserting its old and terrible reputation. Even the fires which gave it its name were at their wildest. Groups of natives had come to the shore to witness their arrival, and now the smoke from their fires gathered in a great cloud and was swept across the sea, obscuring both land and water and adding greatly to their confusion and danger. Although they had experienced many strange and frightening events together, to the women and children among the colonists this was the most nightmarish experience they had endured since leaving Spain.

Sarmiento managed to reform his ships just inside the entrance to the strait, on the north shore a mile or two east of Cape Virgins. Even he had to admit to himself that they could not hope, for the present, to penetrate more deeply, and that 'the people were becoming sad and despondent'. They were some distance from their intended destination on the first narrows where their cannon could destroy any intrepid pirates, but it would have to do. So they anchored with their last cables, and in a brief lull the boats were hoisted out and they began to ship ashore soldiers, colonists, building materials, arms and stores.

The Settlement Is Established

It is a moving moment when Sarmiento first steps ashore to found this new outpost of the Spanish empire, and, knowing what was in store for him, it is impossible not to be affected by his faith and confidence. Here they are, on the most south-easterly point of the Patagonian pampas, an undulating windswept plain of coarse grass and scrubby shrubs, a month's sailing from the nearest settlement. Here nomadic tribes, who have already shown themselves hostile, only just manage to survive. And yet this leader radiates euphoria. The water is sweet, the vegetation favourable. He writes as if there could be no better place in the world to build a town 'Sarmiento carried a great cross on his shoulder, with which, in the name of the most Holy Trinity, he jumped on land, and the others after him,' with eight arquebusiers just in case. With the cross on high they went to their knees and recited a *Te Deum laudamus*. Then, Sarmiento tells us, he took possession in the name of the crowns of Castile and Leon, and made a great heap of stones with his hands, planting the cross as they all sung the hymn of *Crux Vexilla Regis*. There were more speeches, the raising of more flags—all of which gave them a much-needed sense of security in this alien place.

Three hundred had landed, together with a small part of their supplies, when on that first night another gale blew up, driving the ships out to sea. They did not return the following day, nor the next, and Sarmiento was certain that they 'had deserted and gone to Brazil'. He was very philosophical, as always. They had provisions for four days, a few tents, and some of their agricultural supplies, and winter was coming on. Yet he appeared to be quite undaunted by this new and seemingly catastrophic turn of events. There was now no question of fortifying the strait, because none of the cannon and powder had been landed, but the settlement would be built, and it would flourish, with God's blessing. This was the tone of the message he delivered to his colonists when he called them together the next morning; and 'all answered that they were ready to obey and to follow to the end of the world as they had no other father': which was all too true.

As a site for their settlement Sarmiento chose a shallow valley just inland, fed by five springs, which he named the Purification of our Lady after the day on which they had arrived in this land, and the city they were to build he named Nombre de Jesus. The site for the church was traced out, the walls to be built of local stone, the roof of sailcloth, then the town square, with 'streets and houses in squares, building huts made of poles, earth and grass'. While some busied themselves erecting these half-huts, half-tents, others took their spades and worked the unpromising land outside the town, hopefully sowing beans and other vegetables, fruit trees and the vines they had brought with them.

Suddenly, and to everyone's surprise, their ships reappeared round the cape. Nothing was predictable about this armada, and certainly not the loyalty of the crews. At one moment Sarmiento was certain that they had defected, the next here they were again, struggling to gain an anchorage in the inadequate shelter of the little bay. Almost before the colonists could offer prayers of thankfulness in the new canvas church of Nombre de Jesus, it became evident that only a narrow majority among the ships' officers had been in favour of returning, that the ranks were still strongly divided, and that a major mutiny might break out at any time.

By now uncertain of the loyalty of any one, and harrassed by the need to keep his colonists happy and busy on the one hand, and disembark as many of his stores as quickly as he could before his ships were swept away again by wind and current, or simply made off of their own accord, Sarmiento struggled to keep control over events. First he ordered the supplies from his three smaller vessels to be transhipped into his flagship the *Trinidad* and the *Maria*, with the intention of running them ashore at high tide and beaching them. But the captains of the three frigates showed a marked reluctance to relinquish any of their supplies, for the excellent reason that they needed them for the long voyage back to Brazil. Sure enough, a few nights later, 'without any need from wind or current' they sailed away, and this time for good. Sarmiento might have been almost relieved to see their sterns for he must by now have been so wearied of all defectors and insurrectionists.

Certainly the loss of his three ships was a lesser blow than the accident to his flagship, still carrying the greater part of their supplies and all the cannon. Through a mixture of incompetence and bad luck and the vicious qualities of the weather, the *Trinidad*'s beaching operation was clumsily carried out, and the flagship was so badly beaten about on the rocks in a suddenly rising wind that she began to break up. The crew were safely landed through the surf, and Sarmiento, leaving behind at Nombre de Jesus only a skeleton contingent of guards, ordered to the shore every man, woman and child to hold the ship's cables and prevent her half-broken hull from being taken off by the tide and current.

Sacks were made from the ship's sails, and the surviving flour brought ashore in them, together with some salt meat, some grain and barrels of wine. It was a frantic time for everybody, and they were driven on by the knowledge that in six months' time a handful of flour might save one of them from starvation, that one plank of wood might complete the wall of a hut and save the inhabitants from freezing to death. When the ship reached its final stage of demolition by the waves, every bolt and sail, the smallest length of wire and sliver of timber took on a new scale of value and was retrieved for later use.

Then in the midst of all these troubles, the natives attacked. They had kept at a discreet distance up to now, and their proximity was evidenced only by the unnerving columns of smoke that appeared and disappeared about their site, and could even be seen on clear days across the water of the strait in Tierra del Fuego. No doubt the attack was timed to catch the new colonists at a most vulnerable moment, and was preceded by a shower of arrows. One of the guards was wounded, but the rest held their ground and drove off the natives with their arquebuses.

Only a few of the Spaniards had seen these Patagonians before at close quarters, and a very fearsome and intimidating lot they were. Even Sarmiento, one of the few white men who had engaged the 'giants' in combat, knew almost nothing about them, though he was soon to pay heavily for the way he had treated them so roughly last time he was here and had captured 'Felipe'. Sarmiento was content to describe them as 'the race of great people'. Other travellers observed them more closely, before they were wiped out by the Argentinian military and gauchos in the nineteenth century. Seventy five years after Sarmiento's time, an English Captain Wood wrote of them:

'As far as I could observe by these People, they have no Houses nor Habitation, but wander from Place to Place to seek their Food, which consists mostly in Seals and Limpids, with some Fowls and Deer. Having spent the Day in the said Manner, they return at Night, and put themselves behind some Bush, where they may make a small Fire, I suppose on purpose, because they should not be discovered afar off by Night; and they lie upon the cold Earth, without any other Canopy but Heaven. As for the Apparel of these Savages, they have no other but Mantles made of Deer-Skins (guanaco skins) sewed together, wherein they wrap themselves up, and need no other Covering, they being by Nature very hardy, and of an Olive Complexion, as all the *Americans* are, in Conformity to most of whom, these also paint their Faces and Bodies with many Colours.'

They had changed little by Darwin's time (1834), when he wrote of them: 'Their height appears greater than it really is, from their large guanaco mantles, their long flowing hair, and general figure: on an average their height is about six feet ... although they are certainly the tallest race which we anywhere saw. In feature they strikingly resemble the more northern Indians ... but they have a wilder and more formidable appearance, and one man was ringed and dotted with white ... They spend the greater part of the year here (Cape Gregory area); but in summer they hunt along the foot of the Cordillera.'

By the end of February 1584 Nombre de Jesus, if not the city of which Sarmiento and King Philip had dreamed, at least gave the appearance of being a well-found settlement. There was evidence of the colonists' industry in the neatly laid-out dwellings made of stone, cut by the masons, and wood from the *Trinidad*'s wreck; there was a small hospital, a well-guarded store house, and much work had gone into the church. A domestic village touch was lent to the scene by the artificial pond 'where the settlers and their wives could make their arrangements and remain contented', and by the little gardens created about the source of the springs. Nombre de Jesus was defended by a deep ditch with a rampart, on which day and night guard was kept, and four sakers (small pieces of artillery) were mounted as support fire.

It was remarkable what four weeks of intensive work could accomplish. Outside the defence line, something like fields had been scratched from the hard dry soil and thanks to intensive watering the plants were still alive. Backs were bent over the rows of newly planted vines. These peasants might have been working among the terraces of a Spanish hillside for a lifetime, instead of this coarse land of another continent for only a week or two. And Nombre de Jesus, for all the haste of its creation and the unusual nature of its building material, bore a striking similarity to some Castilian village.

The Long March West

Sarmiento was pleased with what he saw, but he was not yet satisfied that he had created a real colony. He saw Nombre de Jesus as a military outpost, blocking the entrance to the Spanish strait. He remembered those sunlit fields of three summers before, thick with orchids and gentians and vetches and giant daisies, the cool streams, the sedges in the marshes about the San Juan river mouth. There the antarctic beech flourished, a tough useful wood, and there were green parrakeets darting among its branches. The hunting was good, too, as well as the fishing. It might rain heavily and snow in the winter, but it was like a tropical paradise by contrast with the windswept, dry scrubland of Cape Virgins. Even the natives had been friendly at Santa Ana. Although it was dangerously late in the year, Sarmiento was determined to take a nucleus force there before winter set in, and by next summer— perhaps there would be reinforcements by then—create there a real city, worthy of this great new Spanish land. He decided to lead a military march overland, and their only ship, the *Maria*, would sail there to prepare the ground for them.

Persevere in your work and good fellowship, Sarmiento told the citizens of Nombre de Jesus in the course of a farewell address, and be true to your God and your King. Then there were vespers and masses, in the church 'with all the solemnity that was possible', before Sarmiento marched out at the head of one hundred of his best soldiers, and one of the friars, leaving Nombre de Jesus in the charge of two captains. Some tears were shed. I will be back soon, Sarmiento promised. And when I do, some of you married people may wish to join us in this new venture.

Every sign seemed to point to the west as the right direction. There the land was greener and more hospitable. Even the livestock seemed to scent this. 'The sheep they had landed, and the dogs, set out also, and it was not possible to induce them to return to the settlement.' Soon the men found that they could supplement their rations with eggs and berries and small fruit. And yet in spite of the favourable signs, it is puzzling that Sarmiento chose to march his men to this Eden of Santa Ana. It was 140 miles as the crow flies, and quite twice this distance along the indented north shore of the strait. He had sailed along it three years earlier and had noted the deep broad reaches and the hinterland that was stark for many miles before the mellower mid-strait region was reached. Why, therefore, risk the lives of so many of his irreplaceable soldiers on this testing route march, especially when the *Maria*, which had sailed three days earlier and not returned, was evidently again proving that the passage by sea held no special terrors?

Many of the soldiers must have asked the same question when, after only a few days, they began to suffer in turn from thirst and hunger and danger from the natives. The streams which could be seen running down from the inland hills, buried themselves and ran underground into the sea; while some of the berries were sweet, others poisoned them. Worst of all was the cunning of the natives. At first there was no sign of them, then the soldiers saw ambushes being prepared ahead. After a while the natives, all of the tall Patagonian Tehuelche tribe, appeared in great numbers, armed with bows and arrows and naked except for guanaco wool twists bound into their hair to give an added impression of height, and beads round their necks and wrists. Their greeting was as unexpected as their appearance. 'Jesus, Maria, Cross, Captain!' cried the chieftain, just like any over-enthusiastic new convert. 'Captain Ho! Ho! Ho!' he continued, raising his hands to heaven.

Above: Port Famine from Fort Bulnes, Mount Tarn in the distance.
Below: Looking down the Magellan Strait from Santa Ana Point towards Canal Magdalena and the mountains of Darwin Island.

The message of the white man's God seemed to have travelled far and made a lasting impression since Sarmiento's religious shore ceremonies of 1580.

These Patagonian warriors gave other impressions of friendship and even warned them that ahead lay tribes in wait who would be more hostile. Come back to our encampment, indicated the chieftain. Instead Sarmiento contented himself with embracing the tall, naked, painted body and offering his warriors the customary beads and combs and mirrors, which gave the usual pleasure. The chieftain replied by swallowing one of his long arrows, until the feathers were hidden in his mouth. 'Then he gave himself a good blow on the chest,' recounted Sarmiento, 'which sounded like the stroke of a timbrel, and immediately after he gave a great leap into the air, with a terrible shout.'

Who could tell whether this was a joyous challenge to battle or a celebratory feat of entertainment? They were soon to learn. The Spanish party had not continued beyond a mile in their march when the natives suddenly appeared again, fiercely attacking the rear of the column with arrows. Sarmiento, in the vanguard, hastened back, attempting to bring order to the confused defenders. One of the soldiers was dead, another ten seriously injured, and the return fire of the arquebuses was wild. Sarmiento fought his way to the chieftain with his sword and shield, felling him with one blow. The fire of the arquebuses was beginning to tell, and the natives started to flee, many of them falling wounded and leaving their chieftain dead on the field of battle.

It was a notable Spanish victory. But this combat close to the shores of the strait marked the turning point in the fortunes of the overland party, and their first casualty the beginning of a long death march. Just inside the second narrows of the strait the northern coastline fragments itself into many deep bays and peninsulas, cut from the bleakest brown land in all southern Patagonia. In summer the temperature is not often below forty degrees, but the wind from the west and north-west and from the snow-clad rump end of the Andes is incessant and makes the temperature feel far below the thermometer reading. It whips up the waters of the bays and the innumerable brackish lakes, and blows the spume into white piles which cling round the stony shorelines before breaking up against the bushes. There is nothing for man here, neither food, shelter nor water—just a few shoots of wild celery and some tasteless berries. For a time they carried the wounded on their backs, but even the fittest soldiers soon became too weak for this, and one by one the wounded were put down and crawled off into the bush to die.

Sarmiento was reduced to killing some of their livestock, although it hurt him to do so. The goat meat was given only to the weakest, its skin divided among those who had worn out their shoes. He calculated that they had now travelled seventy leagues to cover a distance of thirty by water, and the men were falling by the wayside at such a rate that the death penalty was imposed on anyone who failed to report a straggler.

On the pebbly beaches just south of Punta Carreras the survivors reached the lowest point in their spirits and physical weakness. Who can imagine my feelings, asked Sarmiento, 'seeing his comrades whom he loved as himself, quite despondent and without confidence, and hearing the groans and miseries of the sick, wounded and tired? He gave each one a mouthful of meat and some roots, and spoke to them to encourage them, pointing to a cape, not three quarters of a league distant, and promising that, with the favour of God, before they reached it, which was called Santa Ana, they would find the ship.'

The New City

The *Maria* had arrived safely and her captain had sent a boat to search the coast for the overdue party, so that relief came for them the next day with wine and biscuits to give them strength for the final stage of their journey.

They had reached at last the wide hospitable bay where the River San Juan comes down to the strait, 'the good land pleasant to the sight' which had so impressed him on his earlier reconnaissance. Here there were almost tame deer in the woods, fruit and berries in unlimited quantities, timber for building and burning, while fish abounded in the bay. It appeared on this day in late summer, no less than before, to be a pastoral paradise for man and his livestock.

Above the bay, to the south-west and west, rose the heavily forested slopes of Mount Tarn, protecting them from the worst of the winter winds, and the scenic outlook was grand beyond description. The strait had narrowed to a width of seven miles, and the peaks of Dawson Island opposite rose up abruptly from the wooded shoreline. Due south the landscape became still more ragged and spectacular. In clear weather it was possible to make out the narrow mouth of the channel down which Serrano had

Port Famine

sailed the little *Concepción* on his abortive reconnaissance sixty-three
years ago; and in the far distance the curious twin-peaked white
mountain which one day would carry Sarmiento's name.

Pedro Sarmiento's resolution and the strength and resilience of
his men is remarkable. Only the worst sufferers from the long
march were allowed a few days aboard the *Maria* to recuperate.
The remainder were soon hard at work, applying the same skill
and energy which had created Nombre de Jesus out of the barren
pampas in a few weeks to the building of their new town, Don

Felipe. In less than two months 'the church was built of very fine timber, high and strong, the chapel of the high altar being of stone, which all the people brought on their backs'; the royal store house, three hundred feet long 'with thick and lofty forts of oak and beech timber, daubed with clay and roofed with straw'; a hospital and monastery; clay-daubed thatch-roofed wooden houses set out in squares, these were all completed and laid out round the geometrically arranged town square. A palisade surrounded the new town, and four cannon from the *Maria* were brought ashore and mounted to defend the anchorage.

This fulfilment of all Sarmiento's dreams and plans gave him immense satisfaction, and we can imagine him looking down on his new settlement from the raised outcrops of rocks leading to point Santa Ana feeling that at last he was near to completing his duties to his God and King. A fine seed crop was already breaking through the newly-tilled soil—cauliflower and lettuce, radishes, turnips and wheat. This place and its people, he felt, must now certainly flourish. Soon he would return to Nombre de Jesus to reassure himself that it, too, was happy and prosperous. Then he would set about the task of building the fort in the narrows to close this strait once and for all to heretics and pirates. Those were his plans.

A mutiny at this time was therefore a most unexpected and unwelcome event. Such marvellous success and promise for the future should have at last brought contentment to his people. But not a bit of it. There were some, it seemed, who were less optimistic than Sarmiento about their future here, especially when winter arrived—and the first winter chill and first winter gales had already made themselves felt in Don Felipe. The unsettling influence of the strait was stirring doubts in the minds of many of these men—or was it that they could not believe that Sarmiento's reputation for bad luck had finally been broken? Anyway, they had decided not to risk a winter here, and that Sarmiento would first have to be killed, along with any who supported him, before they sailed away in the *Maria* back to warm, lush familiar Rio de Janeiro.

Sarmiento was too quick for them. He got wind of their plans and arrested Antonio Rodriquez, the ringleader, and the other conspirators. Justice was applied harshly and quickly. Rodriquez was executed and his head stuck on a pike as a discouragement to further insurrection.

Mount Sarmiento

Sarmiento Sails Away

We now face an insoluble mystery. Until this moment, with the
first snows of the winter of 1584 settling on the thatched roofs of
Don Felipe, there can be no doubt of Sarmiento's loyalty to the
colonists, the soldiers and sailors under his command, and of his
determination to complete his tasks in the strait. He has already
given nearly four years of his life to the great cause of colonising
and fortifying the *paso*, and it is now so near to a successful
conclusion. In four months two fortified towns have sprung up
on the strait's shores, and it looks as if both will soon be self-
subsisting. The natives have been shown who is master. The forts
in the narrows will make Peru safe against any further attack
from the sea.

And yet, on 25 May Sarmiento embarked on the *Maria* with
thirty men and, just as the frustrated mutineers had plotted to do,
sailed away to Brazil never to return. It was a moonlit night when

he raised anchor and hoisted sail, and as he crept out of the bay by a strange chance there occurred an eclipse. Just as an earlier eclipse at a critical time had seemed to be a supernatural ill-omen to Drake's men, so this eclipse spelled out the eventual fate of these colonists, and conveniently obscured Sarmiento's fleeing ship from any who might have been watching.

Sailing with a following wind, Sarmiento anchored off Nombre de Jesus on the same evening, intending, he has written, 'to give orders for embarkation of things which were to be taken to the city of Don Felipe'. That night, it seems, a gale sprang up, snapping the *Maria*'s single cable and driving her out to sea. It was another odd coincidence.

The storm did not abate for upwards of twenty days, Sarmiento reported, as if to justify his abandonment of his people. We have already witnessed the strait's capacity to toss unwanted caravels and galleons out into the Atlantic. There is no reason to disbelieve the truth of Sarmiento's report of the power and extent of that gale, although it is almost unprecedented in these parts for a westerly gale not to blow itself out in under a week. Perhaps he did, indeed, intend to return to Don Felipe and Nombre de Jesus. And yet one is left with the undeniable fact that Pedro Sarmiento did not succeed in bringing the *Maria* back inside the strait, a failure in seamanship and determination for which he had so bitterly condemned Diego Flores. And Diego Flores had just given up; he had not left two new settlements and some four hundred men, women and children stranded with insufficient supplies to face the Southern winter.

It is a puzzle to know whether to condemn Sarmiento for yielding to a sudden urge for self-survival, or whether to blame those fierce yet whimsical powers of the Fuegian islands to rid themselves arbitrarily of anyone who invaded their shores. Certainly, if Sarmiento had really been storm-wracked under bare masts for all those days off Cape Virgins, he had time to modify his favourable judgement of the *paso*'s climate and to realise that those who had been left behind were in for a hard winter.

Sarmiento reached Rio de Janeiro early in July 1584. Here, with the support of the governor, he arranged for a supply of flour to be sent at once to the colonists. There was little chance of its arriving safely, in the depths of winter, and in fact the vessel did not get far. More ships were despatched when summer came round again. But these efforts, too, seemed doomed to failure. One ship was wrecked almost as soon as it put to sea. A second was got away from Rio de Janeiro on 13 January 1585 'with food and other stores, as well as with munitions . . . and some sheep for breeding'. It reached the 33rd parallel before it 'encountered a gale from the west and south-west, which was so furious that it was judged to be the worst and most terrible we had seen'. Another attempt to send succour to the colonists was foiled by mutiny. And so it went on.

A second southern winter had passed without a single supply ship reaching the strait, and Sarmiento now felt that he had done all that he could for his people, and that it was time to return to Spain and report to his King. Yet one more fateful knot has still to be tied in the confused strand of Sarmiento's career as an explorer-colonist. On the way home his ship fell in with three English men-o'-war, under the command of the notorious Sir Richard Grenville. The Spaniards never had a chance. After a few rounds of cannon and musket fire, Sarmiento surrendered and was brought on board the English flagship as a prisoner.

Here was a fine prize for the English to pick up in the wastes of the Atlantic! And, again, what an extraordinary coincidence! Word had filtered back to England of Spanish efforts to fortify the strait, and now they had the man who could tell them all. The timing of Grenville's arrival at Plymouth with Sarmiento as prisoner was equally fortuitous. Another feared captain, an archetypal pirate in the eyes of the Spanish, had fitted out five ships to sail through the strait in an effort to repeat Drake's Peruvian raid on a greater scale. Only the news of possible Spanish fortification had deterred him. Now that they had the governor of these settlements himself in their hands, with the information that the forts had not yet been built, Thomas Cavendish sailed away, full of confidence, to play out the final and savagely ironical act in the story of Sarmiento's colony.

The Starving Colonists

There is only one eyewitness's report on what happened to Sarmiento's colonists and soldiers after they were abandoned. It is short and lacking in detail. And perhaps that is as well, for it is a melancholy tale.

When winter closed about the two towns, there were probably two hundred and fifty men, women and children, nearly all colonists, at Nombre de Jesus, and rather fewer than one hundred soldiers at Don Felipe. Although the climate is more temperate at Cape Virgins, the colonists suffered worst in their unsheltered situation when the gales tore across the pampas. Their crops had not yet matured, and in any case were almost all doomed to destruction during the winter months. Cold, hungry and abandoned, they determined to make their way on foot along the route Sarmiento had reconnoitred. They would have heard Sarmiento describe the delights of the pasture and woodland of that westerly region, and this straggling party, with some of their possessions on their backs, were buoyed up with the confident hope that there they would soon find warmth, shelter and food.

Nothing has been told of this march, but if Sarmiento's young disciplined soldiers suffered so acutely under a stern leader in summer weather, it must have been a gruelling experience, and many certainly died on the way. Nor were they welcome when they at last rounded Santa Ana point, and saw before them the rows of new houses, the big church and storehouse, all lying under a mantle of heavy snow. It was bitterly cold—much colder than at Nombre de Jesus—and the soldiers were as short of food as they were.

There is nothing to match the bleakness of a winter in the strait. Farther south, and along the Beagle Channel, there is a dry crispness in the air, and although it often snows, there are clear skies, too, which give a healthful feel to the climate. But here, mid-way along the strait, the sky can be grey for weeks on end, mists and low cloud obscure the mountains, and there are days when driving, freezing rain, sleet and snow follow one another in dreary succession. Here, even with shelter, warmth and a full stomach, the will to live is reduced to a low level.

An officer named Andres de Viedma had assumed command at Don Felipe. He knew that his unhappy party could not last out the winter. They were overcrowded in their inadequate wooden houses—they were really no better than huts—and the rations would have to be reduced month by month until they could no longer support life. The only solution lay in reducing their numbers, and to accomplish this Viedma fell back on the desperate decision to despatch a number of his soldiers north along the coast to search for a sign of any relief ships. They were 'to pick up shell-fish, and get food in the best way they could'. Although these were described as 'look out' orders, they were really orders to commit mass suicide. None of them was seen alive again.

Of those who remained behind, enough survived the winter to spend the summer months felling timber and building two boats in which they hoped to escape, although there was not a sailor left among them. By now they knew the truth of this land, and they had learned that the soil was as untrustworthy as the climate. The seed that had been planted and grown at first with such promise had died. The soil was too poor, and the temperature too uniformly low to sustain life. The one witness says that they had no provisions. We must presume that they were living off the land, from deer or rabbits, berries, wild celery and fish, like the natives but without their endurance and experience. They knew they would have to leave or die.

Somehow the two boats were completed and launched, and all who were left alive, including five women, sailed off east up the strait. Their voyage lasted a mere six leagues. These men had never navigated before and one of the boats was smashed up on some rocks. Viedma left thirty-one men and the five women on the shore, and himself sailed back to Don Felipe with the twenty-two more. For the whole of another Fuegian winter, these stranded men and women fended for themselves along that terrible coast. There is the brief record that 'they remained on the beach . . . and wandered about all the winter, picking up shell-fish, at night taking refuge in huts they made, four to each'. With the arrival of spring they staggered back into Don Felipe and rejoined Viedma. Of the four hundred or so colonists and soldiers brought here by Sarmiento two years before, only fifteen men and three women and Viedma were still alive.

There was no purpose in remaining in this ghost town, and by now they must have hated it even more than the interminable beech forests and the stony shoreline. So they began to walk again. There was nothing else left to do. They walked in a dazed condition of misery, scarcely conscious of being alive, along the coast, as if instinctively drawn towards their own distant country, or nearer to the sight of a ship's sail which they now knew would never come. Like the streets of Don Felipe, the shore was scattered with the rotting corpses of soldiers and colonists. For many days, led by Viedma, they picked their way among them, keeping themselves alive on crustaceans and berries, huddling together in crevices or any shelter they could find at night.

Cavendish Sails Through the Paso

Thomas Cavendish, the third European to circumnavigate the world, probably more closely epitomises the romantic Victorian conception of the swashbuckling, fearless Elizabethan mariner

Thomas Cavendish, engraved by J. Horsburgh

than anyone else, with the possible exception of Grenville and Drake himself. He certainly brought home more loot than either. This extract from a letter he wrote to the Lord Chamberlain after he returned briefly summarises part of his activity: 'I navigated alongst the coast of Chili, Peru, and Nueva Espanna, where I made great spoiles: I burnt and sunke 19 sailes of ships small and great. All the villages and townes that even I landed at, I burnt and spoiled: and had I not been discovered along the coast, I had taken great quantities of treasure. The matter of most profit unto me was a great ship of the kings which I tooke at California, which ship came from the Phillipinas, being one of the richest of merchandize that even passed those seas . . .'

Piracy as practised by Cavendish was a desperately dangerous business, and the death risk was appallingly high. Besides scurvy, shipwreck and mutiny, there was always the likelihood of falling into the hands of the Spanish soldiery and Inquisition. But if you were courageous, pertinacious, ruthless, and had good luck on your side, you could, on one voyage, become rich and famous for life, buy a country estate and never do another stroke of work.

But Thomas Cavendish was not to enjoy peaceful retirement. He returned from his great circumnavigation, with his share of the 120,000 gold pieces and other plunder, his sailors clothed in silk (so it was said), 'his sails of damask, his topmasts covered with cloth of gold'. All that, and the fact that he was soon again in financial straits, was in character with the man. He was too late to help break up the Great Armada, whose attack this wholesale piracy had helped to precipitate.

Although it is simple, from the surviving records, to plot the course of Cavendish's circumnavigation, to identify the villages and settlements he burned, to tot up the value of his seized cargoes, it is as impossible as with most of his contemporaries to sketch in more than a hazy outline of the man. Really all that is known of him is that he was born around 1555 at Trimley St. Martin in Suffolk, that he went to Corpus Christi college in Cambridge and came down without a degree. We can be sure of only two characteristics: he was improvident in his affairs and extravagant in his manner. He early recognised that the only way he could live as expensively as he wished was to join the freebooting business, which Drake and others had shown to be so profitable. To gain experience, he went on a short trip to the North American coast on 1585, which was not very productive. In the summer of the following year he organised his own affair, the purpose of which was to repeat Drake's richly successful enterprise.

He sailed on his fruitful circumnavigation from Plymouth on 21 July 1586, confident that there would be no shore batteries to reckon with in the Magellan Strait. He had three ships under his command, the largest of 120 tons, and '123 persons of all sortes with all kinde of furniture and victuals sufficient for the space of two yeeres'. After the expected bloody encounters with Portuguese settlers and natives on the way south via Sierra Leone and the Cape Verde islands, Cavendish's ships reached Cape Virgins on 3 January 1587.

On a favourable tide they beat round the Cape and sailed into the strait. There was no sign on shore of native life, nor of Spaniards. Not even the glow of a fire was seen, from Patagonia or 'the land of fire', such as Drake had seen. But that night, between the first and second narrows, a splash of flame was sighted on the northern shore. At daybreak, Cavendish ordered out a boat to row him in the direction of where the fire had been seen.

Rescue by the Enemy

It was a marvellous achievement of Viedma to have brought his party of eighteen so far, and without a single casualty, retracing Sarmiento's original land route past what is now the town of Punta Arenas, and the indentations of the northern shore to Punta Gregorio. They had already covered nearly three-quarters of the distance back to Nombre de Jesus, now another empty ghost town. The shore here is low and bleak with a stony beach, and the wind rarely ceases, winter or summer. The equally bleak shore of Tierra del Fuego is eight miles away, and in clear weather you can see to the east the closing in of the waters to the bottleneck of the first narrows.

It was late in the evening, probably around eleven o'clock (for days are long here in mid-summer), when Viedma would have seen the broad hulls of Cavendish's three vessels sailing towards them from the west. Such a miraculous deliverance after nearly three years, with fewer than one in twenty still alive! Then almost at once Viedma recognised the awful danger that it was too late for his party to be sighted and taken off that day, and by the morning the relief vessels might have passed out of sight through the second narrows. So all the men and women who had the strength gathered brushwood from above the beach, and the fire was kept alight all night.

When the boat came at dawn it rowed past them, as if still searching, and Viedma despatched three soldiers—Martin Chiquillo, Juan Fernandez and Tomé Hernandez—along the shore to intercept it from a promontory. The boat's crew saw Hernandez and his two companions (and we can imagine the grotesque sight they made after their months of nomadic starvation) and turned towards the shore.

'What people are you?' asked Hernandez in his native tongue.

'We are Englishmen, bound for Peru. Do you want to be taken off?' a Spanish-speaking sailor demanded.

The news came as an unpleasant shock. These were the very pirates against whom they had once been expected to defend the strait. And what a time ago that seemed! Three years. Three years since Sarmiento had landed them just up the coast from here, full of high hopes, bursting with activity, planting crops, laying out streets for the great new city, dragging ashore the brass cannon. And now it was three worn-out, ragged, hungry soldiers with one arquebus—and three well-armed English pirate ships!

'No', replied Hernandez. 'If you take us on board you will only throw us into the sea.'

'Please yourself. But you might just as well. We're better Christians than you are.' And the Englishmen began to row back to their ship. They did not get far. After a few strokes, the voices of the soldiers were heard above the surf pleading for them to return. Cavendish ordered Hernandez to be allowed into the boat and told the interpreter to find out if there were any more of this Spanish party.

'Twelve more men and three women', he was told.

This was hardly welcome news. Eighteen unproductive mouths to feed, and Catholic at that, and three of them women. Women always brought bad luck and trouble.

'Send the other two soldiers for the rest of the party', ordered Cavendish. 'Tell them that they should assemble on the beach here.' The boat turned about, oars were dipped into the choppy waters of the strait, and Cavendish and Hernandez were rowed back to the anchored flagship.

Once on deck again, Cavendish had second thoughts about those grubby, lousy, starving Spaniards. Why should he have them in his ships? What had the Spanish ever done for him anyway? And they were the Queen's enemy. What was more, the wind was getting up nicely from the east. For the strait, this was too rare weather to miss.

Perhaps Cavendish never really intended to take off more than one Spaniard, as a sample, just as Sarmiento had once seized Juan and the other local natives. Hernandez himself, in his sworn declaration said simply that 'when Thomas Candi went on board, seeing that it was good weather for navigating, he made sail without waiting for the rest of the people to whom he had sent'. That was all.

So the three ships slipped away down the strait, hove to off Elizabeth Island where they took in water and six casks of penguins, then south again. Their Spanish soldier pointed out the landmarks, the wreck of their amateur-built boat, Santa Ana point, and beyond, in the wide bay, the city. Here they anchored and went ashore. It was just as Hernandez had described it; the forts, the church, the houses and streets—and the corpses. Francis Pretty, one of Cavendish's officers who contributed to Hakluyt an account of this voyage, wrote:

'They had contrived their Citie very well, and seated it in the best place of the Streights for wood and water: they had builded up their Churches by themselves: they had Lawes very severe among themselves, for they had erected a Gibet, whereon they had done execution upon some of their company. It seemed unto us that their whole living for a great space was altogether upon muskles and lympits: for there was not any thing else to bee had, except some Deere which came out of the mountaines downe to the fresh rivers to drinke. These Spaniards which were there, were onely come to fortifie the Streights, to the ende that no other nation should have passage through into the South sea saving onely their owne: but as it appeared it was not Gods will so to have it. For during the time that they were there, which was two yeeres at the least [three years], they could never have any thing to growe or in any wise prosper . . . Their victuals grewe so short, (their store being spent which they had brought with them out of Spaine, and having no meanes to renew the same) that they dyed like dogges in their houses, and in their clothes, wherein we found them still at our comming, until that in the ende the towne being wonderfully taynted with the smell and the savour of the dead people.'

What other name but Port Famine could Cavendish give this terrible city of ghosts? Port Hunger—Puerto del Hambre—is the name of this bay and stretch of coastline today, and on the charts of the strait, this passage over which the people had once looked from their dying city of Don Felipe, is marked Paso del Hambre. There is nothing left of the settlement, for Cavendish pulled down many of the houses for their wood and the rest were soon destroyed by the natives, or burnt.

Cavendish remained at Don Felipe for four days before sailing with a favourable wind round Cape Froward, up the narrow part of the strait and out into the Pacific. His ships took the usual hammering up the Chilean coast, but made safe landfall at the port of Quintero near Valparaiso. Here Hernandez, sent ashore with a party and with orders to deceive a group of suspicious mounted Spanish soldiers that these were friendly ships, succeeded in escaping on the back of one of the horses. The next day he conspired with his countrymen to spring an ambush on Cavendish when he came ashore for water. There was a pitched battle, Cavendish lost a number of his men, and others were captured. After biting the hand that had fed him in this way (though no doubt he remembered his friends and the women now dying near Nombre de Jesus), Hernandez was taken to Santiago with the prisoners, most of whom were hanged. Later he went to Peru to live, and that is all that is known of this soldier, the first man to sail through the strait under two different flags, and the only survivor of that tragic and misguided colonial enterprise.

There is a brief epilogue. Two years after Cavendish left those men and women on the Patagonian shore, the *Delight* of Bristol happened to anchor off Port Famine and a party was sent ashore for water from the river San Juan. There, among the ruins, they found a white man, a Spaniard, who had walked all the way back to where the last death march had begun. We can only guess at his condition and his state of mind. He was taken on board the *Delight* but died soon after, and there is no record even of his name.

It might be thought that Cavendish had broken the Fuegian spell at last by sailing through with little trouble, and gaining vast riches in the Pacific at the expense of Spain—plus a knighthood from Queen Elizabeth. But the strait really killed him in the end. He returned with five ships in 1591, intent on repeating his triumphant pillaging circumnavigation, and battled his way beyond Cape Froward, where 'wee were inforced by the fury of the weather to put into a small coove . . . where wee remained until the 15 of May. In the which time wee indured extreeme stormes, with perpetual snow, where many of our men died with cursed famine, and miserable cold, not having wherewith to cover their bodies, nor to fill their bellies, but living by muskles, water, and weeds of the sea . . .'

It had been a terrible voyage almost all the way from Plymouth. Cavendish had quarrelled with everyone, and shown himself brutal beyond even the broad standards of that time. He was probably already going mad when he entered the strait for the second time, far behind schedule, at the beginning of winter. The three and a half weeks in that small cove on Clarence Island finally and incurably bent his mind. If he was not mad when he doubled Cape Virgins on the way in, he certainly was when—accepting temporary defeat at last—he was hurled back into the Atlantic, still blaming his troubles on those of his men who still lived for their 'mutinie against me'.

The strait had become an obsession with him. Regardless of the condition of his ships and their provisions, he attempted again and again to beat south from Brazil, crying that he would rather be left to die on an island than to return defeated to England.

Sir Thomas Cavendish had his last wish. He died—probably of a brain tumour—on the island of Ascencion, to the relief of his officers and crew. His last act was to write a letter to his executor denouncing as traitorous, and the cause of 'the utter Ruin of us all', one of his captains, John Davis, the most gentlemanly, compassionate and brave navigator of his day, whose reputation suffered for many years as a result.

4

'Cape Hoorn . . . rounded 8 p.m.':
The Dutch Sail South

THE new maritime self-confidence in northern Europe, which had brought first Drake and then Cavendish to the strait, received another thrust forward by the defeat of the great Armada sent against England and the Netherlands in 1588. Spanish sea power was not destroyed, nor even crippled, by this catastrophe. But it was proved to be vulnerable, to the Dutch as well as to the English, as Drake had already shown.

Francis Drake had demonstrated to the Dutch what a good corsair could accomplish, and they no doubt admired him for it. But the Dutch captains were never as piracy-minded as the English or French, and in many ways were shrewder, as the record of Dutch trading and shipping figures was soon to prove. The Dutch thought that trade (by all means under pressure, if necessary) was more productive in the long run than piracy, or colonial conquest in the Spanish tradition. As well, they wanted to keep some sort of *modus vivendi* alive with their late conquerors because it was better business that way.

In the last years of the 16th century several large and carefully prepared expeditions left the Netherlands for the Magellan Strait, bound for the East Indies, where the power of Portugal was already in a decline, and where Spanish strength was vulnerable and her trading areas penetrable. The attractions of the short route, if not irresistible, were tempting enough even for the cautious Dutch to take a chance.

Like the Spanish, these Dutch seamen had no certain knowledge of any great channel south of the Fuegian islands. Drake's discovery of the end of the continent was a closely guarded one, and if rumours even reached the ears of the Dutch merchants (or

Spanish merchants for that matter), they would at first be judged as rough seamen's alcoholic tavern chatter. Drake had sailed through the strait. So had unlucky Sarmiento, and Cavendish, and others. The strait was now charted with some degree of accuracy, and on the latest maps—like that of Ortelius of 1587—Tierra del Fuego was still shown as part of the great land mass of *Terra Australis*. Magellan's *paso* was still the way through, of that there seemed little doubt.

At first these Dutch navigators received the same rough treatment as Camargo, Drake and others had suffered, and the fleets of Simon de Cordes and Oliver van Noort in 1598 experienced in turn the annihilating gales and seas, then the mutinies and courts martial, which seemed to afflict all who sailed south of the 52nd parallel. After breaking through the strait, two of de Cordes's ships were thrust back into it again, another got to Valparaiso and was promptly taken by the Spaniards, and only one survived the passage home. Van Noort, though he became the first Dutchman to complete the circumnavigation, came back with only one ship, too, and no profit.

After these disasters, Dutch traders for a long time continued to sail only east, on the long route round Africa, to their flourishing new trading stations in the Moluccas and the East Indies. Only when the African route became as menaced by the Portuguese and Spaniards as the route through the strait by the elements, did the Dutch make one last attempt to prove that the short cut need not be disastrous. In August 1614 Admiral Joris Spilbergen sailed with six fine Dutch ships from the Zuider Zee. It took him three years to get round the world. When he arrived home again he had triumphed over the Portuguese in battle, broken two mutinies, traded and fought with the Fuegians, and survived a tempest as great as Drake had met off Cape Desire.

Spilbergen's victory brought about a paradoxical situation. It confirmed to the Dutch authorities, as first Magellan and later Sarmiento had seemingly proved to the Spanish crown, that the *paso* opened up a new golden route to the East; and at once set the seal of success on the recently formed Dutch East India Company, the monolithic private trading monopoly which laid the foundations of the great Dutch eastern empire. Soon the Dutch East India Company had become so powerful that it was able to lay down laws, at least as far as Dutch shipping was concerned: and one of these was that only Dutch East Indiamen would be allowed to sail to the East to trade, either round the Cape of Good Hope, or through the Magellan Strait.

This sloppily-drafted piece of legislation caused Dutch merchants and seamen outside the Company to reconsider whether there might not be other routes to the Spice Islands, the East Indies and India itself, either through a passage to the north of the American continent, or by some new route far to the south, through some new strait, or the mysterious continent of *Terra Australis*. The result was (and this is one of the least appreciated facts in exploration) that the world learned that the American continent came to an end only when enterprising Dutch mariners were prohibited from using Magellan's *paso*—not by Spanish guns, as the Spanish had intended, but by the orders of their own countrymen.

'There is great reason it might be found'

The channel between the most easterly tip of America at Cape San Diego and Staten Island, had no name when Camargo's unidentified captain sailed through it safely in 1540. Today this strait carries the name of a Dutch navigator, le Maire, the son of the man who broke the Dutch East India Company's monopolistic trading trust by being the first navigator to sail from the Atlantic to the Pacific by open sea.

In 1613 the Dutch East India Company had experienced a decade of immense and ever growing profit. Wealth and power acquired on this scale and at this speed was bound to lead to internal divisions, and although everyone was doing very nicely out of the monopoly, others thought they could become even richer by breaking it. As the narrator, John Harris, put it in 1745, 'prohibition gave very great distaste to the many rich merchants, who were desirous of fitting out ships, and making discoveries, at their own cost'.

Another historian, James Burney, wrote of the frequent consultations among 'some enterprising merchants in the United Provinces' who were becoming increasingly confident that it would be possible to find another way through to the Pacific than Magellan's; so that 'they formed the design of fitting out ships to make the experiment, which, if successful, would open to them a trade to India by a passage not interdicted, and, it was hoped, amply repay them for their risk and expense'.

The merchant who drew together these ambitious speculator-merchants and welded their power, their wealth and their disenchantment into a new company was Isaac le Maire, once a

Qui facta lustravit Batavis incognita Nautis,
et non visa priùs per Gallos, atque Britannos,
ac Lusitanos Indorum nomine claros,
Christicolasvè alios, sulcantis æquora velis,
sic sua Jacobus Lemarius ora ferebat.

Le Maire

native of Antwerp, who had become a refugee from the fearsome
Spanish occupation of the United Provinces. He had been one of
the founder directors of the East India Company, and during his
best years, had contrived to make a fortune and bring up a family
of no fewer than twenty-two children. He split with his fellow
directors because, after what he had suffered as a young man under
Spanish occupation, he favoured company expansion by knocking
out the Spanish competition instead of making give-and-take
trading agreements. When he began to consider this question of a
new way into the Pacific, le Maire also gave much thought to the
Callao-Panama Spanish gold-and-silver route, and how Drake
had made a fortune from it within a few weeks. A wholesome greed
and an undying hatred of everything Spanish were the two chief
sources of Isaac le Maire's driving force.

One of the best captains working for the East India Company
was Wilhelm Cornelius Schouten, who had sailed to the East
round Good Hope three times, gained wisdom with experience
and made a fortune, too. He sounded to le Maire like the right
man, and it is said that le Maire approached him and asked him
if he thought it was possible that there was 'another passage into
the South Sea than by the Strait of Magellan'. 'There is great
reason it might be found,' Schouten replied without hesitation.

The events in the Netherlands surrounding this proposed voyage
followed the same sort of tortuous sequence that preceded the
departure of Magellan, Drake and so many of the important early
navigators, and we need not concern ourselves closely with them;
nor need we worry too much about shrewd old Isaac le Maire,
who was well able to look after himself and his interests. He had a
lot of powerful friends, including the Prince of Orange, Maurice
de Nassau, himself. For months le Maire worked secretly and
energetically, and by March 1614 had persuaded the States
General to grant a decree which in effect loosened the tenacious
grip of the East India Company by stating that 'all persons,
inhabitants of the United Provinces, who should make discoveries
of new passages, harbours, or lands, shall be permitted and entitled
to make the first four voyages to the places by them discovered . . .'
Two months later the Prince of Orange signed le Maire's authoris-
ing licence.

Meanwhile, le Maire's new company, the *Campagne Australe*, an
appropriately disguising and confusing title, was busily seeking
out what little information there was on navigation south of the
strait, sifting records and rumours from French and English as

well as Dutch sources, signing on the best sailors (high pay was the bait), and selecting the best equipment and arms. The Dutch were supremely thorough at this sort of thing. Le Maire decided two ships were enough but they were the finest available, the *Unity* of 360 tons, and the *Hoorn*, after the home town of the heaviest backers of the expedition. His son Jacob, administrative chief and businessman, was given the title of Merchant and President, Schouten that of Master Mariner.

There was great curiosity in Dutch shipping circles about the destination of these two non-East India Company vessels, looking so trim and shipshape and well prepared for a year or two's voyaging as they rode at anchor in the Texel in June 1615. But nobody was saying a word—only that they were sailing south. The rest was all speculation, even to the crews.

The Sea turns Red

It was not until the last days of January 1616 that this small Dutch expedition was able to record new discoveries and Wilhelm Schouten was able to mark a new coastline on his charts. By then except for mutiny they had been beset by all the trials suffered by every south-seeking voyager for a hundred years—the gales and becalmings, the sicknesses and shortage of provisions and navigational miscalculations. The weather had been mainly foul, and two events seemed to confirm the notorious and often incomprehensible hazards that voyagers approaching the strait seemed invariably to experience. At a moment of fair weather and favourable winds, the *Hoorn* was suddenly struck below the water-line with such violence that it seemed as if she must have hit an uncharted rock. At the same time (or so eyewitnesses reported), the sea about her turned red, 'as if a fountain of blood were gushing up from the keel'. Yet the vessel appeared undamaged, was not taking in water, and was able to sail on. The mystery remained unsolved until they called at Port Desire, the anchorage on the Patagonian coast discovered by Cavendish, where Schouten took advantage of the exceptional tides to careen his ships. Deeply imbedded in the hull of the *Hoorn*, piercing three heavy planks, was the tusk of a great narwhal. Once this was extracted and the damage made good, a fire of dry Patagonian scrub grass was lighted to burn off the weed and crustaceans from the vessel's underside. With an inefficiency that was quite uncharacteristic of the Dutch, the fire, fanned by a sudden wind, got out of hand, and roared its way into the ship's rigging and then the hull timbers.

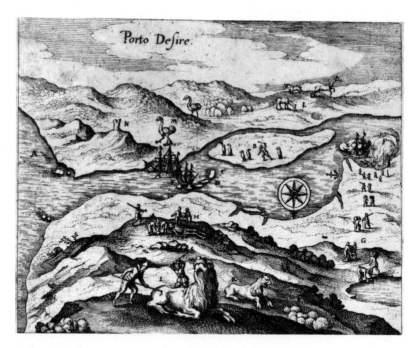

Porto Desire.

Port Desire

The water at low tide was too distant for the sailors to extinguish the flames, and when at last the tide came in it washed hissingly over only the skeleton remains of their second vessel.

The *Unity* pressed on alone, passing well to seaward of notorious Puerto San Julian and far out of sight of the entrance to the forbidden strait. Towards dusk on 23 January, on a south-westerly course and with current and wind in their favour, the look-out called down that there was land dead ahead. They were well below the 54th parallel, the coastline looked stark and dead, little different from Patagonia, and as they neared it, with the light falling fast, they saw that it tended ever farther to the east, confirming Ortelius's map.

For that one night it seemed that the safe, conservative beliefs must prevail, that Magellan's *paso* was the only one, that the rumours of Francis Drake finding that 'the Atlantic and the South Sea meet in a large and free scope' were after all no more than tavern tattle. The *Campagne Australe*, after losing half of its ships, must now, it seemed, utterly fail.

The morning of 24 January was fine and calm, with a breeze from the north. It was midsummer, and absurdly warm. If this

was *Terra Australis*, they could without discomfort have left
behind their thick leather Antarctic clothing. At noon Schouten
took an astrolabe reading which showed they were in 54° 64' S.
To the south the land was seen to break suddenly into rocky
near-perpendicular peaks that were twice as high as the Fuegian
coastline they had been following. It seemed at first a purposeless
disturbance of nature, and then they recognised it for what it was:
the southern continent's last joking deception. This land did not
after all go on for ever. The first peak of this range towered above
a headland and guarded a strip of clear water as wide as the
Straits of Dover. Beyond, it was clear and blue, a glorious panora-
mic snub to every unenterprising defeatist, and to the East India
Company, too. There was another way through, a brief cut into
the South Sea, a mere ten miles long by contrast with Magellan's
hazardous, tortuous *paso*. The next day they sailed down this wide

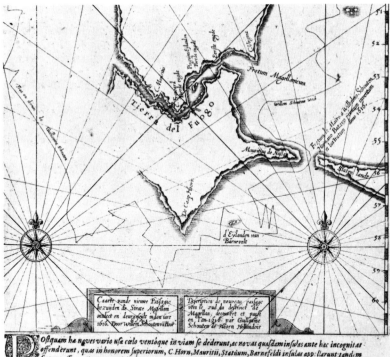

Le Maire Strait

passage, renaming Tierra del Fuego on their starboard quarter
Maurice Land after the Prince who had given them his blessing,
and the rugged, treeless land to the east Staten Land; for without
the authorisation of the States General, they would never have
made this discovery.

And the South Sea was ahead of them. There was a new feel to
the swell, a new blue in the water. That night Schouten noted
with satisfaction and accuracy that Tierra del Fuego was only an
island; less accurately, that Staten Land was the northernmost
coastline of *Terra Australis,* when Camargo's unknown captain
had noted almost eighty years before that it was an island a mere
forty miles long, even if it was the most frightful he had ever seen.
The Spaniards had been luckier with their visibility.

The wind took them far to the south, away from the shelter of
the Beagle Channel. Le Maire and Schouten thought they were
through to the Pacific. But the American continent, though it may
have had its last joke, had not yielded to these Dutchmen its final
secret, its final terminal point. Even these hardy and skilful
Dutchmen in their stout, well-found galleon—heavy guns struck
below, all top hamper lashed to the booms—were not going to
double the tip of the continent without having to fight for every
league to the west. The wind blew from all the quarters, unpredictably switching its direction and strength, from a light breeze
to a full gale. For four days and nights almost every man was on
watch with frozen hands shortening first the topsails then the
mainsails as the wind rose, the rain and hail tearing at them, or
hoisting topsails when it moderated again. Schouten applied all
his skill and resources to holding his high clumsy vessel from being
swept back into the Atlantic, down into the frozen seas of Antarc-
tica, or onto the lee shore of the Fuegian islands, one minute
laying over under the press of sail, then wearing back onto the
opposite tack.

On the fourth morning of this tossing confusion, they sighted
land again, just two islands 'beset round with cliffs', mere rocks
really, circumscribed by a white rim of smashing rollers, twin
devilish hazards in this lunatic corner of this uncharted ocean. Le
Maire named them Barnevelt, after the all-powerful founder of
the Dutch East India Company—perhaps with a note of irony,
for this was the very man who had forced them to search south of
Magellan's route into this terrible new strait.

They were a mere dozen miles east of the last islands in the
Fuegian archipelago, the wicked Wollastons, terminating east-

Wollaston Island

wards in the well-named Cape Deceit, but visibility was poor, and for a while they saw nothing more. Schouten brought the *Unity* round onto a south-westerly course, tacking south of the Barnevelts.

In another hour there was more land ahead, a hump-backed rock that was intermittently splashed over with white foam, a low-lying island beyond, bare and dark-grey against the grey sea. And yet they were still not there, were still clawing their way league by league to find an end to this nightmare of rock—and it now seemed an age since they had hopefully sailed in fair weather through the channel they believed would open into the South Sea.

The daylight was beginning its long sub-Antarctic fade out when a dark shape loomed up on the starboard bow. Its very silhouette, as magnificent in its threatening demeanour as in its size, was at once suggestive of termination. The island began low to the north, lifted higher, then to a crescendo, before plunging into the ocean more than 1,300 feet below: a worthy granite securing pin for the whole American land mass. This, at last, was the turning point, the open sea route from Atlantic to Pacific, and nature had marked it with her greatest signing off flourish.

For Schouten and le Maire, non-Catholic opportunists, Hoorn

Cape Horn

was the only name with which they could honour this magnificent
headland, the home town of those whose speculative interest had
brought them here, and the town to which they hoped one day to
return. The Spaniards or Portuguese would no doubt have given
it the name of a Saint or of the Virgin Mary.

It is right that this Dutch name, Horn, should be retained today,
for Schouten's *Unity* had indeed, for the first time, by carefully
planned intention, unified the world's two greatest oceans; and
'the Horn' was to become for all time the most revered and
emotive maritime landmark. Drake was probably there before
Schouten. This will never be known, for above all in this area
maritime records are more disputable than anywhere in the world.
At least posterity has served out a rough sort of justice, however,
denying le Maire's claim to the great iceberg-strewn sea between
the oceans, and limiting it to the channel between Tierra del
Fuego and Staten Island. Here the name of Francis Drake
prevails, for today it is marked 'Drake Strait' or 'Drake Sea'.

In the *Unity*'s log for 29 January 1516 Schouten wrote the

entry, 'Cape Hoorn in 57° 48′ S. Rounded 8 p.m.' He was more than one hundred miles out in his reckoning, which shows that no glimmer of sun could have broken through the storm clouds on that day, or probably the day before and after. But he was round the continent, and soon the world was to know, thirty-seven years after the *Golden Hind*'s company had seen where 'the Atlantic Ocean and the South Sea meet in a large and free scope', that there was another passage from the old world to the East, as free as that around Africa, below the southern tip of America.

Two Brave Brothers

The *Unity*'s reported discovery of Cape Horn brought equal

Great men of 'the uttermost south', and their discoveries

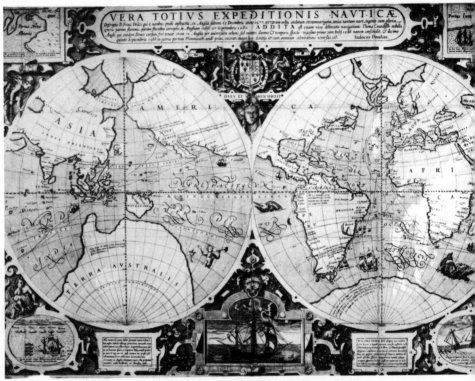

The world as reshaped by Drake and Schouten

dismay to the Dutch East India Company and the Spanish crown. Once safely across the Pacific, the vessel, now full of the fruit of trading in the East Indies, was impounded as soon as she arrived at one of the company's ports, and cargo and crew were seized. The officers told Schouten it did not matter which way he had come, the *Unity* was not flying their flag, and that was enough. It took him two years of fighting in the Dutch courts to retrieve for the backers of the *Campagne Australe* the value of ship and cargo. By then the full narrative of their voyage had been published and translated abroad. Now, more than a century after Magellan had dug the prow of a European ship into Pacific waters for the first time, a new shape could be drawn on the map of America, fining it down at its southern tip to a point, with a clear break on the eastern side before *Terra Australis*.

In Seville, the officers of India House read Schouten's report, and did not dare either to believe or disregard it. If this Dutchman, in a well-armed vessel, had entered the South Sea from the east, why had he not attacked Spanish trade off Peru, like the English pirate, Drake? Yet if it was true that 'the South Sea and the North Sea are one', the implications were hair-raising. This time there was no use in sending a Sarmiento with colonists and cannon. A dozen powerful forts could not control the short twenty-mile-wide strait through which le Maire and Schouten had sailed, and the corsairs of Spain's enemies could now range freely up and down the golden route out of Valparaiso and Callao. Since the catastrophic raid of Francisco Draquez, the sea routes to Panama had remained undisturbed, but those terrible months of January-February 1579 were still remembered with horror in the vice-royalties of Peru and Chile, and in the Royal Council of the Indies back in Old Spain.

The officers of India House were as quick to react to this new threat as they had been forty years earlier when they heard the news of Drake's depredations. This time they decided to look into the matter themselves by sending out two of their crack sea captains, not to colonise and fortify but merely to reconnoitre—to confirm the disturbing new geographical claims of their first rivals, the Dutch, who might have made up this story of a new easy route into the Pacific just to frighten them. This time they chose the right commanders, the right ships, and luck was on their side. The voyage of the Nodal brothers was a family affair, and was a success from beginning to end.

Bartolomé and Gonzalo de Nodal had a common birthplace with Pedro Sarmiento, the town of Pontevedra in Galicia, the 'seed-plot of illustrious sailors'. Apart from an inherited instinct for navigation, there was no other similarity between the failed colonist and the two brothers. The Nodals had been fighting seamen since their 'teens. They had none of Sarmiento's intellectualism, nor his weakness for introspection, and certainly none of his self-doubts. They appear to have been entirely indifferent about their humble origins. They were simple, loyal, stout fighters, who had amassed an impressive record of wounds and prizes by the time they were twenty. This is the sort of thing they enjoyed:

'In the middle of the night, after leaving the bar of Lisbon, the flag-ship sighted a vessel, and Don Diego ordered Captain (Bartolomé) de Nodal to reconnoitre her in a small boat with oars. It was a calm and serene night: and when the captain saw that the vessel was an English man of war, he boarded her and fought until he had cut to pieces nearly all the gunners and musketeers who fired from below. The captain with the rest held out on the poop, while the boat was disabled with the continual battering, which increased the temerity of the action. The captain animated the few wounded men to resist, and dashed onwards to the assault, clearing the way with sword and shield, to enable his men to follow. This they did, renewing the fight until the English surrendered, being hindered from attempting flight as they wished. But the weight of the water in the boat sent her to the bottom with conquerors and conquered.

'Few Spanish survivors remained available, all being wounded. Captain Nodal had three wounds, one of them in the right eye, of which he lost the sight . . .'

His brother Gonzalo led an equally enterprising and eventful life. On his third voyage, off the Scilly Islands, 'he attacked and took a ship of the Rochelle pirates, having killed the master and some gunners and soldiers who resisted. Passing the Lizard, where he had taken a vessel before, he now captured a Dutch ship. Further up the Channel he took an English ship, both being men of war . . .'

This was the very stuff of success, sweetened always by good luck. And they were both known to exercise toughness without brutality, to be superb mariners and navigators who also enjoyed the loyalty of their men.

There were no delays in the Nodals' enterprise, no nonsense about court intrigues, plot and counter-plot, no sabotage by interested parties, no purloining of stores. Bartolomé was summoned to Court by the Royal Council of the Indies within weeks of the publication in Amsterdam of Schouten's narrative of his voyage, was appointed Captain-General, and chose his brother as second-in-command. He at once hastened to Lisbon, selected and fitted out two excellent little caravels, each of 80 tons, provisioned them for ten months, armed them with four pieces of artillery, and impressed eighty Portuguese seamen—'because the destination was so remote and difficult to reach that, for want of confidence, no one would go willingly'. For their cosmographer they took one Diego Ramírez. By 27 September 1618 they were away from Lisbon.

The Brisk Voyage South

There is a reassuring brisk self-confidence about the Nodals's narrative of their voyage to the south. They had to put up with their share of adverse winds and currents, were storm-tossed as severely as Camargo or Magellan, and witnessed as many strange and sinister sights as Drake's men. The Nodals took everything in their stride with a fine matter-of-factness. They noted with precision everything they saw, and wasted no time when they were obliged to go ashore. At Rio de Janeiro just ten days were spent strengthening the caravels' decks against the expected storms ahead, and 'the other five or six days were occupied in getting water, ballast, and other necessary things on board'. A threatened mutiny (not even the professional Nodals could silence all mutterings before the last leg down to the uttermost south) was put down by leaving the three ringleaders in prison in charge of the Governor. Then they were away again.

The weather was foul until they were south of Cape Virgins and progress exasperatingly slow, for unlike some of those before him, Bartolomé de Nodal was determined to reach the highest latitudes in their January midsummer. It was not until almost the end of the month that they sighted le Maire's channel beyond the eastern tip of Tierra del Fuego; and 'God knows the joy and satisfaction that all felt that day', the Nodals noted. 'We displayed our banners, fired our guns, and gave thanks to God for the great mercy which He had shown us.' So now they knew that the Dutchman had not been lying. All they had to do was to follow the course he had taken.

In trying to get through le Maire's Strait, the Nodals's luck temporarily left them. The strong adverse current and wind prevented them from making any progress. The two caravels were forced to find a sheltering bay until the weather eased. It was typical of these joyous, ever-optimistic mariners that they should name this bay on this Godforsaken headland Bahia Buensuceso—Good Success Bay. And it lived up to its name, bringing them much of interest, too, while they waited for the weather to improve. There were shoals of sardines to be caught, wood for fuel, and water from little freshets coming down through the dense beech forests to the shore. Then there were the natives.

The natives of the main island of Tierra del Fuego were the Onas, and were related to the Patagonian 'giants'—the Tehuelche —who had attacked Drake's party at Puerto San Julian and Sarmiento at Nombre de Jesus and on his march along the north of the strait. One of the Onas' tribal practices was to smoke and mummify their dead and leave them in raised barrows, as Magellan's men had discovered on that weird day back in 1519.

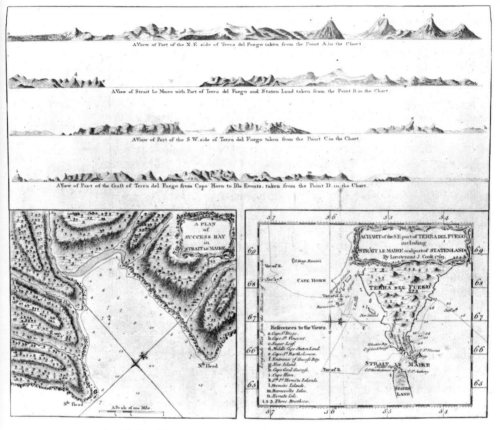

Le Maire Strait and Good Success Bay

The Onas were a nomadic tribe who hunted, fleetly on foot, in small and often mutually hostile groups. Their chief quarry was the guanaco, on which they mainly depended for food and its skin for protection from the winter cold. They hunted the deer and the rhea, too. They would also eat tussock roots and wild celery and berries, but unlike the Yaghans of the south and the Alakalufs of the western islands, they were not fishermen and did not build canoes. The Onas were the feared aristocrats of Tierra del Fuego, as Sarmiento had found the Tehuelches to be north of the Magellan Strait. They were fierce and aggressive, and deadly shots with their bows and stone-tipped arrows. Physically they were greatly superior to their neighbours, too, the men averaging nearly six feet, with muscular arms and legs. Their skin was light

Ona Indians

copper in colour, their hair long, black and straight.

Gonzalo de Nodal first sighted these splendid looking Ona natives on the first day he went ashore in Good Success Bay when he was searching for a freshet. 'When we saw them we fell back on our people to take up arms', he wrote. Bartolomé, watching from the flagship, saw the natives following his brother's party and fired a warning shot from a cannon. It had no apparent effect. The natives came on in larger numbers.

The men of Camargo's ship which wintered in the Beagle Channel eighty years earlier may have had communication with the Onas, but the Nodals's is the first written record of contact with this fierce hunting tribe. The Nodals's intentions were not entirely innocent by present day standards (like Magellan and Sarmiento they wanted to take some home for curiosity but judiciously restrained themselves).

As Gonzalo watched them advance on his watering party in increasing numbers, he noted that 'they were without arms, and that they came in their skins, quite naked. Some had caps of birds' feathers (rheas), and others had skins of sheep (guanacos) with long wool like those of Spain, or a deer skin worn as a cloak, with woollen thread. Their shoes were of leather tanned with red ochre. They came with their arms outstretched, and calling out in their manner *a a a*, throwing up their caps as a sign of friendship. On this we came to them and soon afterwards three others arrived together. They looked particularly at our clothes, and were especially attracted by those who wore red apparel, asking for it by signs. We gave them some glass beads, needles, and other trifles. They had no beards, and their faces were all painted with red ochre and white . . . They did not trust us much,' Gonzalo concluded his account of this first confrontation, 'and presently departed, especially the young ones.'

From the security of the caravels, the Portuguese seamen and their Spanish officers watched the antics of the Onas on shore. They saw that they liked to jump high in the air, with their arms and legs extended, apparently as a sign of joy. They noted cautiously the size and number of their arms, and that they seemed to have no fear of the arquebus. They observed with awe that they ate whole and uncooked the sardines (eschewing the bread that had also been left for them), and 'pulled up the wild grass and ate it, as if they were bullocks or horses'.

Four days before the Nodals left this bay, there was the most threatening incident with the Onas. Gonzalo had again gone ashore for water and the natives had been assembling in greater numbers. Gonzalo posted sentries and went about his work, always a difficult business with the heavy barrels.

'The natives arrived and we let them come unarmed, leaving their weapons hidden . . . We saw that one or two went away calling to others who had remained behind with bows and arrows. We hindered them when they retired and, as the sentries would not let them pass, they began to climb the hills like goats so that, if we had wished, we could not have caught them. Some of us thought it would be well to destroy those who were on a great rock, whence they might be able to do us harm with their arrows. But it was agreed that, unless they began, we should not attack them, and thus we should be on friendly terms another time.'

It was this practical wisdom, firmness and restraint of the

Nodals which made their voyage the most unqualified success of
all these early expeditions to the uttermost south. Unlike Sarmiento
before them, if their vessels had later been smashed on the shore
in a storm there is a reasonable chance that they would have been
given succour by the natives.

It took the Nodals between the 27 January and 5 February 1691
to claw their way across the one hundred miles between Good
Success Bay in le Maire's strait to within sight of the Horn,
negotiating cautiously round the Barnevelts and noting the
hazards for the charts of future navigators. For the Nodals there
was to be no tidy doubling of the Horn, with celebratory toasts in
schnapps. From the time they sighted its ominous black face ('the
mountains are very high' was their only comment) they were hit
by a series of gales and squalls as bad and as prolonged as Drake
had suffered in these waters. They had with them no Pigafetta
nor Fletcher to embellish their account with adjectival extravagance. But their log tells the story well enough: 'very cold with
rain and snow', 'blew a gale', 'strong gales every day, with furious
squalls, much cold and snow'. On some days it was impossible to
take an astrolabe reading, but by dead reckoning and occasional
glimpses of the sun, they were able to plot the progress of their
frantic gyrations south, south-east and south-west of the Horn,
sometimes under mizzen, at others under fore and mizzen sails,
but always managing to keep company with one another.

The End Beyond the End

During this period the Nodals made the discovery for which
they will always be remembered, if only by their names on the
charts of the few who navigate these waters today. From time to
time during these storms they caught sight again of the rock face
of the Horn, sometimes from one bearing, sometimes from another.
On 10 February they plotted their position west of the Cape. From
here they were taken west by south by a strong wind, and in the
teeth of the south-westerly Cape Horn current. In the afternoon
they sighted land, 'and from what we were able to make out', ran
the Nodals's narrative, 'we were satisfied that the land we had
seen out to sea was an island, and near it there were two other
small rocks. We were braced close up during the night with little
wind, that we might get a better view in the morning.'

The island and rocks were lost to view by daylight as they had
been driven too far west and north. But these canny Spaniards
and their cosmographer—in spite of bewildering currents and

winds and ever-varying visibility—knew that they had not been mistaken. Schouten and le Maire were indeed right about the new strait and the clear way through into the Pacific. But Cape Horn was not after all the end of the American continent: there was an end beyond the end. The name of their discovery they generously gave to Diego Ramírez. But they were not content with that brief glimpse between the storm clouds, and determined to plot the islands more accurately before they sailed on.

From west of Diego Ramírez they were driven to the north again and found the two islets—the Ildefonsos—probably the place where Drake stocked up with albatross eggs and penguins. But two days after their first sighting of Diego Ramírez (destined for more than 150 years to be the most southerly recorded land in the world) a strong wind blew them from the Horn south-west again. Late that evening they were in sight of the islands and during the hours of darkness 'we steered south under fore and mizen, intending to return to the island and anchor off it if this proved possible'.

All that they could record in the half-light of the antarctic night and buffeted by a fresh gale was that Diego Ramírez was a group of islets and rocks, the most exposed and inhospitable in the world, and yet for all that the last visible volcanic eruption of the giant Andean range, and of the American continent itself. Although ships have been battered to pieces against the Diego Ramírez, and men have died there, for more than two hundred and fifty years few explorers were able to plot them precisely on their charts, let alone land on them, and no naturalist has ever been there.

The First Circumnavigation of Tierra del Fuego

The Nodals saw only the grey green-capped outline of this last fragment of America. The gales seized their little caravels again and tossed them south-west as far as 58° 30′ S. They battled their way north again when the wind swung through 180°, picked up the western Fuegian coastline, and on 25 February sighted Cape Desire and the western entrance to the Magellan Strait.

They sailed through speedily and uneventfully, carefully noting all that they saw, clearing Cape Virgins on 13 March, thus completing the first Fuegian circumnavigation (a most difficult voyage requiring skilled pilots today) in less than two months. The two brothers were back at San Lucar by 9 July 1620, just over nine months after they had embarked on the most unwarlike yet most notable of all their voyages. They had accomplished it with marvellous skill and promptitude, and had carried out efficiently all that had been asked of them. It was, in fact, a near-miracle of able seamanship and navigation—a family triumph. As they wrote themselves on their return, 'The time in which we have made this voyage is very exact, neither too long nor too short, as we had vessels well suited for it. The one never had to wait for the other. They made such a pair when sailing that in all the rains and fogs we met with, they were never separated one from the other.'

The note of self-satisfaction is justified. Of their impressed Portuguese crews, they claimed that all returned in good health, those in poor health at the start were better when they got home. Certainly no one had died—unless a poor fellow who leaped into the sea for fear of what lay ahead at Rio de Janeiro and could not be found is to spoil this statistical record.

Bartolomé and Gonzalo de Nodal, stout Galician mariners, gallant fighters (their total score was 76 enemy vessels burnt or captured), stern disciplinarians, brilliant navigators, made one new mark on the southern maps and charts, refined many more, and confirmed an equally brave Dutchman's claim to have found the clear way through. They were properly commended and rewarded for their services. But their fund of luck ran out with their return from the Horn. Soon they were off together on more regular naval service, this time to the West Indies. There was not a fight the whole way, or in the Caribbean. On 5 September 1622 the ran into a fearful hurricane, and they both perished in their ships.

5

'Foulweather Jack' Byron

A strange doom is thy father's son's, and past
Recalling as it lies beyond redress,
Reversed for him our grandsire's fate of yore,
He has no rest at sea, nor I on shore

Byron, Epistle to Augusta (*alluding to his grandfather*)

T HE history of the uttermost south is as untidy as its geography,
and the sequence of events is as disorderly as the archipelagic
islands that stretch from Cape Desire to Cape Horn. This historical
account could have been more neatly sewn together if, say, the
imaginary predictions of Spain's India House had become reality,
and convoys of galleons, bound for the Spice Islands, had followed
Magellan through his *paso*; or if the fears of the viceroys of Chile
and Peru had been realised and half England's fighting ships had
sailed in his wake to raid Callao. These would seem to be the
predictable consequences. Instead, after each voyage, carried
through at frightful cost in lives and suffering and ships, men
tended rather to flinch away from the south than exploit its
advantages. Now that the Dutch had discovered the open sea
route to the Pacific—the new short cut to the spices—you would
expect a heavy Dutch traffic to build up round the Horn. After
the Spaniards had confirmed le Maire's discovery, why did they
not now at last switch from their slow and clumsy trade route
across the Isthmus to the direct route from Old Spain to the
viceroyalties? And what about the French and English privateers?
Why are they not now beating round the Horn in droves, to burn
and pillage their way up the rich soft strip of the west coast of
South America?

The answer, of course, is fear. Superstition has played its part
in the past, and will do so in the future. But the simple physical

fear of the worst climate in the world is what keeps the traffic down in Magellan's and Drake's straits. Only the boldest and most desperate will dare to run 'South to the blind Horn's hate'.

The 17th century merchant studied the odds, just as if he were a Lloyd's underwriter today, and decided they were unacceptably high. So did the seaman. His judgement was based more on gossip and rumours than hard statistics, but he had a well-developed regard for his survival, and his decision was right, too. A few pirates got away with it, either round the Horn or through the *paso*, and showed that the prizes were as high as the odds against survival. They usually recovered from the ordeal of the passage at Juan Fernandez before sailing off up the golden coast, picking clean the carcasses of a dozen or more merchantmen. Not all of them reached home. Those who did bought great estates or squandered their wealth in their lifetime.

In the one hundred and twenty years after the Nodals' successful reconnaissance the shifting balances of power in Europe brought new pressures on many parts of the world opened up in the age of reconnaissance. The pressures were strongest in the East, where first the Dutch and then the English East India Companies secured an ever-mounting share of the trade with India, China, the Malaysian archipelago and the East Indies. Both these Protestant nations found that, regardless of their intentions to trade rather than conquer, force and then possession were increasingly required to sustain their trading. The Dutch especially became monopoly and territory minded in the East, brooking no competition in the Moluccas, setting up colonies in Batavia and Java, and even at the Cape of Good Hope, in 1652, to support their lines of communication. Their trade in the Atlantic became equally predatory and prosperous during the 17th century, muscling in on the Portuguese West African slave business and the Portuguese Brazilian sugar trade. Dutch West Indies Company trading posts on the east coast of South America became armed trading posts and then strongly defended colonies. Long stretches of the Brazilian coastline slipped from Portuguese into Dutch hands, or were fought over before succumbing. By the 1650s the old Dutch scruples were finished, just as the Bull of Demarcation had become a laughable piece of paper, an outmoded remnant of Catholic arrogance. The Protestants were everywhere on the march.

The richest and most vulnerable Spanish possessions were the viceroyalties of Chile and Peru. Every year their gold and the silver from Pitosí sailed north for Panama and thence to Old Spain in the bottoms of carracks and caravels from Callao and Valparaiso. This line of communication, and the sources of the riches themselves, were an irresistible temptation to the Dutch and the English who were determined to break the Spanish trading monopoly and the Spanish hold on this western strip of South America. The attack could come only from the sea. An approach from the west, *via* the Cape of Good Hope, India and the vast wastes of the Pacific, was out of the question. A mass assault must come—as Drake had come with his single ship—only from the south: and that meant braving the hazards of Magellan's *paso*, or the le Maire Strait and Cape Horn. For one hundred years from the mid-17th to the mid-18th centuries the uttermost south, the turning point from Atlantic to Pacific, from the Western to the Eastern worlds, was to become the toll-gate for those seeking power and wealth. And the toll to be paid was as high as ever.

The Dutch Invasion Armadas

Thirteen miles north-west of Cape Horn there lies a wildly shaped island, all peninsulas and narrow bays, with a crinkled silhouette that rises here and there to above fifteen hundred feet straight from the sea. A recent edition of *South American Pilot* describes them as 'composed of greenstone, in which hornblende and felspar are more or less conspicuous, and the presence of iron very apparent. The mountains rise in peaks to elevations of 853 to 1,693 feet, and being thickly clothed to within 200 or 300 feet of their summits with different shrubs and evergreen trees, they are difficult to ascend.' If anyone has ever climbed them in clear weather (and only in favourable conditions is it possible to get ashore) they would see to the west the string of islets off Hoste Island along which Drake was driven by that fearsome storm in 1578, and to the south east the full length of Horn Island rising to the cape at its tip. You are only fifteen miles from the end.

A hundred years ago, families of Yaghans still paddled their way down here across Nassau Bay, following the penguins in their search for fish. This island is marked 'Hermite' even on Spanish charts, after Admiral Jacob l'Hermite, unluckiest of all Cape Horners, an experienced and admired navigator, the commander of the first of these invading Protestant fleets, and one of the three

Cape Horn seen from the north

men who might have destroyed Spanish power in South America for all time.

L'Hermite sailed on his voyage of conquest from the Netherlands on 29 April 1623, with a fleet of eleven ships, the largest of 800 tons, and with 294 cannon, over one thousand officers and sailors, and six hundred soldiers. This great force was to be followed by another, intended simultaneously to attack Brazil, and thus secure control over the whole sub-continent—and, by bringing about a union between the Dutch West Indies and East Indies companies, control of the Pacific Ocean, too. So l'Hermite's responsibilities were on a Genghis Khan-like scale.

The Nassau fleet, as it later came to be called, made slow but satisfactory progress south, and the weather was generally favourable. The greatest fleet ever to face the Horn doubled the Cape peacefully on 15 February 1624. It was then caught in a dense fog, and was actually becalmed for a while before finding safety in a wide bay (where Darwin later anchored) on the north coast of the island that was to bear l'Hermite's name.

Perhaps it was in this mournful spot with its appalling climate ('certainly wretched', wrote Darwin of it, ' . . . not cheered by a gleam of sunshine') that the Dutch admiral first realised that he

had been struck by a fatal illness. Certainly from this time the
deterioration from a condition of robust health set in at an
accelerating pace. (There is no record of its nature.) The fleet's
fortunes at once began to decline at the same pace as the powers
of its leadership. The incident which followed immediately on
their arrival at Hermite Island signals the beginning of a succession
of disasters which made the admiral's last weeks a miserable
agony.

A watering party was put ashore on the west side of the bay,
without escort or arms, although natives had been seen. The boat
crews were caught in a squall while ferrying the replenished barrels
and were unable to return until the following day. They saw at
once that it had been a nasty night on shore. 'The natives, it
seems, without other cause of quarrel than the Hollanders being

L'Hermite's landfall

unprovided with means of defence, had attacked them with clubs and slings, and killed all but two, who had the good fortune to conceal themselves. 'Five of the bodies,' concludes Burney's reference to the incident, 'were found cut into quarters, and mangled in a strange manner'.

After this sanguinary event, the fleet made its way haltingly up the Fuegian and Chilean coasts, its progress always delayed, not by bad weather (though it was bad enough) but by trifling ineptitudes. One day eight men were carelessly washed off the flagship in a squall. At Juan Fernandez so many seals and sea lions were clubbed to death 'by way of diversion' that the stink of their putrifying bodies made it almost impossible to go on shore again.

L'Hermite, who had been lying on his bunk incapable of exercising his command for weeks, died at last, and things went from bad to worse under Admiral Gheen Hugo Schapenham. For the next week the Nassau Fleet, which was meant to conquer the richest area in the world (and could well have done so) sailed aimlessly up and down the coasts of Chile and Peru, sometimes together, sometimes in smaller groups, behaving like a disorganised gang of vandals. There was no plan. They were dilatory and indecisive and undisciplined and pointlessly destructive. When they found them, they hanged Spaniards on the slightest provocation, burnt a lot of ships in Callao harbour when there was a strong off shore wind blowing and had to retreat from these self-inflicted fireships, and missed the Treasure Fleet en route between Callao and Panama. A number of the seamen and soldiers deserted. Moreover, the Spaniards fought back with surprising tenaciousness.

This desultory affair faded out like an ill-conceived and dispirited orgy, and was altogether very un-Dutch. In the end, they drifted up north to Mexico, and in November 1624 steered out to sea and headed for the Moluccas.

The Nassau Fleet was the first expedition to break through from the Atlantic to the Pacific in strength. Everything at first had seemed so promising. By the standards of Cape Horn, the weather had been favourable and the Spanish colonists had certainly been in no condition to withstand a well-organised assault. It was the extinction of the vital spark of leadership which doomed the Nassau Fleet. Twenty years later this dismal episode was repeated, almost incident by incident, thus seeming to demonstrate to the superstitious that even if the Fuegian weather relented and spared

the ships, you could not escape so easily the powers of evil of this
broken land. For if it spared a fleet's ships, it was still capable of
killing its leader.

In 1642 the determination of the Dutch States General to
destroy Spanish power in Peru and Chile was as powerful as ever.
After all, they argued, Admiral l'Hermite had just been unlucky,
like that unfortunate Spaniard, Sarmiento, in the 1580s. This
time the first target was Chile, so that (in the words of Prince
Maurice) 'we can root out our enemies and keep the best and
most valuable part of the New World for ourselves'. This was
plain speaking all right, and as the Dutch at this time were by a
wide margin the greatest trading and naval power in the world,
and were buoyed up by decades of success and affluence, and the
Spanish viceroyalties were still in a very unsettled condition, how
could it fail? It turned out a disaster because, like the Nassau Fleet,
its able leader was struck down by a fatal disease somewhere
around 'the southernmost point'.

There was never a more serene passage round the Horn than
that of Captain Hendrick Brouwer with his 'five sail of stout ships'
in March 1643. They even rediscovered the fact, unrecorded on
the maps since Camargo's day, that Schouten's Staten Land was
not a northern cape of *Terra Australis* at all, but only an island,
and not a very big one at that. 'On the 5th [March]', wrote
Burney, 'They came in sight of *Strait le Maire*; and it being a very
clear day, the people . . . saw distinctly the whole extent from
West to East of the *Staten Land*, by which it appeared that this land
. . . was an Island of very moderate extent'. Brouwer found it
more convenient to sail round the island, doubled the Horn, and
by 30 April had reached the appointed place of rendezvous, the
island of Chiloé, far up the Chilean coast.

Brouwer did not die for another nine weeks, but by then all
leadership had gone, and the second Dutch expedition strong
enough to wrench control from the Spaniards had fallen into the
same condition of decay and corruption as that of the Nassau
Fleet twenty years earlier. Aimless pillaging and burning alter-
nated with clumsy attempts to side with the disaffected natives
against their rulers. In October 1643, short of provisions and
sickened by the futility of their life in this hostile land, the fleet
sailed south again, round the Horn and safely back to Holland.

Two disasters on this scale were enough for the Dutch. The
dream of Pacific conquest died. They left the Spanish Pacific
viceroyalties in peace, and for another eighty years there was to

be no large scale expedition from the Netherlands for the south.

Robert Jenkins's Ear

In England the dream of repeating Drake's exploits off Callao was still alive. Far from becoming discouraged by Dutch disasters, the idea of taking possession of these rich Pacific viceroyalties, instead of just raiding their harbours, appeared increasingly attractive to the English. Just as much as the Dutch, English trading had suffered from Spanish arrogance and monopolism. Trading in the East or the Caribbean was still a hazardous business in the 18th century, and in fact became worse as the century advanced. As if already seeing the future decline of their imperial power, the Spanish navy was hypersensitive to the sight even of an unarmed foreign sail—although, in fairness, for more than a century they had also had to cope with ever-growing numbers of pirates, and the protection of their own trade was a dangerous full-time job. During the 1720s and 1730s indignation increased among English merchants and seamen about Spanish interference with their shipping. A typical petition presented to Parliament, in this case by the merchants of Bristol on 3 March 1738, reads: 'That for some years past, the British trade and navigation, to and from the British colonies and plantations in America, hath been greatly interrupted and exposed to the continual insults and depredations of the Spaniards in those seas, where they have taken and made prizes of great number of British ships and vessels.'

A few weeks later there occurred a curious incident in the Palace of Westminster. A master mariner named Robert Jenkins was summoned to appear before a committee of the House of Commons to tell the members about an incident that had occurred seven years earlier. Sailing back home from Jamaica in the brig *Rebecca*, Jenkins recounted how on 9 April 1731 he had been boarded by the crew of a Spanish *guarda costa*, commanded by one Captain Fandino. The brig was later released 'after using (Jenkins) in a most barbarous inhuman manner', ran one account of the affair, 'taking all his money, cutting off one of his ears, plundering him of those necessaries which were to carry the ship safe home, without doubt with the intent that she should perish in her passage'.

Jenkins had kept that ear as proof, and now held up the black withered lump of flesh before the members.

'What were your feelings when you found yourself in the hands of such barbarians?' he was asked.

Jenkins answered humbly, 'I committed my soul to God, and my cause to my country.'

Although Jenkins had taken his case to the King immediately on his return, the incident had then been forgotten. Now it was used to inflame public feeling in England against these continued Spanish depredations, and was a contributory cause of 'The War of Jenkins's Ear' in 1739; for both belligerents one of the most unprofitable and ill-conducted and generally muddled wars of all time.

This was to be fought mainly at sea, and the English started off without any clear-cut plans and with the uneasy feeling that the Royal Navy, their only shield against invasion and their only offensive weapon, too, was poorly equipped and low in morale after too many years of peace. Harassment of Spanish shipping and raids against Spanish harbours and colonies seemed likely to be the most profitable lines of attack, and all sorts of ideas were put forward for raids on Buenos Aires and Havana and large scale attacks on Spanish shipping in the Caribbean. Panama, the narrow and vulnerable funnel through which most of the Pacific treasure still passed, was mooted as a rich target, and a more sensational project was an assault on the Philippines and the capture of the Manila treasure ship off Acapulco.

The final agreed plan, which suffered a long and painful gestation between October 1739 and June 1740, was more ambitious and sweepingly grandiose even than those of the Dutch a century earlier. It was, like earlier Dutch plans, to send a powerful fleet with adequate marines and artillery round Cape Horn, and up the Chilean coast. The fleet was to employ its strength to stir up the Chilean natives to overthrow their Spanish overlords, and then proceed to Peru, take Callao and Lima and enter into a treaty with the most powerful Spanish emigrés (who were known to be disaffected) in order to overthrow the viceroy and enter into an exclusive trading arrangement with the English. Next, the fleet was to break the Spanish trading route from Peru to Panama, and at Panama 'to make an attempt upon that town and endeavour to take it, or burn and destroy it, as you think most for our service'. No half measures, in fact. After that it was to attempt to discover a passage north of the American Continent.

These, in essence, were the instructions given to Captain George Anson R.N. at the beginning of 1740, and the despatch of his fleet to the Horn marks the culmination of the series of armed

George Anson (after Reynolds)

predatory raids and invasions into the Pacific, beginning with
Drake's in the 16th century. Anson's voyage proved that no other
region in the world could match the power of the Fuegian
archipelago to decide the fate of men bent on plunder or conquest.
Here it was shown, once again, how climate and geography in
their extreme forms can be the most violent arbiters of history.

George Anson was ill-equipped in *matériel* and experience in
war to effect this monumental undertaking. His experience of war

was limited to long anti-piratical cruises, notably off the coast of the English colony in South Carolina, where he served from 1723 to 1730. Like Magellan and Drake he was up against powerful political cliques who did not want him to go, believing that the defence of the homeland and raids into the Caribbean were the first priorities, and that the despatch of a fleet round the notorious Horn was far too hazardous an undertaking. There were not the ships or men to spare.

Whatever may be said of George Anson—and he has been described as generous and humane as well as cold, calculating and single-mindedly self-interested (he was certainly handsome, a ladies' man, and very musical) he acted with heroic determination against all the obstacles planted in his way to prevent his fleet from sailing. The essence of success of the invasion was surprise, yet every power in Europe discovered the destination of the fleet during the eight months from January 1740 until its eventual departure in September.

The Chelsea Invalids

The fleet was made up of five men-of-war, ranging from the flagship *Centurion* (60 guns) to the little *Tyral* with eight guns, and two supply ships. But in June plans for the urgently needed repairs to the largest ships had not yet been put in hand. Seamen for the vessels were as elusive as new spars and masts and sailcloth. Sailors and soldiers assigned to his fleet were suddenly switched to vessels whose needs the Admiralty decreed were more important. Promised a smart regiment of foot soldiers, Anson was offered instead a party of no less than five hundred invalid pensioners from Chelsea Hospital. Few were under sixty, many over seventy. One of them was a sort of veteran veteran: he had been wounded at the Battle of the Boyne fifty years earlier. The greater number of them carried the scars or infections of past foreign campaigns. Brought out of a deservedly tranquil retirement, these old men were marched out of London down the Portsmouth road. Those who had the strength and courage, and these were the best, deserted in large numbers.

Now almost at his wits' end, Anson sent a message to the Admiralty saying, 'I am sorry for the occasion of complaining that fourscore of the . . . invalids have been suffered to desert the night before they were embarked, and that as many more are unfit for service by infirmities and extreme old age . . . I hope his Grace (First Duke of Newcastle) will despatch orders for the changing the defective, which will enable me to proceed instantly on our expedition.' For replacements, Anson received 210 raw recruits at the other limit of the age range—most of them had never fired a musket nor set foot on board a ship before. So, to destroy Spanish power on the Pacific coast of America, instead of the eight hundred crack troops he had been promised, Anson could muster less than five hundred pathetic senile wrecks and inexperienced youths. Of the embarkation of these old pensioners, it has been movingly recorded in the narrative of Richard Walter, who sailed in the flagship:

> They were themselves extremely averse to the service they were engaged in, and fully apprized of all the disasters they were afterwards exposed to; the apprehensions of which were strongly mark'd by the concern that appeared in their countenances, which was mixed with no small degree of indignation, to be thus hurried from their repose into a fatiguing employ, to which neither the strength of their bodies, nor the vigour of their minds, were any ways proportioned, and where, without seeing the face of an enemy, or in the least promoting the success of the enterprise they were engaged in, they would in all probability uselessly perish by lingering and painful diseases; and this too, after they had spent the activity and strength of their youth in their Country's service.

Not one of these unfortunate old warriors survived the voyage.

Ill-manned, ill-victualled, in ships ill-equipped for this gigantic undertaking, Anson sailed—as all the world knew—down the Channel in the last days of September 1740. As a final delaying encumberance, the Commodore (his new rank as C.-in-C.) was given the task of convoying no fewer than 150 sail of merchantmen for the first leg of the journey.

The Spanish admiralty had had more than six months to prepare counter-measures. Like Magellan two hundred and twenty years earlier, Anson not only had potentially mutinous crews, but was to be shadowed on his way south by a powerful enemy force, playing a wide-dimensioned, slow-paced game of tag all the way. For the Spanish Admiral Don Jose Pizzaro, 'a man of great reputation, and generally esteemed an experienced sea officer', had received orders to take five powerful men-of-war to Madeira, Anson's first port of call, and to intercept and destroy the squadron *en route*.

The loss of any one ship of his inadequate force by storm, or at the hands of Pizzaro, would have greatly jeopardised Anson's chances of success. His most valuable ship was not the *Gloucester*, a fourth-rate of 866 tons, with fifty guns, or even the *Centurion* herself, but a storeship of 560 tons, a converted three-masted East Indiaman with a crew of 120 (including some of the lowest scrapings and press-ganged drunks and layabouts in the squadron) and about forty of the aged Chelsea Pensioners and green young soldiers. With her conversion to military use the ship had also changed her name, to *Wager*, after the First Lord of the Admiralty, Sir Charles Wager, whose weakness and incompetence had contributed to the delay of the Squadron's departure. The *Wager* had in her holds the field guns, mortars and small arms for the land assault on Valdivia, Valparaiso, Callao, Lima and Panama, quantities of ammunition and small arms, and a great part of the provisions for the whole fleet, including most of the brandy, rum and wine. She was even more valuable to Anson than the *San Antonio* had been to Magellan.

On the protracted voyage south to the Horn, three men in turn served as commander of the *Wager*. The first was Captain Dandy Kidd, who was transferred to another vessel at Madeira, and was replaced by Captain the Hon. George Murray. The name Dandy Kidd suggests a swashbuckler, an extrovert, a man calling cheerfully for action. He was in fact a sick voice of doom. He was on his deathbed before the squadron reached Puerto San Julian, where he was heard to say 'that this voyage, which both officers and sailors had engaged in, with so much cheerfulness and alacrity, would prove in the end very far from their expectations, notwithstanding the vast treasure they imagined to gain by it; that it would end in poverty, vermin, famine, death and destruction'. A few days later, when they were anchored off the port, the water was seen to be 'tinctured to that degree, that it look'd like blood': another fateful augury, though in fact it turned out to be nothing more than a massive invasion of shrimps.

Here at Puerto San Julian the *Wager*'s third commander, Captain David Cheap, took over. Cheap was to prove himself a brave, petulant, indecisive commander, unpredictable in his application of authority, and as weak-willed as he was physically resilient. He inherited from Murray and the unfortunate Dandy Kidd, besides a rag, tag and bobtail crew and the aged pensioners, a mixed bag of officers, including the devious and untrustworthy Lieutenant Robert Beans, a loyal and straightforward young surgeon, John Elliot, Midshipman Alexander Campbell, Henry Cozens—a wildly undisciplined young man—and the Hon. John

Byron, son of the fourth Lord Byron and grandfather to Lord George Gordon Byron, who celebrated his seventeenth birthday on the voyage out from England.

Death by Fever

After disposing of its giant convoy of merchantmen, Anson arrived at Funchal Roads, Madeira, and learned from the friendly Portuguese governor (Portugal, now an independent kingdom again, was neutral) that a large number of sail—believed to be Spanish—had been seen hovering on the horizon as if expecting the arrival of the English. Anson sent out a scout to reconnoitre. Nothing was seen. The Spanish ships had already left, believing that the English must have by-passed the roadstead. Pizzaro was as impatient as Anson was plodding, which made the pursuit all the more interesting. At Madeira the two squadrons had missed one another by less than twenty-four hours. But they would come closer together than that, and Anson (no more than the pursued Magellan had been) was not in a fit combat condition.

The first of the Pensioners had died before they were out of the Channel. Their living conditions were appalling beyond description. For the healthy young sailor they were bad enough. With the coming of the three-master in the 15th century, the new skills of the shipwright, the better understanding of hull design and sail, as well as of the art of navigation, which had begun in the days of Henry the Navigator, little thought had been given to the comforts and conveniences of life below decks: not since the time at sea had grown from a week or two of sailing close inshore from port to port, to the long ocean voyages which could entail many weeks out of sight of land. The diet had scarcely altered in the past two hundred years. Fresh fruit and meat were taken on board whenever possible, and livestock were carried in pens in the welldeck, leading a few miserable days of existence before a merciful death. Nothing was understood about diet. The surgeon's twin panaceas were brandy for the sick and the saw and knife for the wounded.

By contrast with the speedy and efficient Nodals and the Dutch navigators, and even with Drake, the voyage south of Anson's squadron was disastrous all the way. The *Wager*, like its consorts, was desperately overcrowded. The sailors did not even refer to the soldiers as soldiers, or marines, or even as the Chelsea Pensioners. They were 'the invalids', and they made life miserable for everyone else, too. There was nothing for them to do. Enforced idleness

ADMIRAL BYRON.

made them sick more quickly than if they had some function or duty on shipboard. Seasickness struck them down during the first weeks, and here in the fetid lower decks, jammed hammock to hammock, much closer than the regulation fourteen inches apart, these old men swung to and fro, dying one by one. Younger men, in the open air on watch for much of the time and hardened to the smells and overcrowding below decks, could survive on hard salt meat and even tougher ship's 'biscuit'. Besides, a generous daily ration of rum or brandy and wine helped to anaesthetise them against the worst rigours and discomforts of their life. Later, in the heavy swell of the doldrums, with the ports of the *Wager* and other ships closed because they were so heavily laden and with the temperature in the nineties, the stench from the immobile sick and dying old men in the unventilated air spread to the raw young soldiers as did the infection.

When the mortality rate had reached such a level that every day the squadron had to hove to for the decent disposal of its dead, and the surgeons and their untrained assistants, the 'loblolly boys', were almost dead from fatigue too, Anson realised he would have to take some drastic steps if there was to be anyone left to work the ships, let alone to make an armed assault on Spanish fortresses still 3,000 miles distant. He ventured below decks in his flagship, and what he discovered was so appalling that he ordered scuttles to be cut in all his ships to try to get some air to the sick and dying.

Most of the old pensioners in the *Wager* were dead before the Brazilian coast was sighted, and the survivors were carried ashore to the island of Santa Catherina to recuperate in tents. 'As soon as we had performed this necessary duty, we scraped our decks, and gave our ship a thorough cleaning; then smoked it between decks, and after all washed every part well with vinegar. These operations were extremely necessary for correcting the noisesome stench on board, and destroying the vermin; for from the number of our men, and the heat of the climate, both these nuisances had increased upon us to a very loathsome degree, and besides being most intolerably offensive, they were doubtless in some sort productive of the sickness we had laboured under for a considerable time.'

Calenture fever had been the worst killer, 'a disease', according to Walter's narrative, 'which was not only terrible in its first instance, but even the remains of it often proved fatal to those who considered themselves as recovered from it. For it always left them in a very weak and helpless condition, and usually afflicted with fluxes and tenesmus's.'

The Treacherous Governor

The Governor of the little Portuguese settlement at Santa Catherina gave them as hospitable a welcome as they had received at Madeira. He appeared friendly and helpful and even sent out a pilot to guide the ships to their anchorage. But the spell ashore failed to have the recuperative effects on the invalids that Anson had hoped for. The sandy beach on which the hospital tents were erected looked healthily inviting, and the diet of fresh fruit and water should have been curative. Instead, the old men continued to die in the same numbers as on shipboard, and seventy in all were buried in the graveyard. After a few days, the death rate actually increased. This was ascribed to the 'great numbers of muscatos' and the sand flies which pestered the sick and those who tended them. The high temperature (they were only a few degrees south of the Equator) and damp tropical air could not have helped either, and the mosquito net had not yet been invented. So Anson determined to be away as soon as he could, judging that the colder, drier air of the sub-Antarctic would be more likely to restore the survivors. And he was, in any case, weeks behind his timetable.

This slow progress of the squadron had again upset Admiral Pizzaro's interception plans. After missing Anson by no more than a few hours at Madeira, he steered across the South Atlantic for the River Plate. There during the month of January 1741, while Anson was still far north in Brazil, he awaited the arrival of the English squadron, or for some news of its whereabouts. The intelligence arrived first, direct from the Governor of Santa Catherina, an old crony of Pizzaro's, who had despatched a speedy vessel south to the Spanish colony with the most minute details of the English squadron while he was smilingly helping Anson to settle in. Pizzaro put to sea with the intention of doubling the Horn and meeting Anson on the west coast while he was still in a weakened condition from his passage, and probably with his heavy guns stove below.

But this time Anson was too quick for him, weighing from Santa Catherina on 18 January, four days before Pizzaro got away impatiently from the River Plate without waiting to take in a proper store of provisions. Anson made such a swift passage down the coast that both squadrons were off the Patagonian coast at the same time, and almost in the same place.

On 10 February Pizzaro made contact, and believed that he must soon be in action with his quarry, when he sighted the fifth rate *Pearl* (40 guns). This ship had become separated from the squadron during a fog as bad as that experienced by Drake off the Brazilian coast, and for several weeks had run south on her own, searching all the way for the *Centurion*. On that morning the *Pearl*'s captain made out five men-of-war, and closed innocently with them. One of the ships looked just like the *Gloucester* and the flagship was wearing a red broad pennant, a replica of Anson's. Just short of gunshot, the *Pearl*'s officers began to feel uneasy, then recognised the trap into which they had so nearly fallen, and made good their escape.

The *Pearl* rejoined the squadron off Puerto San Julian, where they were delayed for several days while storm damage was repaired. The bleak anchorage had the same melancholy effect on Anson's men as it had had on every ships' company, since the mutinies and executions of the 16th century. No one liked the place, all were anxious to get away as soon as possible. It offered them nothing. Hunting parties quite failed to discover the guanaco and rheas which had once abounded here. Nor, presumably because of some freak drought, was there a drop of fresh water to be found—a failure for which they were to pay dearly in the trials that lay ahead. For the same reason they saw none of the now notorious Patagonian 'giants'.

On 27 February 1741 at 7 a.m. the squadron stood out to sea again. Anson believed he was still in time to catch the best of the summer weather at the Horn. He was as ignorant as all those who had attempted the passage before him that he was choosing the worst time of the year rather than the best. All the summer months are bad, with almost unremitting westerly gales. In June and July, though the days are short and the weather bitter cold, the wind sometimes swings to the east, almost the only time of the year when it does, and the seas are less fierce. The worst time of all are the equinoctial months of March and October. Anson had chosen March. And for the last of the invasion fleets to attempt the passage into the Pacific, Cape Horn had prepared a truly malevolent reception.

'Our most sanguine dreams'

For a while the weather feigned tranquility. Even as far south as le Maire Strait, the weather remained fair, and the squadron

advanced through the wide passage in good order, bowled along
by a brisk wind and tide. Walter's narrative sets a tone of cheerfulness, tinged with forebodings.

As these Streights are often considered as the boundary between
Atlantick and *Pacifick* Oceans, and as we presumed we had
nothing now before us but an open sea, till we arrived on those
opulent coasts, where all our hopes and wishes centered, we
could not help flattering ourselves, that the greatest difficulty of
our passage was now at an end, and that our most sanguine
dreams were upon the point of being realised; and hence we
indulged our imaginations in those romantick schemes, which
the fancied possession of the *Chilean* gold and *Peruvian* silver
might be conceived to inspire. These joyous ideas were height-
ened by the brightness of the sky, and the serenity of the
weather, which was indeed most pleasing; for tho' the winter
was now advancing apace, yet the morning of this day, in its
brilliancy and mildness, gave place to none we had seen since
our departure from *England*. Thus animated by these delusions,
we travers'd these memorable Streights, ignorant of the dreadful
calamities that were then impending, and just ready to break
upon us; ignorant that the time drew near, when the squadron
would be separated never to unite again, and that this day of
our passage was the last cheerful day that the greatest part of us
would ever enjoy.

A few dozen leagues to the south-east, beyond the crenellated
silhouette of Staten Island, Pizzaro's squadron, now closer to their
quarry than they would ever be again, was enjoying a similar
balmy day. Combat was as remote as storms in the minds of the
Spanish as well as the English seamen. Then all must have
sighted, within minutes of one another, the darkening sky ahead.
That would have been soon after noon on 7 March 1741.

Scurvy and Storm

The timing of this first gale could not have been calculated with
a more refined cruelty. It was bad enough that the deceit was
sustained until everyone thought that the worst of their sufferings
were over, and that it struck just as they were about to begin the
long, dangerous haul up the Fuegian archipelago. As the sky
clouded over and the men went aloft to reef the courses, the scurvy
also began its fearful and decimating attack.

With every league recorded by the ships' logs on the passage
south from Santa Catherina to Tierra del Fuego the health of

A View of Streight le Maire between Terra del Fuego, and Staten Land, in ẏ Latẹ of 54:47 Sẹ and Longẹ from London 70:04 Wẹ with a Squadron ẏ Ships under ẏ Command of Commodore GEO. ANSON Esqr. a. Part of Staten Land. b. Cape Sṭ Bartholomew. c. Part of Terra del Fuego. d. Iṣ. Maurice. e. by some taken for ẏ Bay of good Success, by others for Valentines Bay. We Steer'd thro' ẏ Streights Sẹ within three Leagẹ of Terra del Fuego, and found ẏ rapid Current set ẇ ẏ Southward, till past ẏ Streights, then it set to ẏ Eastward along Staten-land agreable to Monṣṛ Frasier's account. We had soundings from 54 to 65 fathoms small Stones and shells between two and three Leagẹ from Terra del Fuego. Variation of ẏ Compass 42:30 Easterly

the crews and the surviving soldiers had improved. The vitamin-loaded diet and the fresh water from Brazil, and then the first chill drafts of the southern air, had cleared away any lingering elements of the calenture fever. The earlier casualty rate had also eased the pressure on space below decks. But there were still many weak from the fever's after effects, even as late as March.

Three hundred years ago almost nothing was known of the disease which killed more people than either shipwreck or war. It was vaguely associated with the unnatural practice of going to sea at all, and with the sea being an alien and hostile medium. The roots of this fear are impenetrably deep in Western man, and by then had been fertilised for centuries by cults, superstitions and religions. More fundamentally, man, being a land animal, was indulging in an unnatural environment by going to sea, and must be expected to suffer the consequences. Greed and cheap gain being the first motive power, death or injury by disease was as natural a risk as by sword or musket shot. That was a part of the gamble.

Scurvy was by far the worst killer. Both those who suffered from it, and those who might have devised a cure, regarded it as a God-sent consequence of being away from land for too long. The vapours of the sea alone, and especially when inhaled for long periods, were thought to be noxious; only a land environment (the smallest island would do) could bring about a cure. It took nearly four hundred years before it was understood that it was the fresh vegetables and fresh water, which were so avidly seized on at any port of call, rather than the inhalation of the air of the land, that alleviated the sufferings of those afflicted with scurvy.

There was also a deep-seated (and contradictory yet convenient) theory amongst officers that 'none but the idle and indolent are thought ever sick of this disease'. One contemporary writer tells of the 'very great prejudice and hardship from which the unhappy persons who labour under this affliction have too long severely and most unjustly suffered . . . This so generally received, though vilely mistaken opinion, has caused many poor sufferers to endure more from their commanding officers than from the distemper itself; being drubbed, kicked and cuffed, to do their duty, when utterly incapable of it, and often when ready to expire . . .'

Walter wrote of its symptoms as being 'inconstant and innumerable, and its progress and effects extremely irregular', and continued to describe its manifestations among the unfortunate soldiers and seamen of Anson's expedition:

'Scarcely any two persons have the same complaints and where there hath been found some conformity in the symptoms, the order of their appearance has been totally different . . . Yet there are some symptoms which are more general than the rest . . . These common appearances are large discoloured spots dispersed over the whole surface of the body, swelled legs, putrid gums, and above all, an extraordinary lassitude of the whole body, especially after any exercise, however inconsiderable; and this lassitude at last degenerates into a proneness to swoon on the least exertion of strength, or even on the least motion.

'This disease is likewise usually attended with a strange dejection of the spirits, and with shivering, tremblings, and a disposition to be seized with the most dreadful terrors on the slightest accident. Indeed it was most remarkable, in all our reiterated experience of this malady, that whatever discouraged our people, or at any time damped their hopes, never failed to add new vigour to the distemper; for it usually killed those who were in the last stages of it, and confined those to their hammocks, who were before capable of some kind of duty, so that it seemed as if alacrity of mind, and sanguine thoughts, were no contemptible preservatives from its fatal malignity.'

The *Wager* was one of the first to suffer from the sudden onset of scurvy, and the least able to deal with it. Seamen and pensioners were especially close-packed in the supply-ship, and Anson had ordered Captain Cheap to transfer one of his surgeons to the flagship to replace his own, who had died of fever in the tropics. Not that any surgeon could offer much more than moral support and encouragement when the scurvy began to spread after its first attack. He could do nothing about the wretched cramped and damp conditions, the bitter cold, the unchanging diet of salt meat

(cold when the fires could not be lit) and biscuit, and the shortage
of water—two pints a day, three for invalids—since leaving
Puerto San Julian.

The *Wager* was the sternmost ship when the squadron passed
out of the le Maire Strait, and the closest to the hideous rocky
face of Staten Island's southern shore. Deeply laden with her
heavy cargo, she responded sluggishly to the helm and was least
capable of sailing close to the wind. And now, suddenly, they no
longer had a following breeze but faced a fierce south-westerly
gale. This was not the only danger. For at the southern exit from
the strait through which, an hour before under a clear sky, the
tide had thrust them, they met the eastward current that sweeps
from Pacific to Atlantic round the Horn. Under storm canvas,
through the rest of that day and all through the night the *Wager*
clawed off those black cliffs. By dawn, although they had been
steering south south-west since the storm had broken over them,
they had lost thirty miles and were almost east of Staten Island on
whose rocks, according to Midshipman Byron, 'we were very near
being wrecked'.

The *Centurion* off Cape Horn

Lost in the Uttermost South

Like Drake's squadron nearly two centuries earlier, they never
knew for sure their position for the next weeks, and the surviving
charts showing the squadron's changes of course are highly
speculative. For some two weeks they forced their way south,
Anson believing that the strength of the Horn current would
diminish with distance from the Cape. It was a dreadful fortnight
of suffering and labour. Those off watch in the *Wager* were often
at the pumps, the rigging and spars were constantly needing
repair, the men were wet day and night, the seas washed continu-
ally over the decks, and even the heads (the latrines) were unusable
for days on end. Below decks, the first boils and sores were breaking
out on the skins of the old men. 'On the 10th,' a diarist in the
Wager cryptically recorded, 'we lost sight of the *Anne* Pink [another
supply ship], on the 12th carried away the rails and timbers of the
head on both sides.'

The duration of the storm was astonishing. No one had believed
it possible for gales as fierce as this to last for so long. Not until
23 March did they abate. By then the *Wager* was somewhere south
of the 58th parallel, and everyone was in a state of misery and
despair. One officer, stationed aloft to search for icebergs (as if
they were not already sufficiently tormented) told how he 'had to
endure such fatigues from the severity of the weather . . . that
really life is not worth preserving at the expense of such hardships'.

On that same day 'the gale re-awakened in a frantic squall', and
the flagship herself was disabled. The battered squadron, still
miraculously together, struggled north-westwards, each watch
more rigorous than the last as the scurvy began to decimate the
seamen, too. By 8 April the *Wager* had lost her mizzen mast, and
there were only some fifteen fit men left to work the ship. The
ship's gunner, John Bulkeley, later recorded that 'we had very
hard gales at west, with the largest swell I ever saw . . . between
six and seven in the morning, holding by the topsail hallyards to
windward, there broke a sea in the ship, which carried me over the
wheel, bilg'd the cutter, and canted her off the skeet's bottom up
athwart the barge'.

They were almost driven ashore near Noir Island off the
Fuegian archipelago before another hurricane seized and turned
them about as if they were ocean flotsam, hurling them south
again, further south than before and below the 60th parallel.
Now at last the squadron began to break up. The *Severn* and *Pearl*

(two of Anson's most valuable ships, representing half his fighting strength) disappeared on 10 April in a squall of mixed hail and snow. They had been lagging behind for some time, and were gone when the squall cleared.

The *Wager* was to hold her station for a little longer, although she was now in desperate straits, sometimes half filled with water and with almost all control gone. Captain Cheap was too ill to move from his cabin, and the gunner was in charge of one watch. Byron, a fit and strong young man, was standing up well to the rigours and demonstrating the tenacity of body and spirit which was to preserve him through the months of horrors that still lay ahead.

The Wreck of the Wager

The *Wager* had her last communication with the flagship on 13 April. Even in these tumultuous seas, when survival appeared doubtful, Anson remained aware of the other enemy, and of the risk of being discovered by Pizzaro with his force which must now be several times more powerful than his own. For this reason, he was determined to keep together the squadron's survivors. In a brief lull, the battered *Centurion* bore down under the lee side of the ship, and Anson called out across the water to Cheap, who was brought up from his cabin to answer.

'Why do you not set the main topsail and make more sail?' the Commodore demanded.

Cheap's reply revealed the pitiful state of his ship, although this must have been evident to Anson.

'My rigging is all gone, and broke fore and aft, and my people almost all taken ill and down', he answered. 'But I will set him as soon as possible.'

'Please do so, and make what sail you can after me.'

The ship's carpenter, John Cummins, did what he could, fitting a cap on the stump of the shattered mizzen mast and getting up a lower studding sail boom. A new mainsail was bent, so that the *Wager* was able to regain for a time her place with the squadron.

But the *Wager* was now a broken ship—crippled in her rigging and hull, her company shattered in health and spirit. Among those still capable of keeping a watch, there still remained a will to live. But with the breaking of each flooding roller over the welldeck, the tearing of each sheet of canvas as it was bent, the hurling overboard of each corpse sewn roughly into its canvas shroud, the will to stay with the squadron on its westerly suicide course was gradually eroded away. There is no evidence of a spoken conspiracy, with its mutinous overtones. This pressed crew from the gutters and taverns of Portsmouth had been too deeply indoctrinated with fear of the awful consequences of outright rebellion. But there is a point in the sufferings of every sailor beyond which he knows he cannot continue to function. (In the *Severn* and the *Pearl* this limit had already been passed, for, as Anson was later to discover, the commanders of these warships had yielded to the temptation first to lag behind, and then when out of sight to swing over the helm and with the wind at last in their favour, to sail for safety and home.)

Already there was a growing body in the *Wager* who favoured giving up while there were still enough crew alive to sail their ship. For the *Wager*'s Master this limit of endurance had been reached by 19 April, when he took over the evening watch from Gunner Bulkeley. They were already far astern of the *Centurion*, and the new officer of the watch 'could not see the Commodore's light, tho' it was visible to every one else on the quarter-deck: the Master still persisted he could not see it; on which I went and acquainted the Captain, who came upon deck, and seeing the light, ask'd the Master where his eyes were?'

It was already too late to make up the lost distance, and who was to tell how hard they had tried to do so? By dawn only the *Gloucester* and *Anne* were distantly in sight, and they were both soon gone. Yet Cheap, unlike his ship's Master, was not a man to tolerate deliberate defection. 'Shattered and disabled' they might be (in Byron's words) and with now only twelve fit men in all to work the ship, the sick captain ordered a heading to the squadron's appointed rendezvous up the Chilean coast at Guamblin Island, three hundred miles south of Valdivia, their first objective.

The mutterings continued and spread. The *Gloucester* and *Anne* had got away from it all (no one had believed they had sunk in that snowstorm) so why should not they? And why should they not have better rations now that—as one seaman put it—'the Commodore was parted'. The men were becoming insolent and threatening. Cheap ordered a brace of pistols with a brace of balls to be given to every officer in the ship to be ready for any trouble.

There was dissension among the officers, too. With the *Wager* in this broken condition, most of them considered it foolhardy to steer for Anson's first rendezvous, which would entail searching a notoriously dangerous lee shore for a single island. These officers wanted to set course for another rendezvous, far out from the

coast at Juan Fernandez, where there was timber for repairing
the ship and water and fruit to restore their bodies. John Byron
was among the dissentients. He was to come to know every aspect
of David Cheap's character over the next months and years; this
was his first taste of the man's obstinacy. Byron complained at the
time of his captain's 'rigid adherence to orders from which he
thought himself in no case at liberty to depart', and his 'stubborn
defiance of all difficulties'. They were going to Guamblin Island
and that was that.

During the early days of May 1741, in terrible winter weather,
the *Wager* was swept up the uncharted broken Chilean coastline
north of Cape Desire. No one knew within any useful degree of
accuracy where they were, and those still capable of keeping on
deck spent most of their time anxiously searching for a sign of
land. The seas continued boisterous and they had almost no
control over the ship. On 5 May Byron spotted from the quarter
deck masses of kelp which suggested that they could not be far
from land. Cheap, who was better now and on deck, reckoned
they were twenty leagues from the shore, others sixty leagues.
No matter what the margin of error might be, it was certainly
wide enough to keep doubly alert those in the ship who still had
any interest in staying alive.

It was not until the morning of 13 May that the warning cry
of land ahead to the north-north-west was heard from the
forecastle, although they must have been sailing perilously close
inshore in poor visibility for several days. The cry came from
John Cummins, who was in the forecastle inspecting the chain
plates. At first the Bosun's mate who was with him could not see it,
and when the lieutenant of the watch was informed he discounted
the possibility. Captain Cheap was not even informed. If land it
was, it would be to the east, on their starboard quarter. In fact
they must already have been in the Gulf of Peñas, a deep bay cut
into the confusion of coastal islands 350 miles north of the western
entrance to Magellan Strait, and the land that Cummins had seen
briefly through thick mist and low scudding clouds was the
Peninsula of the Three Mountains at the northern entrance to the
gulf.

At 2 p.m. John Bulkeley ordered the fore yard lowered and the
fore sail up. 'Notwithstanding I was officer of the watch,' he
wrote in his account, 'I was oblig'd to go upon the fore yard,
where was Mr. Campbell midshipman, one bosun's mate, four
seamen, and the master's servant; which were all the hands we

could get out of the ship's company to assist. Whilst on the yard I saw the land very plain, on the larboard beam bearing N.W. half N. nearest high land, with hillocks, and one remarkable hommacoe [hummock] like a sugar loaf, very high. At the sight of land I came off the fore yard and acquainted the captain.'

They were now in a dangerous situation, with a rocky shelterless shore on three sides, and a gale blowing of such strength that even fully rigged and with a fit crew they would have been unlikely to survive. Cheap left his cabin to see for himself, slipped, fell heavily with the roll of the ship and dislocated his shoulder. He was carried in acute pain to the surgeon's cabin, where he ordered the lieutenant and John Bulkeley to attend on him. 'It is necessary for us to make sail,' he told them through his pain, 'and to use your utmost endeavours to crowd the ship off the shore. You see, gentlemen, my misfortune will not permit me to continue on the deck.'

That night it was too dark to see even the length of the ship. Byron was on deck, struggling with those who still had strength left to get up the fore sail. 'Which done,' wrote Byron, 'we wore ship with her head to the southward, and endeavoured to crowd her off from the land: but the weather, from being tempestuous, blowing now a perfect hurricane, and right in upon the shore, rendered our endeavours . . . entirely fruitless. The night came on, dreadful beyond description, in which, attempting to throw out our topsails to claw off the shore, they were immediately blown from the yards.'

The *Wager* first struck the rocks off a small island on the south side of the Gulf of Peñas in the Guayaneco Archipelago at 4 a.m. on 14 May. She was driven off within a few minutes, struck again much harder and was thrown on her beam ends, the seas washing clean over her.

This second shock created a galvanising response among all those still alive in the ship—and these still numbered above one hundred and fifty. In the ghastly minutes that followed, the *Wager* might have been a long-rotting piece of timber full of secretive insects that is unearthed and is struck a searching blow. From the deepest bowels of the doomed ship the frightened, the sick, and dying, the shammers, all emerged from the hatchways—some shouting in fear, some hauling themselves up painfully or helped by their shipmates—and gazed about in the darkness at the scene, searching for some means of escape.

Byron observed them in amazement. 'Instances there were . . .

of behaviour so very remarkable, they could not escape the notice of any one who was not entirely bereaved of his senses; for some were in this condition to all intents and purposes; particularly one, in the raving despair brought upon him, was seen stalking about the deck, flourishing a cutlass over his head, and calling himself king of the country, and striking everybody he came near, till his companions, seeing no other security against his tyranny, knocked him down. Some, reduced before by long sickness and scurvy became on this occasion as it were petrified and bereaved of all sense, like inanimate logs, and were bandied to and fro by the jerks and rolls of the ship, without exerting any efforts to help themselves. So terrible was the scene of foaming breakers around us, that one of the bravest men we had could not help expressing his dismay at it, saying it was too shocking a sight to bear; and would have thrown himself over the rails of the quarter-deck into the sea, had he not been prevented.'

But bravery and resolution were witnessed, too. The man at the wheel refused to leave his station while the ship held together, and was still trying to get some response to the helm. Then there was one seaman Jones, who attempted to instil some courage into his shipmates. 'My friends,' he cried out above the sounds of the storm, 'let us not be discouraged: did you never see a ship amongst breakers before? Let us try to push her through them. Come, lend a hand; here is a sheet, and here is a brace; lay hold; I don't doubt but we may stick her yet near enough to the land to save our lives.' What is more, the efforts he inspired succeeded in freeing the *Wager*, and, steering by the sheets and braces, she was got nearer shore, jammed tight between two great rocks, one of which sheltered her from the worst of the gale.

Daylight broke, the mist and cloud momentarily cleared, revealing the dramatic change in their situation. There was a beach not far distant, a few minutes' rowing away, and the *Wager* now seemed as if she would hold together after all.

The Disembarkation

The realisation that they were safe from the tempest brought about a reaction amongst the *Wager*'s company as startling and un-explained as if the crucial act had been left out of some epic melodrama. At one moment the decks of the vessel presented a scene of terror and panic, with the cries of pleading and prayers overwhelmed by the shrieks and curses of those determined that their lives should end in noisy hysteria. Now the stage, lit by a

Cape Horn

grey dawn light, had become the setting for a new demonstration
of uproar. The sick, the malingerers, young men who had dutifully
kept a watch through two months of storm, even some of the
surviving old pensioners, burst into an orgy of vandalism, looting
and drunkenness as if the pressure of discipline, confinement,
deprival and fear had been building up to this moment of irresistible explosion. The armoury was the first target of these wild men.
Seizing swords and pistols with which they threatened anyone
who attempted to restrain them, they got into the ship's hold,
which was already half full of water and the corpses of some of the
desperately sick who had been swept there from their hammocks
and drowned by the first onrush of water, and broached the wine
casks—and there were many of these.

Drunkenness took them in different ways. Some prised open
locked chests and plundered the officers' cabins for money and
valuables. Others—the inevitable showmen of any drunken
party—raced up onto deck, shouting, screaming, laying about
them with their swords, until the worst cases succumbed and
tumbled unconscious into the flooded welldeck. (Their bodies
were still washing gently from side to side days later.)

Then there were the comics. The pillaging had produced an
unexpected store of formal wear intended for the victory ceremonies in newly-conquered Spanish cities. A group of drunks,
the hard core led by the Bosun and an old bruiser, James Mitchell,
seized these with glee, donned them, and joined the bedlam on
deck, 'imagining themselves Lords Paramount', as one eyewitness
described their arrival. It provided the last macabre touch to this
grand guignol scene, through which, like scene-shifters over-
impatient for the fall of the curtain, the non-participants struggled
to lower the boats and then tumbled pell mell into them.

The disembarkation was as riotous as the orgy, even if there was
a purpose behind it. The remaining masts—the main and foremast—had been cut away earlier in an attempt to steady the ship,
and this handicapped the efforts of those lowering the barge, the
cutter and the yawl. The barge was got away first with the mate
aboard, with orders to reconnoitre and return. Once ashore, he
decided to remain. The ship's lieutenant was the next away with
a second party. He did not return either, but at least he sent his
crew back with the boat.

Captain Cheap, at his wits' end and in agony from his shoulder,
determined to be the last to leave. He was still issuing orders from
his cabin when Byron begged him to get ashore in the yawl, if

The barren island

only to escape from the more murderous of his drunken crew. 'Get the men out as soon as possible,' Cheap begged, and asked to be kept informed of events—no mean demand under the circumstances.

But Byron got his way, and with help carried his captain up onto deck and lowered him into the yawl. Then he returned to the wardroom in the hope of salvaging some of his clothes and personal possessions. Before he could get to his chest the *Wager* gave a great lurch as if to break the revels on deck with an intermission, the hull was broken through by a rock and the water came pouring in. Believing that the *Wager* must soon break up, Byron made his way quickly back to the quarterdeck and joined Cheap, the army officers, Midshipman Campbell and the other officers in the yawl. They rowed to the shore, leaving behind them the sounds of the men's 'luxury and riot, feast and dance' from the broken ship.

The Barren Island

Byron rightly considered their safe arrival on shore, in his own restrained words, 'a desirable event'. But there were other considerations which seemed to suggest that an alcoholic end in the breaking-up *Wager* might be preferable to the fate that seemed to await them on this stark Chilean island in mid-winter. 'Which ever way we looked,' Byron wrote of this moment, 'a scene of horror presented itself: on one side the wreck (in which was all that we had in the world to support us), together with a boisterous sea, presented us with the most dreary prospect; on the other, the land did not wear a much more favourable appearance: desolate and barren, without sign of culture, we could hope to receive little other benefit from it than the preservation it afforded us from the sea.'

The island on which the *Wager*'s company had been shipwrecked is one of a pair at the southern entrance of the Gulf of Peñas. This area of the Chilean coastline, a navigator's nightmare, is geographical anarchy, and on any but a large scale map only a mean average of promontories, peninsulas, deep inlets and fiords, channels and islands and islets and more rocks, lends a general outline shape. The rest is confusion, worse even than that of Tierra del Fuego. A modern maritime chart marks the more easterly of these two islands as Wager Island, and elsewhere commemorates the ordeal of the ship and her company with such names as Byron Island, the more westerly of the two and separated from Wager Island by a half-mile-wide channel, Rundle Passage,

the
scene of the
Wager's
shipwreck

0   10   20
Nautical Miles

South Pacific Ocean

Peninsula de Taitao

P. Esmeralda

Rio San Tadeo

P. de Tres Montes

Purcell I.   P. Forelius

Javier I.

Gulf of Peñas

Canal Cheap

N
W   E
S

Wager I.

Byron I.
Archipelago
Guayaneco

Mount Wager, 2,139 feet, dominates the centre of Wager Island, the peak of Mount Anson, 1,436 feet, is on the north shore, Lake Byron is just a rock-flanked pond at the head of a long narrow channel that all but bisects the island. Rugged Island is no more than an enlarged rocky hazard which the *Wager* must have narrowly missed before being smashed onto the north-west corner of Wager Island. Forty-five miles to the north-east, separating an island from the Cordilleras-dominated shore, is Cheap Canal.

Although farther to the north from the western entrance to the Magellan Strait than Puerto San Julian from Cape Virgins, the islands of the Guayaneco Archipelago have almost everything— climate, natural history and topography—in common with the north-western end of the Fuegian archipelago. At this fining-down point of the American continent, there is more variation in climate and natural life from east to west than from north to south. The Andes, and the land mass beyond them see to that. The same westerly winds beat against the battered shoreline, bringing squalls of rain, hail, sleet and snow through the cold summer and colder winter, with only brief breaks of watery sunlight. Like western Tierra del Fuego, the climate is foul and dampness predominates in every season; but the temperature never gets as low as in its equally dreary northern counterpart, Alaska. The larch and the beech—evergreen and deciduous— are almost the only trees, and these sink at a comparatively early age into despairing senility, collapse, and add to the tangle of rotting timber which makes penetration of the forests almost impossible. There are coarse grasses and moss, bogs and swamps, limpets and mussels and the inevitable kelp on the shoreline, a few foxes and rodents, some disconsolate frogs, and little else. The nomadic canoe natives, who still survived at this time, were similar to the Alakalufs, desperately primitive, treacherous and pathetic, and spent their mean lives paddling from island to island, setting up crude encampments for the time it took to fish the local waters and clear the best of the mussels from the rocks. They were accompanied on their wanderings by their dogs who helped by driving the fish before them in the water, herding them together to be speared; and when times were especially bad, or a change of diet was called for, provided dog stew for the pot.

By happy chance, the natives had been on the northern shore of Wager Island recently, and one of their wigwams had survived and was found close to the shore where the crew landed. On

that first night it probably saved a number of lives. Naval and
army officers, pensioners, seamen and boys who had got away
from the *Wager* on the first day crowded into the wigwam at dusk,
and some others, who could find no room, huddled under a tree.
It rained all night and the cold was piercing. Three were found
to be dead at daybreak.

The day was little less terrible than the night, and it continued
to pour with rain and blow a gale off the sea. Life became a simple,
individual struggle for survival. Their only food was a three-pound
bag of biscuit crumbs, for 137 people, many of whom were in the
last stages of scurvy, and the wild celery which grew abundantly
along the forest fringes. These ingredients were mixed in a pot of
water, to which was added the corpse of a single seagull, and the
whole served up to those with the strength to demand a share.
Unfortunately the biscuit bag had previously contained tobacco,
which caused those who ate the stew to be 'seized with the most
painful sickness at our stomachs, violent retchings, swoonings,
and other symptoms of being poisoned'.

Their only possible salvation lay in the wreck, still being beaten
by the waves offshore, and still occupied by the hard core of the
revellers, whose party had seemingly continued through the night.
These gay drunks had no means of getting ashore, and no desire to
do so, or allowing anyone on board. The crew of the yawl which
rowed out to the *Wager* during the day were driven off; but on the
following day, May 16, the Bosun and his party seemed to have
had enough. The seas were higher than ever, the gale even worse,
and it was clear that the ship must soon break up—and that no
boat could possibly approach the wreck. The Bosun's men thought
otherwise. Now they were calling for rescue, regardless of risk,
and wildly beating the sides of the ship to emphasise their demand.
When this failed to work, they were seen to drag a four-pounder
gun from the quarterdeck, and cannon shots rang out above the
roar of the storm. For drunks, their aim was not bad and one of
the balls passed close over the wigwam in which Captain Cheap
was recuperating, and was clearly heard by those inside.

Several more days passed before the tired, hung-over and
frightened revellers could be rescued, and some of the provisions
salvaged from the *Wager*. It was a dangerous task, not only because
of the high seas, but because the Bosun and his men were still in
an antagonistic frame of mind, and still had access to the ship's
armoury. They were on the quarterdeck, fully armed with muskets
and swords, still in long ceremonial finery with lace ruffs and

cuffs, and were in a noisy mood when the rescue boat came alongside.

Captain Cheap, supported by Lieutenant Hamilton, and armed only with a stick, bravely marched forward to meet them as they came ashore. The confrontation provided the one comic moment of their stay on Wager Island—and perhaps the only light relief the island has experienced in its history.

Captain Cheap marched straight up to his boozy Bosun. 'You are a rogue and a villian,' he said, and struck him on the head with the stick, so that he fell to the ground and lay motionless. After a few moments, the Bosun dragged himself to his feet, and observing that his Captain now had a cocked pistol in his hand, exposed his naked chest. 'You deserve to be shot,' said Cheap, but restrained himself from doing so, and contented himself with ordering him and his men to give up their arms, and their finery. 'It was scarce possible to refrain from laughter at the whimsical appearance these fellows made,' Byron commented as they stripped down to their greasy trousers and dirty checked shirts.

This day was notable, too, for the arrival of the natives. They appeared round a headland in their canoes, at once timid and curious. By this time some provisions and goods had been got out of the wreck, and Cheap and a party of officers on the shore were eventually able to tempt them with signs of friendship and the offering of lengths of cloth. The natives beached their canoes and came ashore tentatively, ready to run—a short, swarthy, greasy bunch of men with lank hair falling over their faces, and naked in the damp, bitterly cold wind except for a skin loin cloth. They were especially fascinated by the mirror Cheap held out to them, searching behind it for another of their own kind, and grimacing and chuckling at it. In return, they left behind some large mussels before departing, each sporting a hat and a red soldier's waistcoat.

They were back again two days later, perhaps feeling that they still had a debt to pay, this time with three sheep, a gift that surprised as well as delighted the castaways. It did not appear likely that there was any grazing within a hundred miles of this God-forsaken spot. The next time they brought their wives and children and dogs, built themselves some wigwams, and settled down as if to become a part of this seemingly friendly community. They even offered the white men some of their dogs, which at once went into the stewpot, though Byron reserved one of them for himself as a companion.

These natives survived by their wigwams, the most crude and

easily erected dwellings imaginable, lined with bark and sealskin; by the seal oil with which they soaked their skin; and by fire. Their fires went with them everywhere, burning in a clay and mud bowl in every canoe, and brought ashore at every landing place. Crouching all the time over these fires when not sleeping or fishing and hunting, gave them a stooped stance, made their eyes stream and caused premature blindness. The women were the fitter and more industrious sex. They spent less time over the fires, while the men, except for bringing in the wood to keep the fires alight, doing household chores and quarrelling amongst themselves, did nothing. Fishing was woman's work. The women went off in the morning in the canoes, with their baskets, spears and dogs, the smoke trailing behind, as if each canoe was some miniature precursor of Fulton's first steamboat. Their expertise and endurance as swimmers amazed those who watched them leap overboard with a basket between their teeth, diving for long periods to five or six fathoms for sea eggs*—'they seem as amphibious as seals and alligators', remarked one eyewitness—often carrying their naked children on their backs to accustom their lungs to the strain. Or they would throw their dogs into the water and wait, like shepherds with their collies, for them to corral the best fish into an inlet, where they could be speared or netted.

These were unreal and uneasy days for the survivors of the shipwreck. Their life had not settled into any routine, and yet those who were fit enough—and the wild celery was rapidly curing the worst of the scurvy—tended to follow the same routine in order to subsist. Muskets were used to hunt wildfowl, the rocks were searched for mussels, and wood gathered for the fires outside the wigwam and beside the three upturned boats, which made temporary shelters for the rest of the men. When the weather allowed, parties were sent to the wreck to bring back wine and provisions for the store tent—closely guarded day and night—which had been set up on the beach. Byron led another party through the dense beech forests and, clambering over the rotting trunks of old trees, reached the top of the nearest high land. No wonder he named it Mount Misery. From the summit he learned only what he had suspected, that they were on an island, surrounded by more islands. If he caught a distant glimpse of the

---

* Byron defined the sea egg as 'a shellfish, from which several prickles project in all directions, by means whereof it removes itself from place to place. In it are found four or five yolks, resembling the inner divisions of an orange, which are of a very nutritive quality, and excellent flavour.'

snow-capped Cordilleras, he certainly was unable to trace any route by land or sea that might lead them to the main; 'our prospect that way being intercepted by still higher hills and lofty woods'.

The Assassination of Midshipman Cozens

A week after they had been shipwrecked and faced imminent death, most were still alive. Any wonder at their escape had long since disappeared. Most of the time was spent in fighting off the hunger and cold, but there still remained hours for nursing discontents and grudges. According to the letter of the law, their pay, and so their liability to naval discipline, ceased from the moment they were cast on shore. There were precedents for this, and 'mess-deck lawyers' to remind the others of it. It was a time for firm, decisive leadership; for all his personal bravery and resourcefulness, this was something that David Cheap was unable to provide.

One of his men described Cheap as 'a gentleman possess'd of many virtues; he was an excellent seaman himself, and lov'd a seaman; as for personal bravery, no man had a larger share of it; . . . no misfortune could dispirit or deject him, and fear was a weakness he was entirely a stranger to; the loss of the ship was the loss of him; he knew how to govern when he was a commander on board . . .' Captain Cheap's troubles began from the time his ship first struck. Ill and incapacitated as he was, it was beyond his powers to control his riff-raff crew and passengers, and he resorted to alternating bouts of extreme severity and lax overfriendliness with some of the worst offenders.

The undisciplined behaviour became worse with the easing of their immediate food problems when the ship began to break up and barrels of beef, flour, and peas, brandy, rum and wine were washed up on the shore. The provision tent on the beach, though guarded day and night, was nevertheless constantly raided, and attempts at severe rationing were strongly resented. There were outbursts of violence against this sensible measure. The thug, James Mitchell, gathered about him a group of nine from the old revellers' gang. On the night of 3 June, they placed a barrel of gunpowder outside Cheap's hut and laid a train to it, with the intention of blowing him up and making off with the provisions in the uproar. The ruse failed, but Mitchell's crowd deserted anyway, and set up a rebel camp a mile or two away. Mitchell, it was believed, had already carried out two murders. The body of one of his victims was reported to be still lying unburied in the forest.

There were other flare-ups over the following days—fights over trifles, drunken disputes (the ration of alcohol was generous: a quart of wine or half a pint of spirits a day), and almost continuous petty violence. If only Cheap had given them some evidence of his leadership, instead of breaking into sudden fits of over-sternness, and had presented them with some definite programme for getting them away, things might have been better. Instead, rival gangs formed under strong-arm toughs, and, like a microcosm of a state in anarchy, each tent and wood-and-thatch hut which sprang up between the forest and the beach represented a clique of varying size, but mutually hostile, some especially aggresive, some mean and jealously husbanding their resources, others known for being drunken rakes, and suspected of most of the thefts.

For a young observer like Byron, it was a sad sight, and to escape he built a little place of his own, and settled in with his dog, who bit anyone who came near. Some of the other more enter-prising individuals built little rafts and coracles and went out fishing and shooting in the nearby bays: for a time this one-man enterprise paid off, and these were the only people who fed really well.

Only a common cause could have brought about some sort of unity, and Captain Cheap did in the end provide this, though not by intention and it nearly cost him his life. One of his more obstreperous officers was Midshipman Cozens. 'When sober,' was Byron's judgement, 'I never knew a better natured man, or one more inoffensive.' He was one of those unfortunate fellows who cannot carry their liquor and become wild in their cups. This, of course, made him popular with all but the senior officers. Everyone else loved him for his frank openness when he was sober, and for making them laugh when he was drunk. From the start of the voyage he had been the *Wager*'s light relief.

There had been many brushes between Cozens and Cheap before. The first serious one since the shipwreck occurred when Cozens was trying unsuccessfully to roll a cask of dried peas up the beach. Cheap advanced angrily on him and told him he was drunk. 'With what should I get drunk, unless it be with water,' Cozens rudely replied. 'You're a scoundrel!' Cheap told him, and struck him with a stick.

That night, still drunk, Cozens abused his captain so loudly, calling him a rogue and a fool, that Cheap had him put under guard.

Cozens's next rows were with the ship's surgeon and purser, both members of a small group of officers who remained loyal to their captain at all times. The quarrel with the purser was the more serious, and began with a dispute about the wine allowance. Cozens was in a wild mood, and this was not the first time the two men had met in conflict. At the height of the quarrel, the purser, loudly accusing Cozens of mutiny, drew his loaded pistol and shot at him at close range. Cozen's life was saved by the purser's arm being canted up by a witness as the pistol was discharged.

The rain was teeming down at the time, precluding any sort of hunting with firearms, so the shot alerted everyone to danger. The captain was one of the first on the scene. He had heard the cry of 'Mutiny!' and was carrying a pistol. 'Where is the villian?' he was heard to shout.

Byron appeared too late to witness what happened then. He heard the second shot as he ran from his hut, and when he arrived Cozens was lying on the ground with blood running from his head. It seemed that Cheap had not bothered with questions, even to ask who had fired the earlier shot. Seeing Cozens standing before the purser, obviously drunk again, Cheap precipitately put the pistol to his head and pulled the trigger, the ball missing his eye and lodging in his cheek behind the jaw.

Word of the outrage spread rapidly to every hut and tent along the beach. The men, carrying pistols, swords or muskets, gathered in the rain about the fallen young midshipman. Suddenly it looked like a full scale mutiny. Cheap stood his ground, surrounded by his surgeon and purser and three of the army lieutenants, all armed with pistols. He spoke to the men with all the authority he could muster, telling them that he would not tolerate mutiny, that he was their commander still, and that they were to return to their tents and huts. They obeyed this time, and even now Cheap might, with wisely applied firmness and decisiveness, have maintained control over them. But instead of accepting the injustice of what he had done, he became more than ever conscious of his slipping authority and behaved with unexpected brutal inhumanity. No one was to move, or even to tend poor Cozens, he ordered. What was the use of preserving his life, anyway, Cheap argued, for if he survived it would only be to face the hangman's noose after his court martial back in England?

This, then, was the situation on 11 June. Captain Cheap and his stout band of loyalists—Lieutenant Robert Beans, the surgeon, Lieutenant Hamilton and the purser—remained in a state of self-imposed siege in their tent. A few yards away lay the wounded figure of Midshipman Cozens, his head resting in his drying blood and covered only by a tarpaulin, with no one daring to give him succour, although before he died several days later the carpenter's mate and the surgeon's mate did at least remove the ball from his cheek. The rest of the camp had forgotten most of their disputes in their newly-found unity, and new determination to get away from this vile island. That fatal pistol shot had done more than federate the antagonistic groups along the seashore by a mutual hatred of their captain. It had also made them realise that, as no one else was going to lead, they would have to fend for themselves.

The Mutineers' Plans

The new leadership resolved itself around an enterprising mixed group including two of the midshipmen, Alexander Campbell, and Isaac Morris, Thomas Clark, the *Wager*'s master, the Bosun, the surgeon's mate, John Jones, and petty officers Bulkeley and Cummins, a mixed bag if ever there was one. Cummins believed that, with his skill as a carpenter, and with unskilled assistance, it would be possible to adapt the ship's longboat, which had been salvaged from the wreck before it broke up, so as to carry up to 81 men, with food and water for a long sea voyage. He would cut it in half and enlarge it by fitting in an additional centre section nearly twelve feet long. There were now only a few over a hundred survivors from the 150 or so who had got ashore, the rest having died from starvation, exposure and scurvy. This casualty rate simplified the accommodation problem, and the rest would sail in the yawl and the barge, making a little three-boat escaping squadron.

Until the last days of July, the direction of their escape, when the work on the boats was completed, had not been discussed. They knew that they were not far—perhaps 300 miles—from Valdivia to the north. They might even be able to find and link up again with the Commodore or one of the other ships. Then on 30 July Byron was seen by John Bulkeley to be reading Sir John Narborough's journal of his voyage in these waters, which Byron had borrowed from Captain Cheap. Bulkeley in his turn borrowed it from Byron, and reached the daring conclusion that they should —no less—sail their open boats back down the Chilean coast to

Cape Desire, through the Magellan Strait, up the Patagonian coast to Santa Catherina in Brazil, where they could be assured of a welcome. Thence back to Europe in the next Portuguese ship.

When this was put to the men, they found the appeal irresistibly attractive. A paper was drawn up for supporting signatures, 'and as soon as the people heard it, they came flocking to sign first, crying all aloud for the Straits, seeming overjoyed, as if they were going to England directly, without any affliction or trouble.'

After the sufferings of the gale, the terror of the shipwreck, the weeks of exposure and starvation during the worst season of the worst climate in the world, hope of salvation had almost died. Now here was the wonderful idea, put to them as a workable proposition, that they could sail back home, just like that. In this new state of euphoria, they quite forgot that they would have to sail in small open boats the same seas that had scattered and disabled a great naval squadron and wrecked their own ship; that they would have to navigate the dread strait through to the Atlantic; and then for another 1400 miles, against contrary winds, up the Patagonian and Brazilian coasts, where they had previously failed even to find water.

When Cheap heard of the plan he was outraged. It was not daring, it was mass-suicide. They would not last a day on this frightful lee shore with its continuous gales. It was also an evasion of their duty, he protested. Even in his leaking tent on an un-charted island with the rain pouring down day and night, the wind screaming through the forest on one side, his vital stores and field guns lost, all his old soldiers dead (the last of the invalids died on 30 July)—through all these miseries and trials Cheap remained obdurately loyal to Commodore Anson and determined to complete his part of the mission. Not that he had any counter-plan, except that he must lead his men north to the nearest Spanish port, seize a vessel by force of arms, and sail off to rejoin the squadron—a proposal which appeared by any rational judgement to be equally lunatic and suicidal, with the added hazard—a dread one to any English seaman—of facing the Inquisition, a Spanish prison, and the torture chamber. Any attempt by Cheap to regain authority was doomed after his expressed opposition to the plan to sail home.

The preparations for the escape from Wager Island were long and arduous and accompanied by more suffering and death. Only this new sense of purpose in their existence preserved the lives of the survivors of those first terrible days. The sea had swept to the shore most of the remaining provisions from the broken-up *Wager*, and by mid-August the ration was down to a quarter pound of flour and three squares of salt beef a day. The rest of their diet was made up from any limpets and mussels still to be found on the rocks, some edible seaweed fried in candle wax, and scurvy grass. That was all, and it was not enough to keep a man alive in this damp, freezing climate, in which, as Bulkeley described it, 'a man will pause some time whether he shall stay in his tent and starve, or go out in quest of food'. The other, dangerous alternative was to raid the provision tent. In desperation, a number of the men attempted this. The price of an illegal gorging of salt meat was appallingly high if you were caught. Two men were given no fewer than four hundred lashes, and others were deprived of all food and expelled into the forest.

The only stores that still seemed inexhaustible were the wines and spirits, barrels and barrels of them. The generous ration of alcohol (a pint of brandy a day at one time) helped to keep out the cold and insulated the minds of the men from their hunger and sufferings. But it also led to the same sort of frenzied wildness which had led to that early orgy and the murder of Midshipman Cozens. Some odd things happened. John Cummins, working away indefatigably on the longboat, one day saw a seaman breaking up a priceless anchor stock for firewood. He was at once thrown into such a state of fury that he lapsed into delirium. They were all finally dependent on the carpenter for their salvation and his condition caused the acutest anxiety. 'All possible methods are used to restore him,' noted John Bulkeley of his friend. Fortunately they proved effectual.

On another evil day of driving rain and wind Byron was surprised in his one-man hut by a determined delegation of starving seamen who ordered him to give up his dog for the stewpot. Byron pleaded with them in vain, and they tore the wretched animal away from him. There is nothing like hunger for making a man a realist, so Byron joined them round their fire. 'It was exceeding good eating,' commented one of the diners at this 'dog-feast'. 'We thought no English mutton preferable to it.' Three weeks later, when the famine was worse than ever, Byron remembered where they had killed his beloved dog, and found there his paws and skin, and was glad to make a meal of the rotting remains.

Men were dying again, some dying drunk, some sober, and the death rate increased through August and September while the

weakened carpenter and his assistants laboriously completed their
work on the longboat and repaired the other boats. Since that
glorious day of decision, the spirit and unanimity of the men had
both diminished as the winter wore on through continued tempests
and downpours. On 11 September John Bulkeley wrote des-
pairingly in his journal: 'The people were uneasy; scarce any
work done for this week past; everything is at a stand; we have
now among us no command, order, or discipline; add to our
uneasiness, the uncomfortableness of the climate, we have been
inhabitants of this island sixteen weeks, and have not seen ten
fair days; the murmurings of the people, the scarcity of provision,
and the severity of the weather, would really make a man weary
of life.'

The natives returned, with their promise of salvation as before—
their giant mussels which had tasted so good, their sheep found
heaven knew where, their idiotic cheerfulness which at least
diverted their minds. But this time the castaways got nothing from
them. The strain of wickedness which had poisoned the spirit of all
ranks in the *Wager* since she had sailed and seemed likely to doom
all to a delayed death—and had been inflamed by continued
alcoholism—this time caused some of the men to act cruelly
toward the only people who might yet have saved them. Some of
the sailors—the renegades who had long ago settled away from
the main encampment and had all the time been an anxiety—
threatened to steal the natives' canoes to sail to the mainland.
Others attempted to seduce their women, in spite of their witch-
like appearance and seal oil-soaked bodies. At this their men
ordered immediate embarkation, and by that evening there was
not a chattering native to be heard.

It was the *Wager* herself—or rather her skeletal remains resting
between the offshore rocks—which finally saved the lives of all
that remained of her company. There were, incredibly, three
clear days towards the end of September, and a party of men were
able to get away in the barge and row to the wreck. Four casks of
beef were found lodged in a corner of the hull, a treasure beyond
the price of a shipload of Potosí silver. That night they all feasted
for the first time for weeks—to such satisfaction that they would
not even look at the peas which had also been retrieved, for 'our
stomachs are become nice and dainty', as one observed in satisfaction.

This beef of old England had a marvellous reuniting and
rejuvenating effect on the men. By the end of the first week in

October the work on the longboat was finished, and the vessel was solemnly and optimistically named *Speedwell*. Rations were calculated and apportioned to the three boats, barrel after barrel of gunpowder was emptied—to Cheap's fury—and filled with water, charts prepared from Narborough's book to indicate roughly their course among the islands to the Magellan Strait; which was really a case of the blind leading the blind.

The Bosun Is Called a Scoundrel

The fate of Captain Cheap was in their hands. All that remained was to decide what to do with him. Captain Pemberton, who seems to have been of a vindictive disposition from the little we know of him, was in favour of taking him by force with them, so that justice could be served on him for the murder of Cozens. Lieutenant Robert Beans, a loyal Cheap supporter until now, had suddenly turned renegade, too, though Cheap had still to learn this. He favoured abducting his captain, and as second-in-command his voice was influential. Others were less certain, and wanted to leave him behind with some provisions. Byron claimed to have known nothing of all the plotting and counter-plotting, which came to a head on 9 October, and presumed that Cheap would come with them as a passenger.

In the early hours of that morning Captain Cheap was asleep in his bunk when Bulkeley, Cummins, the Ship's Master, and the vengeful Bosun broke in and woke him up.

'Do you know what you have done, or are about?' Cheap demanded as they bound his wrists.

'Yes, sir,' he was told. 'Our assistance was demanded by Captain Pemberton, to secure you as a prisoner for the death of Mr. Cozens; and as we are the subjects of Great Britain, we are obliged to take you as such to England.'

'Gentlemen,' Cheap replied pathetically. 'I am still your commander; Captain Pemberton has nothing to do with me. I will show you my instructions.' And as if this might reassert his authority, he searched through his papers for the documents he had brought with him from the wreck, and showed them to the four men. 'What is this for, then? I did not think you could treat me like this.'

Bulkeley repeated the purpose of their mission. 'It is your own fault, sir. You have not done anything for the public good or for finding a means of escape from here. You have acted, instead, carelessly and indifferently, as if we had no leader.'

Above: Canal O'Brien at the western end of the Beagle Channel.
Below: Diego Ramírez; this is an unnamed rocky fragment of the islets south-west of Cape Horn, discovered by the Nodal brothers in 1619.

This all-too-true statement flattened Cheap, and he seemed as if resigned to his fate. 'Very well, gentlemen, you have caught me napping. I do not see any of you in liquor. You are a brave lot of fellows, but my officers are scoundrels. Where is my lieutenant? Is he not your leader? Please call Mr. Beans,' he asked Bulkeley.

When Robert Beans appeared, Cheap burst out in wrath: 'You will answer for this. If I do not live to see England, I hope some of my friends will. Well, sir, what do you plan to do with me now?'

Beans told him that he was to be taken to the purser's tent, where he would be confined with Hamilton and the surgeon. Then he allowed Cheap to dress for the short walk to his temporary prison. As Cheap passed his captors standing at the tent's entrance, he apologised for not taking his hat off to them, 'on account of my hands being tied'—but to Beans he repeated his threat that he would be called to account for this crime.

Cheap's gentlemanly behaviour, so characteristic of the man at a time of stress like this, was favourably noticed by nearly everybody, and only the Bosun—not surprisingly—took advantage of his captain's helplessness. Later that day he went to the Purser's tent, and began shouting abuse at Cheap, reminding him of the time when he had struck him on the beach. 'Then it was your time,' he shouted threateningly, 'but now, God damn you, it is mine.'

Still Cheap retained his dignity. 'You are a scoundrel,' he told the Bosun coldly, 'for using a gentleman ill when he is a prisoner.' The wild Bosun was at length restrained from violence by his friends. Such behaviour would not look well in the records.

The pace of events on Wager Island was accelerating. The longboat, the cutter and the barge were ready, provisioned and watered for launching for their ambitious voyage (the yawl was left behind as unfit). The only remaining subject of dispute was still whether or not they should take Cheap and his two loyal officers with them. Pemberton remained adamant that they must come as prisoners. Cheap was equally determined that he should remain behind, and, if he could not get at the Spaniards, preferred a more dignified—and perhaps more comfortable—death in his tent than in the longboat. 'I do not want to go off in any of your craft,' he kept repeating. 'I never planned to go to England, and would rather choose to be shot by you.' Then, with great earnestness, he told Beans and Bulkeley in his tent-prison the night before they planned to embark:

'Gentlemen, I shall never live to see England, but die by inches on the voyage; and it is surprising to me that you think you can survive this voyage to the south. You will encounter ten thousand difficulties. I am sorry so many brave fellows should be led to a place of which they know nothing, when by going to the northward there is, not more than ninety leagues distant, the island of Chiloe [with its Spanish settlement] where we can be certain of taking prizes, and may even have the chance of rejoining the commodore.'

The next day Cheap appealed for the last time to Bulkeley, begging to be shot rather than taken as prisoner in the *Speedwell*. Majority opinion was coming round to the view that they would be better off without their Captain and his last loyal officers, Surgeon Elliot and Lieutenant Hamilton. They would be packed tight enough, and short enough of food, without adding reluctant passengers. But the question of shooting Cheap was never considered. This might lead them all to the gallows—there were precedents for that. No, they would leave him behind, with a little food.

Only Pemberton stood out against this decision, and even as they were embarking, ordered his few surviving young soldiers to stand to arms in formal array on the beach in order to conduct Cheap on board as a prisoner. On this remote, blustery shore, the scene was like a pantomime parody of some army disciplinary ceremony. Pemberton was determined to see the thing through, like any good infantry officer. The impatient seamen thought otherwise. 'Let him stay, and be damned!' they called out, and Pemberton as a soldier whose authority would be nil once on board, had to accede or be left behind, too, with his men.

One by one the cutter and the barge, each stepped with a single mast and lateen sail, and the *Speedwell*, now rigged as a schooner and partly decked, were launched. Pemberton marched his men through the surf in proper style, and himself climbed over the longboat's gunwale after them. Then the last men gave the boats a heave, hoisted themselves over the stern and they were off.

The flotilla did not get far that day, nor the next, and anchored each night in some nearby sheltered bay. They could not even get away from Wager Island without constant danger from being swamped and suffering damage from storms. On the second day out, it was decided to send a party in the barge back to their old beach to see if some sailcloth could be found, the longboat being already disabled from a split foresail. Byron, now deeply concerned at the abandoning of his Captain, saw that this might be his last chance of rejoining him and volunteered to lead the party with his friend, Midshipman Campbell.

As soon as they were clear of the other boats, Byron told the crew that he had no intention of returning, that their place was beside their Captain. His companions in the barge were by chance mostly young soldiers, who were a good deal less enthusiastic even than Captain Cheap about returning the way they had come in a small boat, and they eagerly agreed to re-settle in their old encampment rather than face any more unpleasantness at sea.

Captain Cheap was overjoyed to see Byron and his contingent. Since the departure of all but two of his company he had resigned himself to starvation and a death that could not be delayed by more than a few days. Now, with the sound barge, and this new accession to his military strength, and freed of all mutinous elements, they could not only escape, but could even put into effect the operation against the Spaniards which he had been nursing for so long. The soldiers had their muskets, so all that was needed was to repair the yawl, get together some provisions, and set sail. His resilience was remarkable. He was already looking forward to a good fight, and for the first time since the shipwreck was at last showing evidence of decisiveness—an unwelcome surprise for the soldiers who now found themselves facing another voyage (and, in an open boat, the north looked as unpleasant as the south), with a fight at the end of it.

The problem of provisioning the two boats was the most difficult to solve. Byron volunteered to return to the nearby bay where he had left the mutineers to beg from them their share of the provisions, but Cheap was not going to risk losing either the boat, or her crew, who might change their minds now they knew what they were in for. Instead, Byron had to make the trip overland—a long and arduous journey through swamp and forest— at the end of which he met with a frosty reception. The cutter and longboat were still anchored, waiting for a clearance in the weather, when Byron appeared on a rocky headland and called out his request. He was told brusquely, from across the water, that they needed all the provisions that they had, that they would come and make him prisoner if he hung around, and that he had better return the barge, or they would recapture it by force.

Byron returned wearily to the encampment, which was now named Cheap Bay, and reported to his Captain. They had meat for about two days, no more, and now faced the most miserable period of their existence since the shipwreck five months before. The unseaworthy yawl had to be repaired without the skilled guidance of the carpenter, and except for the inexhaustible wild celery, the earlier attraction of which had so far diminished that it now made them sick, and a small supply of flour which Cheap had secreted away, there was almost nothing to sustain them. The sea birds had become canny about Cheap Bay, the mussels and limpets had long since been stripped from every rock within collecting distance. Without the strength to repair the yawl, or provisions for their first few days at sea, 'we were doomed to a miserable end', as Byron described their state.

Byron himself, once the fittest and strongest of the party, was laid low with diarrhoea 'by which', he said, 'I was reduced to a very feeble state'.

The word had got around of Cheap's secret store, and in their desperation three men raided it one night. Starving men develop a specially acute and accurate sense of suspicion and the culprits were quickly identified. None of them lived for long. One escaped at once into the forest before he could be flogged, another after, and neither was seen again. The third was taken in the barge and left on a rocky offshore islet. In pity for him, his guards built him a little hut and lit a fire before leaving. A few days later Cheap relented and ordered his release, but it was already too late. 'We found him dead and stiff,' reported one of his would-be rescuers.

But by now none of the survivors expected to live for more than a few days. There was just nothing at all left to eat, the mutineers had long since disappeared into the fogs and storms to the south. Then once again and for the last time, their old ship provided their salvation. In the middle of November the wind died and for just one day they had clear weather. With the last of their strength they got the barge launched and rowed out to the *Wager*. For nearly six months the old East Indiaman had been battered and broken by a constant succession of gales and high seas. There was almost nothing left of her—just a few ribs and a fragment of the bottom of her hull. Yet there, amazingly, providence had preserved what they most needed, the miraculous gift of three casks of salt beef.

The Open Boat Voyage

There were nineteen of the *Wager*'s original complement left on the island on 15 December 1741 when the repaired yawl and the barge were both loaded with the greater part of the beef, their firearms and all that they could carry, and were launched through the surf out of Cheap Bay into the Gulf of Peñas. Their intention was to work up the coast, keeping as close inshore as the wind allowed and taking advantage of any likely looking channels that might give them a sheltered passage. They had no charts, no map, no certain knowledge of the distance to the nearest Spanish settlement where they hoped, not for succour but for the chance—if only in a minor way—of emulating Drake and singeing the King of Spain's beard.

One can only contemplate in perplexed yet admiring wonder the gallantry and optimism of Captain Cheap, now that at last he was a man of action again. He had had nine months' experience of these southern coasts. He knew well enough the unrelenting nature of the climate, the vicious quality of the winds and currents, the destructive powers of the waves—which had tossed him and his ship onto the rocks seven months before. From the summit of Mount Misery he had been able to make out the hostile cliffs, the islands and islets, headlands, precipitous channels and half-hidden rocks—today they are still not fully plotted and demand for every ship the services of a skilled pilot—which stretched as far as he could see to the north. Yet he left Wager Island as if he were the skipper of a Channel packet bound for Calais on a choppy day— with the added stimulus of a brawl ashore at the other end.

On that first day, within a few hours, these brave intentions were forgotten in a struggle for their lives. The wind shifted dead west and increased in ferocity so that the two boats had to sail before the wind to avoid being swamped. The men jammed close together between the gunwales, leaning over so that their backs acted as a shield. Still the seas poured in, threatening to fill both boats. In turn, Cheap and Hamilton ordered their possessions to be thrown out, even the grapnels, and finally in desperation the casks of beef were hurled one by one into the waves. As the dusk closed about them they could just make out the ragged profile of the lee shore onto which they were being driven. But the crazy indentations of this coast which have wrecked so many ships this time proved to be the salvation of Cheap's two boats. First the yawl and then the barge were in turn swept through a narrow opening into a fiord of calm, smooth water.

Their first day at sea and first night ashore set the pattern for the following weeks. They slept on the bare rock in pouring rain without any covering; there was no wood for a fire, nor shellfish for a scratch meal. At first light they arose, stiff and half-frozen,

got into the boats and rowed out to check the state of the sea.
Sometimes they made several leagues to the north and found
another sheltered anchorage for the night. On other days they
were forced to remain ashore, picking their way among the rocks
for mussels and some form of edible seaweed. Their luck was
variable from day to day. Once they shot a fat goose, which gave
them fresh will to survive. On another night they warmed
themselves by a fire of rotting wood, though it snapped sparks on
them while they slept, burning their clothes. On several nights
they could not even get ashore, and rested half-asleep at their
oars, awoken every few minutes by the need to keep the bows of
the boats into the wind. There was never a real break in the
diabolical weather, and their hunger became more and more
agonising until on Christmas Day, of all days, as if the point of
desperation was reached in unison, they all pulled off their
makeshift sealskin shoes and gnawed through them.

From time to time they caught glimpses of a headland, the same
cape they had sighted shortly before they had been wrecked, with
the three mountains behind. They had by now followed the coast
of the Gulf of Peñas almost from the south to the north. This gulf,
they believed, held devilish powers, and in their extremity, they
increasingly believed that they would find calmer waters if they
could once double this cape. Again and again they were driven
back by the prevailing westerly gales.

Recuperating from one of these attempts in a sheltered inlet,
the men went ashore to scavenge along the beach, leaving two
men in each boat as guards. Byron was one of those in the barge,
dozing like the others, when he became conscious of the boat's
renewed agitation, 'and the roaring of the breakers everywhere
about us'. He went on to record of that night of disaster, which
confirmed in all their minds the satanic quality of the gulf that
held them trapped: 'At the same time I heard a shrieking, like
that of persons in distress; I looked out, and saw the yawl canted
bottom upwards by a sea, and soon afterwards disappeared. One
of our men, whose name was William Rose, a quartermaster, was
drowned; the other was thrown ashore by the surf, with his head
buried in the sand . . .'

This was the turning-point of their voyage from Wager Island
and again brought to a fine point of balance the men's will to
survive. It coincided, too, with one of those occurrences, heavy
with sombre symbolism, which so many mariners in these parts
had experienced before, like Drake's discovery of the gibbet at

Puerto San Julian, the eclipse of the moon which signalled the end of the little *Marigold*, that other eclipse which had covered Sarmiento's escape from Port Famine, and, with sinister similarity, the grisly discovery of corpses by Magellan's men when they made their first landing on Tierra del Fuego.

Elliot, the surgeon, was searching the shore without much hope for shellfish when he chanced on a cave whose entrance did not appear entirely natural, as if it had been deliberately cleared of rocks to make an easier entrance. They had seen none of the usual evidence of native life since they had left Cheap Bay, and this coast was more discouraging to human life even than their island. Inside the cave widened out into a large chamber, lit by a hole above, and filled by two layers of elaborate biers carrying in all twelve neatly laid out, solemn-faced corpses. Elliot thought they had been lying there a long time, yet (and this sent a chill of fear through him) the bodies had in no manner decayed. The flesh had simply hardened and dried. He left hastily through the narrow entrance, searching for someone to tell of this ill-omen.

For four at least of their company, death did come soon. Even with the barge laden so that a heavy sea must swamp it, no more than sixteen could leave this cove. Four must be left behind to fend for themselves when the sea became calm enough for them to embark. Cheap had decided that they must return defeated to Wager Island, where at least they had huts to shelter from the endless rain and wind, and where there was still some hope that the natives might return, in forgiving mood, with some of those outsize mussels which had tasted so good—so long ago. For the present, anyway, an armed assault on a Spanish colonial settlement had to be deferred.

The Return to Cheap Bay

The selection of the four men who were to be left as castaways on this coast, with its half-hidden charnel house, was not, after all, such an agonising duty. By now they were all so disheartened and weak that the idea of lying down in peace to die close to those peaceful corpses was almost preferable to facing again the pulverising waves, freezing spume and rain, of another passage by sea. Certainly the four young soldiers whom Cheap picked from the company on the beach appeared to make no objection. They were given muskets, powder and shot, and demonstrated with a sudden burst of patriotic and comradely cheerfulness when at length the barge was launched and put to sea through the breakers. 'God

bless the King!' they called out after the receding boat. 'Hip-hip-
hooray!' They could be seen shortly after, four stalwart young
figures in their torn, sodden uniforms clambering along the rocky
shore, helping each other over the difficult places.

Cheap named the place Marine Bay in their honour. But they
had not yet seen the last of it. At the whim of a renewed tempest
the barge was driven back to the same spot some days later,
although by then they were struggling to return to Wager Island.
From the sea there appeared to be no sign of the soldiers, but
already they had determined to take them on board even though
it meant that they would all certainly be drowned. When the
weather allowed, the barge ground up on the beach again, and
parties went out in search of their friends. All they found was a
single musket lying amongst the rocks.

They returned in the manner they had come, hugging tight to
the coastline when the wind allowed, as close as they dared when
the wind blew on-shore, rowing beneath a bare mast when it
threatened to hurl them against some lowering headland, and at
dusk finding what shelter ashore they could. It was a gruelling
and dispiriting voyage, far worse than the outward passage when
at least they were encouraged by some sort of hope of an improve-
ment in their lot.

Like patients arriving again at a hospital for incurables from
which they had once been released, Cheap, Hamilton, the midshipmen Campbell and Byron, Surgeon Elliot and the mixed
weary contingent of eleven seamen and soldiers landed again in
Cheap Bay in mid-January 1742. None had eaten anything but
seaweed and grass for the past four days, and they scarcely had the
strength to get up the beach. By great good chance, one of them
found a pile of putrefying seal flesh behind one of the huts and they
all set to on this feast. At least it gave them strength to look about
and consider their future in a less melancholy light. Everyone
now began to notice that a change had come over the place.
Nothing was quite as it was. Familiar things had been moved,
others had disappeared, new objects had appeared—that life-
giving seal flesh had not been there before, for instance. There was,
too, a feel in the air that made the seamen—always sensitive to
such things—feel uneasy. Even the officers, who were normally
rather patronising about uneducated seamens' superstitions,
recognised the hostility in the atmosphere.

Everyone heard the cry in the night from the sea, and most ran
from their shelter down to the beach and looked out across the

moonlit waves. The cries were like those of a drowning man. Then they saw a figure in the sea, not far off. He was half out of the water, seemingly swimming (yet who could swim in such an attitude?), and uttering this strange, haunting cry. He disappeared shortly after.

Perhaps their dreadfully weakened physical condition had made them over susceptible to superstitious fancies. Yet it was crystal clear to all of them that a restless spirit was abroad and must be placated. They remembered, then, the corpse of the seaman Mitchell had murdered before he set up his own camp of desperadoes along the beach. The spirit of this dead man must be put to rest by burial: their failure to do so, they now realised, had been the cause of all their miseries since his murder. The next day a party went into the forest up the slopes of Mount Misery, located the remains of his corpse, and buried it. Now, surely, their fortunes must change for the better.

A measure of relief was, indeed, now close at hand. One of the discoveries they had made on their return to the encampment was that all the huts and tents had been pillaged of anything of value. The natives had obviously been back again in their absence, but a curious aspect of the robberies was the disappearance of anything of metal. Even the nails from the *Wager*'s wreckage which was still strewn along the shore, had disappeared; yet previously the natives had shown no interest in metal objects. Then it was discovered that one of the huts had been securely nailed up. They forced an entrance, and inside was a pile of all the missing metal, stored as if for later collection. This seemed to suggest that their visitors this time were not from the primitive tribe who had once been so friendly and then fled in disgust at the attempts to seduce their wives. Was it even possible that a party of Spaniards had called at Cheap Bay, with the intention of returning to collect their spoils?

The Cacique

The mystery was explained a few days later—days of desperate starvation on the beach when it had even been suggested that one of their number might volunteer his body for the support of the remainder. A sailor died of starvation, a soldier accused of theft ran off into the forest. On the fifteenth day after their return, two canoes were sighted, edging their way along the coast and then paddling through the surf and up onto the beach. At first the occupants appeared as primitive as their earlier visitors. But this time among them was a leader of obviously superior caste—a *cacique* proudly carrying the emblem of office the Spanish authorities conferred on chieftains to secure their loyalty, a silver-headed stick. He had also a personal native servant and his wife.

This *cacique* could talk a little Spanish, enough for the surgeon, who was fluent in the language, to understand him. It seemed that word of the shipwreck and the camp on Wager Island had been passed from tribe to tribe, far up the coast, until it reached the Chonos tribe near Chiloé. This chieftain had come to see for himself, for where there was a wreck there were always pickings—in this case only some metal scrap, but to his superior tribe a priceless possession.

The past two months had brought about a remarkable change in the expectations of Captain Cheap and his men. Once, they had set forth hopefully, with ample provisions and arms for an assault on some Spanish harbour, with every hope of soon sailing off up the coast in a captured Spanish vessel. Briefly, the spirit of the corsair commander had been reawoken in Cheap's breast. Now as an alternative to cannibalism and then a slow and painful death they found themselves bargaining with a half-naked savage to lead them away to the enemy they had come to destroy: A Spanish prison, even the Inquisition, seemed like a golden haven.

The *cacique* appeared to have a poor estimation of the only thing they had to offer, the battered barge. But in the end agreed to take them, perhaps calculating that there might be some reward from his Spanish rulers for delivering up a party of enemy Englishmen. And with the simple terms agreed a new vision of relief from their distress filled the men's minds. This chieftain became a prophet of hope, a guide who had found his way to them and, as an expert in navigation and survival along the fierce and perplexing coastline, would lead them unerringly back to civilisation.

The Long Journey North

New sufferings and dangers began to disillusion them within hours of their embarkation, with the two canoes leading the overloaded barge along the same route they had followed two months earlier. For they failed to understand that these scattered native tribes all lived at the narrowest measure above survival level. Their wigwams were no more protective than the tents and huts in which the castaways had lived since the previous May,

and their canoes were even worse designed than their barge for
facing the open sea. Life continued at all only because of the
natives' inherited resilience to the wet and the cold, their skill at
fishing and locating the best places for collecting mussels, and
their nomadic existence. You kept alive by fishing and seal
hunting, occasional forays against enemy tribes, and crouching
over fires when you were doing nothing else. Then you moved on.
You starved if you stayed for more than a few days in one place.

For much of the time as they made their way northwards from
inlet to sheltered bay and river estuary, the surviving sailors and
soldiers suffered as fearfully as they had when they were alone.
The *cacique* offered them no special guarantee of privileged
treatment from the natives with whom they camped. Rather, he
treated them all except Captain Cheap as if they were below the
level of the lowest canoe native, refusing them a share of the food,
or even a place by the fire or in a wigwam. Only the *cacique*'s
servant and his wife, and some of the native women, showed any
evidence of humanity. Byron was several times kicked and beaten
like the tribal dogs, and was only saved from starvation by the
kindness of the women, who no doubt took a fancy to his youthful
good looks. Several of the seamen died during the early part of the
journey, and Surgeon Elliot—who had appeared the strongest
among them when they left—now began to show that he could
not last for long.

With each further stage in their sufferings and hunger, the last
vestiges of humane conduct began to disappear. Instead of abject
surrender to inevitable death, or the glorious sacrifice of those
four soldiers, the determination to survive, as they approached
nearer and nearer to civilisation, took a turn to madness. Captain
Cheap was known to be sitting on a private store of seal meat while
he watched one of his men sink into oblivion at his feet in the boat.
His own life, he knew, depended on his privileged relationship
with the *cacique*, and he emulated this chieftain's despising
treatment of the common native with his own officers and men.
In turn, the natives gave the Englishmen all the lowliest tasks,
including dragging about the *cacique*'s wretched pile of rusting
iron.

By now everyone was a little mad, Cheap was just madder than
his officers, and all mutual help was at an end. The *cacique* and the
natives suddenly disappeared, supposedly on some seal hunt, and
they were left quite alone on the most woebegone shore on which
they had yet landed. This was typical of the treatment they had

suffered ever since they had embarked. On one terrible day here
(and it seemed as if it must be the last of so many terrible days)
when they lacked even grass or seaweed for a meal, they decided to
take the barge along the coast in search of mussels—or anything
to ease the agony in their stomachs. The seamen and soldiers
were the first to climb aboard, with the muskets and all their
personal possessions. Before the officers could join them, in one
concerted movement they pushed off and began rowing—stoutly
for starving men—away from the shore. They were soon gone
round a headland and were never seen again.

Who is to judge how much treachery and how much madness
lay behind this act? Or were the fates having a final fling?
Whatever the cause, the results, in a place where nothing was
predictable, this time brought salvation to the abused—and almost
certain death to the absconders.

As soon as the barge disappeared a gale blew up in which,
they were certain, no small boat could survive. And yet, falling
and rising on the mountainous seas, there soon came into view,
momentarily on the crest of these waves, a small dark object.
Byron was the first to spot it, but could not believe that it could
be a canoe, the natives being so cautious about choosing their
time to launch their boats and canny in predicting a storm. He
ran to the others, who joined him on the shore. Byron himself
described the events that followed:

The despondency they were in would not allow them to give
credit to it at first; but afterwards, being convinced that it was
as I reported it, we were all in the greatest hurry to strip off some
of our rags to make a signal withal, which we fixed upon a long
pole. This had the desired effect: the people in the canoe seeing
the signal, made towards the land at about two miles distance
from us; for no boat could approach the land where we were:
there they put into a small cove, sheltered by a large ledge of
rocks without, which broke the violence of the sea. Captain
Cheap and I walked along the shore, and got to the cove about
the time they landed. Here we found the persons·arrived in this
canoe to be our native servant and his wife . . .

This amiable, courageous couple proved to be their salvation.
By now their party was reduced to an all-officer contingent
consisting of Cheap, Byron, Campbell, Hamilton and Surgeon
Elliot, who expired a day or two later, but at this time still just
had the strength to act as interpreter. The servant agreed to take
them overland to join the camp of a large tribe of natives where a

rendezvous with the incorrigible *cacique* had been arranged.

This lucky event did not mark an end to their troubles, and at the time they were not in a position to recognise the importance of that exchange of their barge for a crude native canoe which had appeared out of the same storm which would have drowned them had they been allowed to accompany the defectors. They again suffered terribly at the hands of the natives—all except Cheap who, in spite of his unbalanced condition and the loss of the promised barge, had somehow managed to ingratiate himself even further with the *cacique*. Over the next weeks they were starved, sodden, frozen and driven almost mad with the vermin, which had now got a firm grip on their emaciated bodies. They lay down without covering at night, were made to paddle by the lowest caste of native men until they collapsed, and portage the canoes with their loads of rusty scrap across swamps and over mountains down to the next stretch of water.

But all the time they were progressing north, and such was their resilience that all four of them survived until they arrived at an island just south of Chiloé.*

By the time they were approaching this most southerly point over which the Viceroy of Chile had any direct jurisdiction, and of which the *cacique* was the tribal chieftain, Cheap was so ill and deranged that he could not have lasted a day longer. Nor was the *cacique* in much better shape, and by now had lost all his dignity and illusions of grandeur. When the first habitation on Chiloé hove into sight, he became quite beside himself with excitement and anxiety to show his subjects that he would soon be with them

---

* After careful study of this region and its available maps and charts, and surviving records, the author has retraced the route of Captain Cheap and his officers as follows: from Wager Island in 47° 45′ S., 75° W., N.W. up the coast of the Gulf of Peñas, through Canal Cheap between Isla Javier and the mainland to Isla Purcell. Thence to Peninsula Forelius, Peninsula Esmeralda to the mouth of the Rio San Tadeo. Up this river and down to the north side of Istmo de Ofqui into the Iaguna de San Rafael (46° 45′ S., 74° W.). From this point, they followed the sheltered channels to Isla Guancanec in the Guaitecas Islands (43° 50′ S., 74° W.). Their only exposed passage in their canoes was across the Boca del Guafo to Chiloé. Byron described this crossing: '. . . There ran a most dreadful hollow sea, dangerous indeed, for any open boat whatever, but a thousand times more for such a crazy vessel as we were in. [The cacique] at length mustered up resolution enough to attempt it, first having crossed himself for an hour together, and made a kind of lug-sail out of the bits of blankets they wore about them sewed together with split supple jacks. We then put off, and a terrible passage we had . . .'

again, and demanded the loan of Byron's musket in order to give notice of his arrival. Byron had no shot left, and just one charge of powder, with which he primed his gun. The *cacique* had never fired it before, and as they closed with the shore, he stood up in the canoe, holding the weapon high above his head, no doubt pleased to celebrate his return to his subjects with an impressive bang. The explosion had two unexpected results. The recoil caused the *cacique* to fall back heavily into the bottom of the canoe, and the natives on the land, instead of rushing to welcome their chieftain, ran in fear for cover and hid themselves in the woods.

This was an unpromising overture to the return to civilisation of the *Wager*'s company (just four of the two hundred or so who had left Portsmouth). Events and circumstances soon improved, and on this green, mellow island they were provided with a surfeit of all the food and clothing and shelter of which they had so long been deprived. Even the *cacique* seemed quite pleased with the results of his long plundering voyage, and almost the last they saw of him was of his back bowed over a hole in which he was secretly burying his iron loot.

Chilean Holiday

We are now far away (some 800 miles to the north) of the area with which this book is mainly concerned, and we must briefly summarise what happened to Captain David Cheap, Lieutenant Hamilton, and Midshipmen Alexander Campbell and the Hon. John Byron after their surrender into Spanish hands. From the pathetic, emaciated and verminous condition in which they landed, they rapidly regained their health and mental stability. At first Cheap preserved the stand-offishness which was so untypical of the man, in his unbalanced condition of mind continuing to act the same role before his own officers as the *cacique* had played in front of his people and the primitive tribes of the Gulf of Peñas. Byron seems to have accepted this status of inferior caste with the same philosophy which had sustained him through his nine-months-long trial, and was always the last in the line for the food and comforts which were suddenly thrust upon them. Campbell was not prepared to be so yielding, and a quarrel developed between him and Cheap which neither ever made up. Cheap's greed was the root cause; Campbell could never forget how his captain had watched men die when he still had his own hoard.

When they became prisoners of the Spanish authorities at Castro, the centre of Spanish government in the island, the four officers were regarded with the same fear and caution as if they had been the vanguard of some massive invading force of heretics instead of a foursome of emaciated wrecks, and a contingent of guards with drawn swords escorted them to their cells. Their confinement lasted only a few days. This settlement was remote from European chancellory disputes and religious acrimony. The Jesuit priests were curious about any valuables they might be carrying and persuaded them to give up what they still possessed. But they were not even seriously interrogated by the civil authorities, who had heard little of Anson's designs, and certainly knew nothing about Jenkins's ear. They soon all felt more like new arrivals who are welcome as diversions from the routine tedium of life in a remote outpost than as dangerous enemies.

After nine months of starvation their appetite could not be appeased. 'We were never satisfied,' Byron recalled later, 'and used to take all oportunities, for some months after, of filling our pockets when we were not seen, that we might get up two or three times in the night to cram ourselves. Captain Cheap used to declare that he was quite ashamed of himself.'

The four officers remained in Chiloé until January 1743, living the comfortable life of indulged colonialists. Then they were sent north to Valparaiso, where the two midshipmen had another brief spell in confinement. Soon they joined their captain and Lieutenant Hamilton in Santiago—there was 'nothing but extravagance, vice and folly' in that wicked city according to their mule-driver—and here they led an almost hedonistic existence in the house of an expatriate Scottish surgeon, one Patrick Gedd, who introduced them to all the delights—the fandangoes, the banquets, the fine wines and spirits and exotic foods of this distant but well-served Spanish outpost. They loved the hot climate, the beautiful dark women, and their self-indulgent existence.

In this place of sun and wine and fruit and beautiful women, they were reminded only twice of the outside world, and of the circumstances which had brought them here. Soon after their arrival they were invited by the governor to meet Admiral Pizzaro, who had come so close to catching them on the long voyage down to Cape Horn. Byron's first memory of this meeting was the embarrassment in preparing for it. They had not yet acquired any proper clothes, and this was obviously to be a very ceremonial occasion, which could certainly not be refused. One of Pizzaro's officers came to the rescue, and none of them forgot his generosity for he offered to lend them a sum of money so that they could all buy the formal wear they required on the strength of a draft on the English consul in Lisbon—precarious enough security at any time, most especially in a time of war.

Pizzaro had had an even worse time than Anson, and had reached Valparaiso only shortly before Cheap and his party. Now that Pizzaro and Cheap could discuss their experiences, they learned that they had been almost within cannon shot of one another during that fearful storm off Staten Island. But while two of Anson's ships had been hurled back at the Horn, it seemed that not one ship of the Spanish squadron had made it. Of Pizzaro's five big men-of-war, one had foundered, one had been deliberately run ashore by her mutinous crew, and the other three had been driven back to the River Plate, smashed in their structure, dismasted, and manned by only a small surviving proportion of their original crews—all of them mutinous. Only 58 of the *Esperanza*'s company of more than 450 were alive. Famine, exposure, fatigue, and above all the scurvy accounted for this ghastly toll. It was largely Pizzaro's fault for attempting a passage round the Horn without adequate provisions. Yet the admiral made up for his impatience which had caused the catastrophe by a marvellous doggedness. Anson was far away in the Pacific when Pizzaro tried again, after repairing his two soundest vessels. One of these was smashed before she got to the south, and Pizzaro's flagship was again dismasted and blown back under a jury rig to the River Plate. A year later he tried again, and after a dreadful passage, doubled the Horn late in 1742. At Santiago all that he discovered of Anson's squadron were four officers of one of his ships, recovering from an ordeal that made all the Spanish sufferings seem trifling. It was, one imagines, a good evening of nautical reminiscence at the palace of the hospitable governor.

All that Cheap and his fellow officers could learn of their commodore and the rest of their squadron was pieced together from conversation with released prisoners of captured Spanish ships. They were relieved to hear that these prisoners had been treated well by Anson, and 'some of them told us', Byron later recalled, 'that they were so happy on board the *Centurion* that they should not have been sorry if the commodore had taken them with him to England'.

Things had changed since Drake had plundered this coastline

160 years ago. Only the spoils were the same, and after recovering strength at Juan Fernandez, Anson had made a highly successful passage up the coast. With only 18 soldiers still alive of the 400 who had embarked in England, and with the loss of the artillery and ammunition, there was no question of an invasion. But they took many rewarding pickings from captured merchantmen, and sacked and burned the rich town of Payta on their way north. Like Drake, their biggest prize, the capture which seemed to justify the losses of all their shipmates and their own sufferings, and made every one of them rich for life, was taken far to the north, off Acapulco, where they intercepted the Manila galleon.

Byron's Return to Soho Square

It took Cheap, Hamilton and Byron sixteen months longer to reach England. The governor made no attempt to restrict their movements, and even paid his prisoners-of-war a regular salary for doing nothing. Byron at least seems to have been quite sorry to leave when he was told that a French ship, *en route* from Lima to Spain, would pick them up at Valparaiso at the end of December 1744.

Campbell, who had not been on speaking terms with his captain since their arrival on Chiloé, refused to sail in the same ship with him. He had detached himself from his old shipmates, and in Santiago hobnobbed with the Spanish officers, arousing

A view of CAPE ESPIRITU SANTO, on SAMAL, one of the Philippine Islands, in the latitude of 12:40 N. Bearing WSW distant 6 leagues. In the position here represented his Majesty's Ship the CENTURION engag'd and took the Spanish Galeon call'd NOSTRA SEIGNIORA DE CABADONGA, from ACAPULCO bound to MANILA

'they intercepted the Manila galleon'

Cheap's suspicions that he had become a Papist. Pizzaro, who was himself about to leave the viceroyalty, seemed to have taken a fancy to the lad, and promised to get him back to Europe quicker in a Spanish ship. This meant an overland journey across South America, for Pizzaro had had enough of the Horn. So Campbell became a part of the Spanish admiral's *entourage* over the Andes, across the Pampas to Buenos Aires. From Montevideo, Campbell embarked in a Spanish man-of-war for Cadiz; thence to Madrid, and to London, where he arrived in May 1746.

For all Pizzaro's good intentions, he failed to meet his promise to Campbell. Cheap was already there, still as vindictive as ever against Campbell, spreading the story that he had turned mutinous as well as Papist; and, according to Campbell, 'rendering me odious among my brother-sailors'. His blackened reputation prevented him from being offered further service at sea, and nothing more is known of this young midshipman after his private publication of a pamphlet attacking Cheap's greed and vengefulness.

By the time Byron arrived back in England, after many more adventures, in November 1745, his family had long since given up all hope for their boy, now a dishevelled 22-year-old young man. He was penniless and hungry again when he at last arrived in London. 'I found the house shut up,' he wrote. 'Having been absent for so many years, and in all that time never having heard a word from home, I knew not who was dead, and who was living, or where to go next; or even how to pay the coachman. I recollected a linen-draper's shop, not far from thence, which our family had used. I therefore drove there next, and making myself known, they paid the coachman. I then enquired after our family, and was told my sister had married Lord Carlisle, and was at that time in Soho Square. I immediately walked to the house, and knocked at the door; but the porter not liking my figure, which was half French, half Spanish, with the addition of a large pair of boots covered with dirt, he was going to shut the door in my face; but I prevailed with him to let me come in.

'I need not acquaint my readers with what surprise and joy my sister received me . . .'

The Mutineers' Passage

Captain Cheap, Lieutenant Hamilton and Byron believed that they were the first survivors of the *Wager* to arrive safely back in England. Nor did they expect any others. This was not the case, as they soon discovered. The longboat had, after all, survived her seemingly suicidal enterprise—the passage south, the lee shores of those islands, the gales off Cape Desire, the treacherous currents and williwaws of the Magellan Strait, and the long passage up the coast of Patagonia. Only a handful of the toughest and most ruthless had escaped death by drowning, scurvy, starvation and exposure. A mixed complement of 72 sailors and soldiers, from boys barely in their teens to an 82-year-old cook, had embarked. A dozen disappeared when the cutter was lost before they reached Cape Desire. Eleven more, deciding that anything was better than a confined death by starvation in the bottom of the longboat, became volunteer castaways on the island of Madre de Dios. Thirty in all were still miraculously alive when the battered longboat sailed into Rio Grande, in safe Portuguese territory north of the River Plate. Among the survivors, not surprisingly, was that wily, shrewd and ruthless pair of petty officers, Cummins and Bulkeley. Lieutenant Beans was also fit and well; and of course, Captain Pemberton.

It was a rancorous passage as well as a remarkable one. The quarrels, between the soldiers and the sailors, the officers and the men, and individual seamen, like the wind never abated—all through the channels of the Chilean archipelago, the month-long (and decimating) passage through the Magellan Strait, and all up the Patagonian coast.

Perhaps fifteen (the number is not recorded) finally made it back to England.

Beans was among the first to arrive, and reported to the Admiralty. There was a lot to tell their Lordships, most of it disagreeable and some of it possibly compromising. Was he, or was he not, the leader of a mutiny? His captain was believed to be lost. There had been no word of him since they had left him on Wager Island. Beans could reasonably claim that he had invited Cheap to accompany them, that he had refused and had been left with provisions, arms and a boat. This was not mutiny. He had, rather, acted decisively (unlike his captain) by seeking for the *Wager*'s company a means of escape from the island, and though many had unfortunately been lost, they had made it.

The Lords of the Admiralty listened to Beans's explanation and account with sympathy, congratulated him and exonerated him from any charge of mutiny. They listened, too, to his account of the behaviour of some of his subordinates. At Rio Grande there had been an attempt to usurp his authority by the gunner and the carpenter, and Beans recommended that disciplinary measures should be taken against these two when, and if, they should arrive back in England.

Bulkeley and Cummins arrived at Lisbon on 28 November 1742, more than a year after they had sailed from Wager Island, and here they heard hints of their likely reception when they arrived home. Beans had been there before them, blackening their names 'with the greatest calumnies; and by an imperfect narrative, has not only traduced us but made the whole affair dark and mysterious'. Sure enough, on reaching Spithead, a message was sent out to their ship that they were not to be allowed ashore until their case had been investigated. For two weeks they remained prisoners within sight of their homes and to the great distress of their families.

The diary which Bulkeley and Cummins had been far-sighted enough to keep, even during their worst experiences in the *Speedwell*, was examined by an Admiralty committee set up to investigate the loss of the *Wager*, and was found to be sufficiently convincing to allow their release. It brought a fresh light to bear on Beans's case, too, and it was decided that none of the triumverate of naval leaders who had so quarrelsomely completed the greatest voyage by longboat in the annals of the Royal Navy should receive any pay, or employment, until either Anson or Cheap returned.

According to their own account, Bulkeley and Cummins had a hard time keeping their families alive while Captain Cheap spent two years of well-deserved comfort in Santiago. They made a little money, and helped to clear some of the public suspicion behind their part in the *Speedwell*'s voyage, by publishing their 'faithful narrative'. They chose an apt enough quotation (from Waller) for the title page:

> Bold were the men who on the Ocean first
> Spread the new sails, when ship-wreck was the worst:
> More dangers NOW from MAN alone we find,
> Than from the rocks, the billows, and the wind.

The Aftermath

Another two years passed before Cheap, Hamilton and Byron arrived home. After hearing the captain's account of the events leading up to the departure of the *Speedwell* their Lordships showed wisdom and compassion by exonerating everyone of any disciplinary charge, even the charge of murder of Cozens against

'to cultivate a Friendship with the Inhabitants'

David Cheap. Bulkeley and Cummins resumed their naval careers, but Beans, like Campbell, decided to take up a new career. Cheap remained unemployed for only a short time, and was soon at sea again, his warlike spirit undiminished in spite of the hospitality he had received from the enemy in Santiago. Off Madeira one day he sighted and captured a deep-laden Spanish prize. The proceeds set him up in comfort. On his return he married a widow from York and settled down to enjoy the life of a country gentleman.

John Byron, too, went back vigorously to war with Spain, as commander of a sloop, and for the next thirty-five years, whenever war with Spain or France offered him the chance of action, he was out there fighting and taking prizes. By 1779 he was a very rich admiral, ripe for retirement.

Long after his return from Santiago, Byron revisited once more the uttermost south and sailed close to the islands where as a young midshipman he had so often nearly starved to death. He was now a venerable Commodore of 41, and his secret mission was, like that of his late Commodore, to explore the passages to the north and the south of the American continent. But instead of harassing Spanish trade in the Pacific and attacking the cities of Chile and Peru his object was to discover new lands, and there 'to endeavour by all proper means to cultivate a Friendship with the Inhabitants—and take possession of convenient situations in the Country, in the name of the King of Great Britain . . .' He was also instructed 'to make enquiry after the People who were shipwrecked in His Majesty's Ship the *Wager* and left upon that Coast, and use your best endeavours to bring them home with you . . .'

Byron's voyage took him to the Falkland Islands, though he was beaten at the post here by the French, and through the Magellan Strait. In Byron's eyes the Chilean islands were as hauntingly nightmarish as he remembered them, and he described them as making 'the most dismal appearance in the world', while the gales were, if anything, worse than ever; thus confirming the appropriateness of his nickname, 'Foulweather Jack'. After more than twenty years, it was hardly surprising that they found no trace of the volunteer castaways, only shreds of evidence that Englishmen—possibly from the *Speedwell*—had once lived close to the two places where the people had asked to be put ashore. On the Patagonian coast they picked up the barrel of an old musket, rusted almost to pieces but with the King of England's broad arrow clearly identifiable on it. And at the western end of the strait there occurred a curious incident. A native family—an old man, his wife, two sons and a daughter—approached them, and made it clear that they were offering the daughter to them as a gift: 'as being of the same country.'

On closer inspection of the girl they saw that she had 'tolerable features, and an English face'. Did these savages, with their curiously severe attitude to sexual misconduct, wish to be rid of this embarrassing reminder of the mother's past? Byron could not know the answer, but standing here shyly before them was possibly the child of Captain Cheap's personal servant, Joseph Turner, or the cook's mate, George Smith, or John Russel, armourer, who had been left on Isla Madre de Dios on that November day back in 1741? Byron refused the natives' offer, but with the kindness and courtesy he always displayed to them. After all, his life had once depended on them.

Commodore Byron wisely refrained from exploring the Gulf of Peñas in search of Wager Island. This dangerous business was not included in his brief. Instead, he made for Mas Afuero off the Chilean coast, and then headed west across the Pacific. He failed to search for the north-west passage and hurried home *via* the Cape of Good Hope. He did not discover any new lands of significance, and his voyage was afterwards judged a rather perfunctory business, as if he was only bent on making the fastest-ever circumnavigation, which he succeeded in doing.

Admiral Byron died on 10 April, 1786, and in spite of the failure of his two most important voyages—both as midshipman and commodore—'with the universal and justly acquired reputation of a brave and excellent officer'. Two years after his death George Gordon Byron was born. When he grew up he sometimes spoke of his grandfather's adventures and sufferings, and drew on the wreck of the *Wager* for his shipwreck scene in 'Don Juan'.

6

'Hope Deferred, Not Lost'

Motto of Patagonian Missionary Society

COMMODORE Anson's voyage and the trials of H.M.S. *Wager*'s company marks the end of the first stage of Western man's contact with the uttermost south, and concludes it with a climactic finale. Never had 'the blind Horn's hate' so decimated a squadron bent on conquest or piracy as Anson's. Every degree of suffering, every form of death by violence and disease, which navigators since Magellan had experienced, were included among the catalogue of Anson's catastrophes. After two centuries when the Fuegian archipelago and Cape Horn had been no more than a passage or turning point for opportunists—and, briefly and tragically, for would-be colonists—there followed a third century when the fighting seamen and exploiters were increasingly replaced by the scientists and map-makers, the peaceful-minded explorers and missionaries.

When Anson's squadron doubled the Horn, no more was known of *Terra Australis* than when Schouten sailed round the Cape almost a century and a half earlier. By the 1760s, 'the advancement of trade' in the Pacific had become a necessity for Britain and for France in order to level up what we call today their balance of payments. Hard cash was being paid for the products of the East at a time when the increasing output of industrial products at home badly needed new markets. French and British merchants visionaries and explorers saw a network of commercial outposts extending from the South Atlantic, through the South Pacific, to the new lands they intended to discover.

Byron's unproductive circumnavigation had been intended as one stage in the British plan of exploration, a peaceful one, of course. There was no longer war with Spain, and he had been urged to take 'all possible care to avoid giving any kind of Umbrage or Offence to the Spaniards'. Louise-Antoine de Bougainville, the French master-navigator who just beat Byron to the Falkland Islands and set up an establishment there, went on to explore and chart the Magellan Strait and the Fuegian archipelago. James Cook on the first of his great voyages of discovery anchored off Good Success Bay in le Maire Strait, noted the native life and the botany of this south-easterly corner of Tierra del Fuego, 'doubled the Cape on this occasion as if it had been the North Foreland on the Kentish coast; the heavens were fair, the wind temperate, the weather pleasant; and being near the shore they had a distinct view of the coast.' On his next voyage Cook sailed south-east along the lee shores of the archipelago down which Drake had been bowled by those fearful gales of October 1578, charting for the first time islands and headlands which Anson and the Nodals had seen only as grey menacing shapes, leaving behind, as fair winds drove them to the Horn, a string of evocative names—York Minster, Cook Bay, Christmas Sound, where they dined off roast geese and Madeira wine. They even found a quiet bay—Puerto Cook on today's charts—ten miles from the eastern tip of Staten Island, and anchored cosily there on New Year's Day. For those who came on peaceful scientific business, it seemed that 'the blind Horn's hate' could turn to benign tolerance of the intruder. Cook was the luckiest Cape Horner of all.

Cook spent only a few weeks in Fuegian waters, bringing home a report of kindly seas which his predecessors had found hostile and terrifying. His great accomplishment lay elsewhere: the destruction of the myth, and the discovery of the reality, of the continent of *Terra Australis*, which had eluded le Maire in the 16th century and so many others since.

Then the Spaniards, in their waning power, made one last peaceful assault on the passages they had once pioneered. The *Santa Maria de Cabeza*, under the command of Captain Cordoba, brought back a chart of the strait which superseded that made by Sir John Narborough and followed by John Bulkeley in the little *Speedwell*, but failed to show any of the intricate channels which connect Magellan's strait southwards into the Pacific. The first modern survey of the uttermost south had to wait another half century after Cook, when, in 1828, the British survey ships, *Adventure* and *Beagle*, returned from a two-years-long scientific commission under Captain Parker King, with Captain Robert

Fitzroy as the *Beagle*'s commander.

Now at last the great hazily-outlined land mass of Tierra del Fuego, once marked with only a few inlets where fighting seamen and explorers alike had sought shelter, began to show its true splintered shape. Scientists equipped with dip circles and magnetic cylinders for magnetic observations, accurate chronometers, sextants and station pointers, began the Herculean task, still incomplete today, of charting the multitudinous creeks and inlets and channels of the thousands of islands and islets and tide-washed rocks, noting the currents that surge between them, the hectic rivers and waterfalls that pour into them, the incandescent-blue glaciers that inch their way down the valleys from the perpetual snows. They measured the height of the mountains, and the tides, took chippings of the rocks, tested the soil, identified the trees and plants and mosses, drew the animals and birds and found new breeds.

Imbued with a dedicated enthusiasm, equipped with all the instruments and implements that they needed, and sailing in well-provisioned, well-found stout vessels, these scientists of the 1820s and 1830s left little for their successors to pick over. There were few failures in their reporting and plotting. That peerless young naturalist, Charles Darwin, recorded that 'the trees all belong to one kind, the *Fagus betuloides*: for the number of the other species of *Fagus* and of the Winter's Bark is quite inconsiderable'; and that 'the gloomy woods are inhabited by few birds: occasionally the plaintive note of a white-tufted tyrant-flycatcher (*Myiobius albiceps*) may be heard, concealed near the summit of the most lofty trees . . .' Fitzroy reported on his geographical observations that the rocks over which Sarmiento had led his soldiers were of sienite, of greenstone in the islands of the Alakalufs, of porphyritic claystone where Doughty and Quesada had been executed, that the summer night temperature where Nombre de Jesus had once been built 'frequently fell as low as 29° Fahrenheit'. Their findings filled many volumes.

These zealous scientists also reported in the most minute detail on the characteristics and habits of the natives. After examining a party of Yaghans for the first time, Darwin wrote that they were 'the most abject and miserable creatures I anywhere beheld . . . Viewing such men, one can hardly make oneself believe that they are fellow creatures, and inhabitants of the same world.' Their nature and condition remained to the end one of nature's puzzles this scientist failed to resolve. He resented their presence in this

Charles Darwin

scientists' paradise, their smell, their appearance, their manner of eating and their diet, their covetousness, their shrill speech. 'While in the boats I got to hate the very sound of their voices, so much trouble did they give us. The first and last word was "yammerschooner" (give me). When, entering some quiet little cove, we have looked round and thought to pass a quiet night,

Yaghan Indians

the odious word "yammerschooner" has shrilly sounded from
some gloomy nook . . .'

Darwin could stoically endure the worst privations, the most
intense seasickness, and would gladly spend uncomfortable hours
struggling through swamp-ridden beech jungles to reach the
summit of a mountain, all for the truth. But he regarded the
Yaghans as an affront to the human race and was thankful to
leave them behind, confining himself to a last philosophical
question: 'Whilst beholding these savages, one asks, Whence
have they come? What could have tempted, or what change
compelled, a tribe of men to leave the fine regions of the north . . .
in invent and build canoes;' and consoled himself with the
conclusion that 'we must suppose that they enjoy a sufficient share
of happiness, of whatever kind it may be, to render life worth
having . . .' The scientist who could spend so many hours examining a new form of globular, bright yellow fungus, naming it
Cyttaria Darwinii, flinched away in revulsion from the highest
forms of Fuegian natural life.

The need for conservation was not fully understood until long
after Charles Darwin's death, but the last century of Fuegian
history was to prove that it was the human species which was to

Fishing

suffer most from the assault of man into the archipelago, more
even than the guanaco from the gauchos, or the seal from the
predatory sealers. For all his sharp curiosity and boundless
imagination and intellectual honesty, Darwin failed to compre-
hend the fatal trail of damage that he and Captain Fitzroy were
unintentionally to inflict on the Yaghan, Alakaluf and Ona tribes
of Tierra del Fuego.

'This gentle chastisement'

Until the middle of the last century the impact of white man on
the natives had been light and sporadic. Since Magellan's first
mild assault, generations had been born and died who never saw
a white bearded man nor their great vessels that moved through
the channels silently and without paddles. In their struggle for
survival their fear was for the raids of the bounding Onas and,
north of the strait, for the tall Tehuelche. Gradually, one imagines,
tales of the white man spread, and sometimes they were good
tales, sometimes bad tales. Like a once deprived group in a
liberalising country today these natives must have been confused
by the widely varying treatment meted out to them—sometimes
kindly and generous, at others severe, or even viciously cruel.

The catalogue of the white man's outrages and kindnesses was
probably about equal. But relations were always sensitive.
Admiral Olivier van Noort in the Magellan Strait in 1599
mistook what was certainly a curious gathering of natives as
hostile opposition to a landing. His men waded ashore in hot
pursuit. They cornered their supposed enemy in a cave, shot the
men first, and then the women to silence them, taking away half a
dozen children as specimens. There is no record of what happened
to them.

One of the crew of an English man-of-war in the strait in 1690,
hove to for fish, water and wood, reported the sad outcome of an
innocent fishing expedition among the islands of the Alakalufs.
'These natives were amicable with us till our people went to fish
where some of them were. They had also some small nets with
which they supplied and contented themselves, till unfortunately
they saw our people fishing with our seine which was 80 fathoms
long. The great number of fishes we caught raised first their
amazement, and then their indignation, which increased to that
height that they began to give our men disturbance by pelting
them with clods.' The English fishermen replied with musket fire
'by which some of the natives were wounded'.

But there are also records of mutual contentment and co-existence. The fierce Tehuelches, who had plagued Sarmiento and his Spanish colonists, worked for months alongside the shipwrecked crew of another Spanish ship in the 1760s, helping them fell the timber and carry it to the shore where the white men built a great vessel in which at length they sailed away. The Tehuelches were certainly well rewarded for their labours with lengths of cloth and silk and satin from the hold of the wrecked vessel. But this event proved that it was possible to come to terms with the natives. The Governor of Buenos Aires, Don Pedro de Cevallos, was informed when the Spaniards at length completed their voyage from Peru, that the natives in Magellan Strait were 'very humane and hospitable'. It is a pity the report was not more widely read.

Confusion and misunderstanding on both sides, rather than hostile intentions, were the usual causes of conflict. Those Spaniards were led by an unusually wise and understanding commander, for he must have had to put up with a lot of pilfering. Pilfering was the first problem. And from the highly educated scientist Charles Darwin, to the roughest corsair captain, the reaction was almost invariably angry resentment, particularly after the savages had just accepted, without much of a show of gratitude, beads, mirrors or perhaps some strips of red cloth. No one seemed to understand that the natives had no moral code about theft. Darwin deplored their egalitarian society, and was righteously indignant about it. 'At present', he wrote, 'even a piece of cloth given to one is torn into shreds and distributed; and no one individual becomes richer than another. On the other hand, it is difficult to understand how a chief can arise till there is property of some sort by which he might manifest his superiority and increase his power.' Darwin was quite unsympathetic to their democratic tradition of shared possessions, which would have led them to dividing the very hull of the *Beagle* into equal parts if they had been allowed to, and he fulminated against their pillaging of anything on which they could lay their hands. In the end, he thought it quite proper for his captain to fire his cannon above their heads to keep off the pests, and went back to his study of *Macrocystis pyrifera*, the kelp seaweed, which deeply fascinated him.

In earlier days, Spanish, Dutch, French and English mariners simply shot the pilferers. The new nineteenth century scientists tried to avoid such drastic punishment. A contemporary of Darwin's, James Weddell, who had a much greater affection for the natives than Darwin, 'judged it proper to impress them [the Yaghans] with an idea of the offence of stealing; and accordingly placed this criminal in the main rigging, and gave him a smart lash with a cat of nine tails, making him understand that it was a punishment for the crime of which he had been guilty.' Weddell claimed that 'this gentle (*sic*) chastisement had the desired effect'. It must also have puzzled and bewildered them.

Everything about these white men, who came and went so quickly, was a puzzle—their vast boats, their coverings of cloth, their bearded faces, their drink (they were always offering them stuff that tasted like fire), the way they began by sharing everything out in the normal way, with laughs of encouragement, and then the next minute stringing them up and whipping them when they helped with the distribution.

Another aspect of the white man's behaviour—less painful but just as puzzling—was their evident love of ceremonials. Flags were raised and lowered on their ships; a signal cannon was fired, its boom echoing from side to side of the channel; when they rowed one stood up and called out rhythmically to the others; when they landed they would sometimes kneel on the shore, chanting together before a priest in rich robes. Or they would climb to the nearest headland or hill and erect a huge cross for all to see. To a pagan people, living from day to day, these rites and formalities appeared very odd.

Over the years, various tribes had become directly involved in these ceremonials, and the memory of them was long-lasting. Old men who had not seen a white man since youth could still chant fragments of the *Ave Maria* and give praise to a Spanish king who had long since died. Tribes with their families massed on the shore were glad to swear allegiance to good King Philip one year, and perhaps the next year indulge the whims of these carriers of gifts by honouring the sovereign of another land and faith. When Bougainville arrived to take possession of Port Famine, the Tehuelches were fitted out with red gowns for the occupation ceremony and taught to sing 'Vive le Roi de France'. Bougainville left some time later, and the French flag was still flying on shore; the lesson had not been forgotten, and the natives saluted him all the way back to his ship—'Vive le Roi! Vive le Roi!'. It was an encouraging entry in their log, and read well back home.

Some of the early navigators thought the natives were cannibals. But reports are few. There is a reference in one account by a diarist with the Nassau Fleet back in 1624. 'They more resemble beasts than men,' he exclaims in a shocked tone 'For . . . they tear men to pieces, and devour the flesh raw and bloody.' Darwin, the modern scientist, took these reports seriously. With all his care for the truth, he was gullible enough to believe the story of a little Yaghan boy, transparently eager to impress his audience, that in winter his tribe smoked to death their old women by holding them over a fire before setting to on the tastiest portions, and even imitated their screams as a joke. (Darwin's contention was finally exploded by later and more open-minded 19th century scientists, but the damage was long-lasting.)

By the 1830s the Fuegian natives had experienced many curious and sometimes unpleasant forms of treatment from their occasional visitors, as well as defamatory reports on their character and practices. From time to time, for more than three hundred years, they had been shot at by arquebuses, bows and muskets, had been stared at in curiosity by Pigafetta, measured by Sir John Narborough, begged from by starving seamen. They had been preached to and dressed by impressive looking priests. They had been laughed at, pursued and abducted and beaten.

None of this mattered very much to the Yaghans of the south, the Alakalufs of Desolation Island, the Onas who had rarely seen the white men anyway, or to the Tehuelches north of the strait, now equipped with tough horses and bolas. In 1830 they were still free of serious interference, the sealers had not yet come with their syphilis, the sheep farmers with their rifles, the gold panners with their liquor; and, most devastating danger of them all, the missionaries had not yet come with their tracts and good intentions, their seeds and farming implements, their cups and saucers and piles of germ-laden second-hand clothes. But this last invasion was more determined and sustained, and as fatal in its consequences as it was inevitable.

The Last Letter

On 6 September 1851 a retired Royal Navy captain, Allen F. Gardiner, lay dying of scurvy, starvation and exposure in the bottom of a launch drawn up on a Fuegian beach not far from Good Success Bay. He was too weak to move but he had beside him the paper and pen with which he had recorded the death of all but one of his fellow missionaries, and with what must have been the last of his strength, he succeeded in completing a devout and formal letter to the party's surgeon, whom he thought might still be lying a short distance away.

Allen F. Gardiner

My dear Mr Williams,
   The Lord has seen fit to call home another of our little
company. Our dear departed brother left the boat on Tuesday
at noon, and has not since returned: doubtless he is in the

presence of his Redeemer, whom he served so faithfully. Yet a little while, and through grace we may join that blessed throng to sing the praises of Christ throughout eternity. I neither hunger nor thirst, though five days without food! Marvellous loving-kindness to me a sinner!

    Your affectionate brother in Christ,
      Allen F. Gardiner

Williams was almost certainly dead, and it is unlikely that Gardiner himself survived that day. He succeeded in pulling himself out of the boat, perhaps to search for water, perhaps to kneel on God's soil, but got no farther. Seven weeks later a schooner hove to off this beach in a severe gale, and managed to get a boat ashore. There were no fewer than three captains in that boat, all men who had sailed the world and seen death many times. But they cried at the sight that met their eyes on that Fuegian beach. Such gallantry, such waste!

The Rakish Naval Officer becomes a Missionary

Allen Francis Gardiner was born at Basildon in Berkshire on 28 June 1794. His childhood was severely pious and full of good works. He was especially devoted to his mother. His wealthy parents set up schools for the poor local children, but kept their own son away from the possible corrupting influence of school life and had him 'religiously educated' at home. He is described as a restless, vivacious child. When he grew up he said he wanted to travel, and he liked to sleep on the floor rather than in bed in order to harden his body. He also developed a fine fighting spirit against the French, something that it was difficult for a young lad to avoid at the turn of the century. He was eleven when Trafalgar was fought, and had already made up his mind to enter the Royal Navy. At thirteen he went to the Naval College at Portsmouth, much to the anxiety of his parents, for the navy had as bad a reputation as ever for licentiousness and carousing and drunkenness. However, he was carefully watched over by the Dockyard Commissioner, a friend of Mr. and Mrs. Gardiner, and does not seem to have come to any harm during his two years there.

Young Gardiner was at sea by the age of fifteen, and had doubled the Horn and seen heavy action before he was twenty. His enemy, after all, was American, not French. As a midshipman in the *Phoebe* he helped search the South American Pacific coasts for the American frigate *Essex*, which was playing havoc with British Pacific trade in the War of 1812. The *Essex* was caught off

Valparaiso on 28 March, 1814, and captured after a sharp engagement. Gardiner formed part of the prize crew which sailed the battered American corsair half round the world back to England. There was sad news for him on his return. His mother had died.

The loss of her wise restraining influence seems to have caused something to crack in his passionate and volatile personality. He reacted strongly against all his religious teaching, turned the Bible out of his cabin and became a sceptic. 'At one time,' writes his fastidious Victorian biographer, 'he fell among infidel companions, by whose false reasoning and flippancy his mind became so poisoned that, though he never avowed himself an infidel . . . he began to look on the study of the Bible as folly.' Now 'the headstrong passions of youth, the love of pleasure', took over, and Allen Gardiner—reading between these carefully evasive lines— became a bit of a lad.

His reform, and his guilt for his past, stemmed from a serious illness picked up somewhere in foreign parts, and from his marriage to a lovely religious lady, Julia Susanna Reade, in 1823. Ten years later his religious reform was completed by a series of disasters. 'Within the last twelve months', he confided to his journal on 29 June 1833, 'the Lord, in His wisdom and justice, has seen fit to take from me an attached and valued aunt, a beloved child, and a tender and affectionate wife. My earthly comforts have been removed, and I pass my days in sorrow.'

These catastrophes led to his retirement from the Royal Navy in order to give himself up to good works. Now he married a vicar's daughter, Elizabeth Lydia Marsh, and with her enthusiastic support devoted the rest of his life, and most of his fortune, to missionary work: and that meant front line field work, not administration and fund-raising at home. In his travels about the world, he said, he had seen the melancholy consequences of Godlessness among savages—from Bolivia to the heart of Africa.

This seemed a precipitate decision for a man in middle life, so fully equipped as a sailor and ill-equipped and untrained as a missionary. Gardiner does not seem to have fully considered what this new life would mean, especially to his family; nor to have bothered much with preparations. He had heard the call of his Lord, and there was no time to waste. He started off in Zululand, but at a bad time. As he arrived, the Zulu chieftain, Dingaan, went to war with the Boers and he was forced to leave. But before he returned home defeated he made one mark on the Dark

Continent, by which he is sometimes remembered today. While in
Natal in 1835 he got together a few settlers there and laid out a
township for them. He named it Durban after the Governor of
Cape Province, Sir Benjamin D'Urban. Next he tried New Guinea,
but the Dutch made his life a misery. 'You might as well instruct
monkeys as the natives of Papua,' they told him sharply and sent
him away.

Gardiner now decided to give his attention to South America.
Many years before, as a naval lieutenant, he had come into contact
with some of the more primitive tribes of northern and central
Patagonia. Now, drawing largely on his own funds, he formed the
tiny Patagonian Missionary Society, for many years the least
supported of all foreign missions: it was really only Allen Gardiner
and a few friends, and he was its only missionary. Most of his two
years in Patagonia he spent among the fierce Araucanian tribes,
who were being rapidly wiped out by the Argentines anyway. But
his greatest difficulties were from the local priests and friars who
did not care for foreign heretics disturbing the beliefs of their
flocks, and Gardiner found himself 'on every side hemmed in by
Spanish Popery'.

Gardiner's fanatical determination increased with each rebuff.
He knew the Fuegian islands. He had seen the stone age conditions
of the Yaghans and Alakalafs. This was virgin missionary land,
undisturbed by the Roman Church. It was also one of the most
inaccessible spots on earth, and in the end he had to charter a
ship of his own, a crazy old schooner, complete with a drunken
and restless crew, in order to get there. In her he intended to sail
among the Fuegian islands until he found a likely spot; then he
would land with a few stores and, sending the schooner home, get
down to work. The voyage was a disastrous shambles. He had
constant trouble with his crew when on board, and from the
natives when he landed.

The fire in his heart was burning more brightly than even when
he got home: his society's motto was, after all, 'Hope deferred,
not lost'. But he had to admit that two would be better than one
for converting the Fuegians and decided not to go alone again.
With the society's catechist, a Mr. Hunt, Gardiner had himself
put ashore with supplies on the north shore of the Magellan Strait,
by chance or by plan, close to Sarmiento's old landing place.
Where the soil had once been blessed by Catholic priests, and the
city of Nombre de Jesus had once risen with marvellous speed
out of the pampas, these two stout Anglicans began building their

huts and searching for Patagonians to convert.

The Cape Virgins area, where Sarmiento had had so much trouble with the natives in the 1580s, was now a much quieter spot. For some time no one came near the Patagonian Missionary Society's encampment, though they lit fires in the hope of attracting attention.

At last a family turned up, but they were not the sort of people they were looking for. Wissale was the name of the family patriarch, a frightening, unscrupulous fellow already corrupted by white riff-raff, who spoke a smattering of English and recognised at once what fair game these two lonely missionaries were. Wissale settled down with his wives and children and followers close to the huts, and swaggered over with his entire family every mealtime, half begging, half demanding food for them all. 'Mitter Hunt, this your son Lux,' Wissale might say, as he placed an unclean naked child into the lap of the catechist.

As their provisions rapidly diminished and Gardiner and Hunt had to put on a show of firmness, Wissale and his people started to become more aggressive and threatening. The missionaries' lives were certainly saved by the chance appearance of a ship bound for Valparaiso passing through the strait. They signalled it and got on board as soon as it hove to.

These evangelical disasters continued in unabated succession through the 1840s. There was a brief trip to Bolivia—and it was no mean task just to get there at that time—to convert the indians of the Andes. But like the Zulus they were too busy making war amongst each other, the 'Popish monks and friars' were hostile, and there was a revolution going on in this new republic, too. The following year Gardiner went farther south and in greater strength than ever before. With a party of five others, he persuaded the Royal Navy to drop him off in early winter in the Beagle Channel. Gardiner had read his Darwin, and work among the lowest and most savage form of human life in the world—cannibals at that— offered an irresistible attraction.

The Landing at Banner Cove

At the entrance to the Beagle Channel there are three islands, the largest some twelve miles long. They are all heavily forested, for much of their circumference right down to the sea. But there are areas of coarse grass on the lower slopes, too, and in summer brilliant meadow flowers and flowering shrubs give a pleasantly pastoral aspect. As Sarmiento was deceived by the summer scene at Port Famine, so many travellers have mistakenly believed that these three islands offer havens of lush contentment amongst the harsh and hostile Fuegian islands. You find that they are not as hospitable as they seem as you approach the shore in a boat. The kelp seems to be thicker and more tenacious than anywhere else, making rowing laborious work, and dangerous in any sort of a sea. The shore and the cliffs are gloriously alive with cormorants, shags, sheerwater, kelp geese, great skuas and gulls. By contrast you enter a dead world as soon as you penetrate the forests and attempt to make your way through swamps and tangles of fallen and rotting evergreen beech, many tortured by the incessant winds into unnatural shapes and angles. Deep inside the forest nothing moves or can be heard except the branches high above tossing in the wind and scraping out an incessant chorus. Nowhere in Tierra del Fuego as in these islands is there such a difference between the hectic life of the shore and nature's vacuum in the forests. Yet they look so tempting and beautiful.

Today the possession of Picton, Lennox and New Islands by the Chileans is strongly disputed by the Argentines who claim that the frontier line runs to the west of the islands. On each a wood-and-galvanised iron hut is occupied by a pair of Chilean sailors, and the Chilean flag is run up from a mast as nominal confirmation of national ownership. Apart from these lonely watchers, the islands which were once popular with the nomadic Yaghans, are sterile and uninhabited; and they leave their rare visitors with a feeling of acute unease.

Gardiner had chosen Picton as his missionary base. On the north side of the island, looking across the entrance of Beagle Channel to the thick forests and mountains of the main island of Tierra del Fuego, there is a deep bay guarded at its entrance by a pretty looking island, heavily forested but with especially lush-looking areas of verdure. Gardiner asked the naval vessel to put him ashore here, and named the bay Banner Cove in appropriate acknowledgement to the fourth verse of Psalm 60, 'Thou hast given a banner to them that fear thee, that it may be displayed because of the truth.' He named the seemingly enchanted island Garden Island; but today it carries the more ominous name of Isla Gardiner.

A whaler took Gardiner and his party ashore with their provisions for six months, while the man-of-war stood offshore taking on water and keeping a watchful eye on events. Gardiner had their storehouse and living quarters rapidly erected from the

Banner Cove

pre-fabricated parts, and by the next day was, hopeful as ever,
prepared to begin work.

This time there was no lack of potential converts. The curious
Yaghans were soon landing at Picton with their families in great
numbers to see what could be begged for or plundered. Gardiner
was writing up his notes in the hut when they arrived, swarming
everywhere, their thieving hands grasping anything that was not
closely guarded. One of them came up behind Gardiner, lifted up
his inkstand and emptied it over his notebook. Others indicated
by signs that it was time for their hosts to lie down and go to
sleep, a transparent indication that they were eager to busy
themselves with pilfering on a wholesale level.

There was absolutely nothing you could do with thievery on
this scale. There were so many of them and they were so tirelessly
light-fingered that even five men working in shifts could not secure
their irreplaceable possessions, let alone begin to hold services
and begin baptisms.

Gardiner had one more day to decide whether they should stick
it out, or re-embark in the man-of-war which looked so invitingly
safe anchored in the Beagle Channel. It was his sense of responsi-

bility for his companions' lives which decided him to withdraw: alone he would certainly have stuck it out. 'From what I have now seen,' he wrote sadly at the end of his shortest ever mission, 'it is my decided opinion that until the character of the natives has undergone some considerable change, a Fuegian mission must of necessity be afloat.' In a ship, anchored offshore, they would be more secure against aggressive and thieving designs, and could pick and choose their subjects for conversion.

But before leaving this land he carries out a very English task. He lays out a little garden on Garden Island in the hope that it will be flourishing when he returns. As if this country enjoys the mild climate of Kent or Hertfordshire, he plants some soft fruit cuttings—raspberry, currant and gooseberry—and spring bulbs.

Once Allen Gardiner is safely back on board the ship, it is a convenient moment to reappraise the man, his circumstances and ambitions with the objectivity he was able to apply to his own future evangelistic plans when the ship weighed anchor in the Beagle Channel on 1 April 1848 and continued on its interrupted journey to Peru, doubling the Horn two days later.

Gardiner is now 54 years old, tall, austerely handsome, with a long aquiline nose and thick, curly, reddish hair. He holds himself with an air of distinction above the fretful worries of others and remains undismayed, however critical the circumstances. His years of service in the Royal Navy, and his complicated and hazardous travels in so many remote parts of the world, have given his organising powers a professional air, when in fact he is a born non-organiser—although he induces in others a complete faith and confidence in his powers. Like many adventurous gospellers, his appearance of sublime authority attracts disciples. But now, after so many abortive missions, he is finding it more than ever difficult to attract backers.

As he sails away from Picton towards the Barnevelts and Cape Horn, again disappointed but undiscouraged, he writes, 'The only obstacle which I can anticipate to the prosecution of our missionary objects in Tierra del Fuego, is one which I am almost ashamed to mention, *i.e. the expense*. But "let us not be weary in well-doing; for in due season we shall reap, if we faint not".' It was now that he determined not to rest until he had converted every Yaghan to the Anglican faith.

It is impossible not to admire the spiritual strength of this curious and passionate man who has suffered and seen so much, has buried one wife and five of his seven children, has been tortured by his own shortcomings and the memory of his fleshly indulgences and knows (for he is not a proud man) that he has fulfilled none of his missionary ambitions. From this distance in time, one falls back on speculation; but from those of his contemporaries who

Yaghan hunter fixing fish spear

have written about him, and from his own history and journals, one is persuaded to the conclusion that only the pursuit of his self-imposed and hopeless task with undeviating and fanatical energy is preserving him from mental breakdown.

Allen Gardiner understands the hostility of the climate and the natives he must convert to the Christian Church. No power on earth can now halt the strength of his spiritual tide. The question of money is a problem which will certainly be overcome. Just as he believed that those English tulips would flourish, so would he find the supporters for his next endeavour, and return—to admire his blooms and bring clothes and better manners and the word of God to these savages.

Late in 1848, Gardiner returned to his country seat, to his patient wife and the children who saw him so rarely and were brought up to respect his authority and not to be too fearful of his strict ways. The Patagonian Missionary Society was in a state of deep gloom about this new disaster, and funds were low. Gardiner busied himself at once with renewing their confidence and getting the finances onto a better footing.

The trouble was that no one had ever been much interested in South America—'that place of savagery and Popery' was the usual reaction among stout Anglicans. In turn the Church Missionary Society, the Moravian Church and the Committee for Foreign Missions of the Church of Scotland refused their help. So Gardiner began stumping the country on a lecture tour, with his maps and drawings and Fuegian artifacts, picking up a few guineas here, a few guineas there. In Bristol he made a very useful ally in the Rev. George Pakenham Despard, who had never been to the uttermost south, but became overnight almost as ardently concerned about the heathen condition of the Fuegians as Gardiner himself. This was just as well because support in London for the little Patagonian Missionary Society was falling off and it looked as if soon there would be only Gardiner himself left. Despard agreed to become Honorary Secretary, and for his greater convenience the skeleton remains of the society were moved from London to Bristol. Here it had a minor renaissance. New support came from various charities and individuals. Still it was not enough to buy a ship, provision it with food, plants, seeds, household goods and Bibles for the Fuegians, and pay a crew to man her. Gardiner went off lecturing again, Despard busied himself locally.

Gardiner acquires a Backer

It seemed such a marvellous cause that its supporters could not understand why almost everyone, even the normally generous, were so reluctant to contribute. Gardiner remained undismayed; with that serenity which his disciples so admired, he knew that the Lord would intervene on their behalf. Meanwhile, his tall, splendid figure could be seen on the platforms of church and village halls about the country. His audiences were never large, and sometimes no one at all turned up. Gardiner gathered a few more guineas, but hardly enough to pay his own expenses.

The breakthrough came, just as Gardiner had predicted it would. A lady in Cheltenham, that handsome West Country spa for rich old folk, wrote to Despard saying that she was interested in the society's activities, but wished to remain anonymous. Gardiner hurried off to see her, and outlined his plans.

'You wish to enter on this mission to Tierra del Fuego in the present year?' she asked. 'What sum of money is necessary to provide the adequate means for this purpose?'

Gardiner told her he needed seven hundred pounds.

'Is the want of money the only obstacle to your undertaking?' she asked. And when Gardiner confirmed that this was the case, he was told that she would provide it.

Even with this munificent sum, they would have to cut back on their plans. Gardiner had wanted to buy a brigantine, which would require a permanent crew of not fewer than nine. He now proposed to his committee that they should, instead, buy a pair of open launches, deck one of them over and stow their provisions on board, and carry them out in the next ship bound for the Pacific. He even managed to convince himself and the committee that these launches would be better than a brigantine, simpler and more manageable in the narrow Fuegian channels. And he reminded the members what heavy seas Cornish fishermen were able to stand up to in their little boats: in fact, he hoped to persuade some of these very fishermen to come with them. His persuasiveness carried the day—it always did—and the committee members who had so recently listened to his demand that nothing smaller than a brigantine would do, agreed to this rather funda-mental change of plan. He was, after all, a retired naval captain.

Over the following weeks Gardiner collected together his party, which proved easier than collecting the money. In the Cornish fishing village of Mousehole three sturdy, pious fishermen, John

Pearce, John Badcock and John Bryant, volunteered to help man the launches: Gardiner warned them that it might be dangerous but they said that in their life they were used to danger. Two sterling characters offered their services as catechists, John Maidment, the secretary of the Y.M.C.A. in London, and a surgeon from Burslem, Richard Williams. The party was completed by Joseph Erwin, the carpenter who had been on the last abortive expedition, but believed that 'being with Captain Gardiner was like a heaven upon earth, he is such a man of prayer'.

After a farewell meeting and an address at Bristol, this party of seven brave and cheerful men took the train to Liverpool and embarked with their launches, each with its own dinghy, and their supplies in the barque *Ocean Queen*, bound for San Francisco, *via* a diversionary stop at Picton Island, Tierra del Fuego. It was 7 September 1850.

According to Gardiner's plans, the committee was to send out further provisions to Picton within two months of their departure from England. They seem to have had some difficulty in arranging this, or they lacked Gardiner's persuasive powers which had succeeded with the captain of the *Ocean Queen*. But Gardiner had also told the committee he believed that there was a regular timber-collecting ship from the Falkland Islands to the Beagle Channel, so that if the provisions could be sent to these islands, they could then be forwarded to Picton. This sounded a satisfactory alternative, and the stores were at length put on board the brig *Pearl* in April 1851, with instructions for their tranship-ment to the missionaries. The timing was rather fine, but if all went well the food should be received by Gardiner before his six-months' supplies were exhausted. Besides, they had guns and plenty of powder, and Gardiner had told them of the rich bird life in the Beagle Channel, to say nothing of the fish, to augment their rations.

The first letters Despard and the Patagonian Missionary Society received from Gardiner's party were full of joyous enthusiasm. They were getting on well together; their determination to succeed was expressed as if with one voice. 'You will be glad to hear that everything goes on most harmoniously', wrote Gardiner, 'not a jarring word has been uttered . . . one spirit prevails—a desire to serve the good Master, in whose name we go forth, counting it all joy to endure hardness for His sake. May we all have grace to persevere unto the end.'

From Picton Island Gardiner wrote a last letter to Despard, despatched home by the *Ocean Queen*, which remained anchored in the Beagle Channel so that the captain could be satisfied that his passengers were safely settled.

It told a rather confused story, and reading between the touchingly confident lines, Despard must have felt the first faint chill of anxiety about their future. When the mission landed in Banner Cove on 6 December, the Yaghans on the island had at once gathered around as they had before, cadging and grumbling and yelling 'Yammerschooner!' Their numbers were at first few, and Gardiner was this time prepared for the next stage of the assault and ordered Erwin to build a wooden stockade around their tents. But it did not prove stout enough to resist the first assault when the Yaghan reinforcements arrived by canoe the next morning.

From Gardiner's report we are left with the picture, similar to that of an Apache attack on an early white settlement in North America, of a horde of dark bodies swarming over the fence of tree trunks, bent on assault. These Yaghans might be after plunder rather than blood, but it was an alarming situation all the same, especially as the mission was ethically prohibited from using their guns, or answering violence with violence.

The flexible nature of Gardiner's plans is evident from the text of this letter. After reaching the conclusion that they could only operate afloat, and bringing with them the two launches for this purpose, he had decided to settle ashore. But already the hectoring and entreating, the shrill repeated cries of 'Yammerschooner!' which had driven Darwin close to distraction, were unsettling the nerves of the party. If they had the cheek to carry on like this with a British brig just offshore, what would happen when it left?

Gardiner's first decision, he wrote to Despard, was to return to the water. His second was to learn the language. It might seem a little late to begin, but that is what he was going to do, if necessary by 'obtaining two or three boys' and 'retaining them for the purpose of learning their language'. Or he was going to 'take three or four lads' to Staten Island, and 'after their language had been acquired, resume our position here under more favourable circumstances'.

It is difficult to imagine the alternative visions reflecting the mission's future that must have come to Gardiner's mind while he made these plans. Did he see his two launches, now named the *Pioneer* and *Speedwell*, one of them already leaking, sailing up and down the Beagle Channel, through the Murray Channel, perhaps over to the Hardy Peninsula or to the brutal Wollastons just north of Cape Horn, making converts to the Anglican Church among the canoe-loads of accompanying Yaghans? Or were there to be language lessons from the captive lads in the mornings, and evangelism in the afternoons? And of all islands to retreat to, why did he suggest Staten Island, that forty-mile-long hell of inaccessible peaks and unscaleable cliffs above stormy waters? As one pities the plight of these seven doomed men, one stands back in puzzled amazement at such grotesque calculations; and one also wonders how Despard reacted to them when he read this letter months later.

The Missionaries are Left Alone

The *Ocean Queen* had to go about her business. She had been anchored off Banner Cove and Garden Island for nearly two weeks, and was due to leave on 19 December. On the day before, Gardiner and his party sailed out in their launches to take off the last of their supplies and say goodbye. The captain and crew of the *Ocean Queen* assembled on deck and presented the missionaries with an address. Gardiner replied suitably, thanked them for all they had done, and led the way over the side back to the *Pioneer* and *Speedwell* tied alongside. 'Hip, hip, hooray!' cried the crew; and Gardiner, standing with his men in the launches, cheered back.

After all, Gardiner again decided on a different course from any of those he had proposed in his last letter. Now he could not get away too soon from the yammering, grasping Yaghans who were still swarming about Banner Cove. He decided that the mission should find a harbour on the north side of the Beagle Channel, the deserted nature of which had suddenly come attractive to his eyes. He hoped there to find security, to repair the leaking launch, and generally retrench before beginning their work. The next day they all broke camp.

The organising of the day was a rather complicated business, but we can be sure that Gardiner gave no sign of being fussed. First the provisions they had already brought ashore had to be secretly buried in case for any reason they were forced to return to this anchorage. Then they had to pack their tents and their personal possessions in the dinghies—which were almost essential for getting ashore through the thick kelp — and tranship them into the launches before weighing anchor. A further complicating factor was the long spare plank for the repair of the *Pioneer*, which the captain of the *Ocean Queen* had found for them. They had to take this with them, too.

Gardiner decided to lead the way in the *Pioneer*, with Maidment, Pearce and Bryant, towing both the dinghies, while the *Speedwell* followed towing the plank. In this order, then, the two launches sailed out past Garden Island into the Beagle Channel.

This channel for days at a time can be as calm as an inland lake, its surface reflecting the white peaks of the mountains that tower above it. But like the Magellan Strait, it can also be aroused to a frenzy of agitation, and the mountains and steep valleys deflect the wind unpredictably, so that there is no telling whether you may next have to tack or wear. A launch only 26 feet long, with a beam of 8 feet, would be very difficult to manage, even by the most experienced seamen, under these conditions.

This turned out to be a very bad day to search the shores of the channel for a quiet harbour. The wind was blowing hard and the waves were so high that they might have been entering the English Channel rather than an apparently sheltered narrow strip of waterway. Gardiner had never seen it so rough. Both launches

The Beagle Channel

were in trouble before they cleared Garden Island, and became separated. Gardiner sailed on through mist and low cloud, steering west up the channel until he sighted on the north shore a deep cove opposite the eastern extremity of Navarin Island. It looked ideal for their purpose, and, naming it Blomefield Harbour, after one of the mission's past secretaries and most generous supporters, Sir T. W. Blomefield, Gardiner headed thankfully for it; but on looking astern discovered that both the dinghies had been torn away by the force of the wind and had disappeared.

It was the first serious blow the party suffered, and from this time almost nothing went right for them. Gardiner could find no trace of the *Speedwell* either, and after a wet night and day ashore, he took the *Pioneer* out into the Channel again to search for her. The gale had blown itself out, there was not a breath of wind, and the four men had each to take an oar. They rowed the heavily loaded launch the full length of the journey they had just completed, right back to Banner Cove, before they sighted the *Speedwell* in the moonlight (it was now 3 a.m.). She was still hove to off Garden Island, where they had last seen her.

'All was still,' wrote Gardiner of this alarming moment, 'not a sound was heard but the splashing of the oars, and the murmur of the surf on the outward beach. It was an awful suspense, not a word was uttered among us. We were now actually alongside, but no movement or sound was heard on board the *Speedwell*. I confess my blood ran cold.'

Williams, Erwin and Badcock were safe and well, sound asleep as it happened, but they had bad news to tell when they were awoken. The plank they were towing had become entangled with the kelp, almost dragging them ashore in the storm. To save themselves they had had to cut away both this vital item of repair and their own anchor.

Something had gone seriously wrong with the seamanship of the party. The three fishermen had spent most of their lives in small boats, Gardiner himself had been many years at sea and had been fully trained in the art of boat handling from the age of 13. Yet none of them seemed able to avoid these ridiculous accidents. The next day, for example, the *Speedwell* managed to stand out from Banner Cove, and it was the *Pioneer's* turn to become stuck. Worse than this, Gardiner anchored her so close inshore in the evening that the tide cast them up high and dry on the rocks by the next morning. This new mishap led to their most dangerous moment with the Yaghans. They were awoken by the nearby sound of shrill voices, and when they emerged to find that they were no longer afloat, they saw two natives, looking decidedly hostile, standing beside them.

'We united in prayer,' Gardiner wrote in his diary. 'Five more men made their appearance, approaching us by the beach. Taking it for granted that their intentions were hostile . . . we landed with our guns and walked towards them, and when within a few paces, we knelt down upon the beach, and committed ourselves to the mercy and protection of our heavenly Father. They stood still, without uttering a word, while we were in prayer, and seemed to be held under some degree of restraint.'

A Dismaying Discovery

This demonstration of faith, and no doubt the sight of the guns too, seemed to have given Gardiner time to reconsider their plans yet again. The *Speedwell* had returned to offer help to her consort. But now Gardiner had given up hope of ever getting both vessels to Blomefield Harbour. They were, he thought, too heavily loaded to cope with the dangerous seas of the channel and must be lightened. So all that day was spent getting ashore some of their heavier cargo and provisions and hiding it (or so they hoped) in a cave.

This operation revealed the most unpleasant surprise of all. They had never made a proper inventory of their stores, and now they found that the most important item of all—their cask of gunpowder—had never been offloaded from the *Ocean Queen*, now far away somewhere up the Chilean coast. This meant that they could neither defend themselves for long against the natives, if it came to a showdown, nor augment their meagre store of food.

Already, after only two weeks in the Beagle Channel, all except Gardiner knew that this mission could never succeed, that they would make no converts, that they would be lucky to survive the rigours of this climate and the hostility of the savages they had come to preach to and civilise. It seemed strange that only a few days earlier they had still been talking enthusiastically about taking a few lads from the tribe and learning their language. Now the sight of a dark naked body lurking on the edge of the forest made each of these seven men reach for their guns even as they fell to their knees in prayer.

On 4 January it looked as if the natives had determined to make a final assault on Banner Cove. Eight canoes appeared in turn from around a headland along the coast, and there were bundles of spears visible above the stern of each. Another party of Yaghans on the beach were filling baskets with stones (they were great stone-throwers) and when the canoes approached the shore, the baskets were handed aboard. Gardiner at once gave the order to flee. They piled into the launches, cut the cables, raised sail and stood out into the Beagle Channel before the attack developed. Gardiner wrote that night in his diary, 'We offered up our praises and thanksgivings to our gracious God, who had shielded us in the hour of peril.'

For the next few weeks the missionaries followed the nomadic pattern of the Yaghans' own life, though instead of wandering from island to island in search of better mussels and fish like the natives, their search was for a safe spot from their enemies. Wherever they went, they knew that it was only a matter of time before they were spotted. Then they would see the first smoke of the natives' fires, which would slowly come nearer overland, or approach their hide-out by canoe across the water, and they would know that they must again embark to seek a fresh refuge. From Picton they sailed south to Lennox Island, and on the exposed south shore of this island enjoyed a long enough peace to patch up the *Pioneer*, which was taking in a lot of water. From here they headed north again, back to the Beagle Channel, where they sought out Blomefield Harbour, and this time all the party succeeded in getting ashore.

They had only a brief rest. The natives were again soon amongst them, as importunate and threatening as ever. Gardiner may have had a hunch (and it could have been no more) that the farther east they sailed, the less likely that they would be pestered. Or perhaps, like Sarmiento's colonists or the *Wager*'s mutineers, even at this great distance and under such intolerable circumstances, they were guided by the homing instinct.

A Safe Sanctuary

At the end of January they stood out of Blomefield Harbour and sailed east out of the Beagle Channel, leaving behind the great snow-capped mountains, the rocky cliffs and tumbling waterfalls, and hugging the less spectacular shoreline of wooded slopes that darken the dour south-eastern shores of the main island of Tierra del Fuego. Almost nothing was known of this coast, and it is still not charted in detail today. Nobody has bothered. It offers only sterile forests and dank, overhung beaches. At that time even the natives avoided it, for the fishing is bad, the mussels are poor and

Above: Above Wulaia, looking west towards Button Island and the mountains of the Dumas Peninsula.
Below: Banner Cove, Picton Island. Gardiner Island on the right; on the extreme left the rock face which once carried Gardiner's message 'Gone to Spaniard Harbour'.

few, the forest quite impenetrable.

Gardiner followed it for some sixty dreary miles, praying always for some hospitable, peaceful harbour where they could take stock and recover themselves. On almost the last day of the month, the two launches rounded the low headland, Kinnaird Point, and entered a wide bay. At once their spirits were raised and they gave thanks to God, for it seemed that at last their Odyssey was over. For days they had seen no sign of a native or a canoe, and now here was a beach beneath grassy flower-covered slopes that reminded the fishermen of any welcoming cove on the Cornish coastland back home. A clear-running river flowed out of the forest, across the rocky shore into the sea. Gardiner named this place Earnest Cove, and they all waded thankfully ashore to their silent sanctuary. For the first time since they had arrived they felt safe.

They had perhaps two days of contentment before they suffered their next blow. They had got ashore what provisions they had left—some wheatmeal, molasses and oatmeal, a cask of rice and biscuit—and had settled into a cave. They had come as far east as they could, and now, like doomed Viedma and his surviving colonists nearly three hundred years earlier, they could only await the sight of a sail. Gardiner was confident that it would come. His trust in God was as firm as his confidence in his organisational prowess. His instructions to Despard and the rest of the committee of the Patagonian Missionary Society had been explicit. Nor had his catechists lost heart, even if they now knew that they had underestimated the difficulties they would have to face.

There is a touching faith in some notes made by Richard Williams on 2 February 1851, which survived him. 'How evident that we were not in a position to commence with such slight means so arduous an undertaking! But all this is well; the mission has been thereby begun, whereas, had we waited for more efficient means, it never probably would have been.' There is no hint of placing blame on Gardiner, who had been here before and should have known the difficulties they would have to face in only two crazy launches. Moreover, the night before a gale had blown up, and Earnest Cove proved to be less sheltered than Gardiner had estimated. The *Pioneer* snapped her moorings, was driven onto the rocks and then onto the jagged roots of a fallen beech, which tore out her side. They did what they could with the remains, dragging the hull farther up the beach and erecting a canvas covering over it to make some sort of a shelter.

For already the summer was going, the temperatures at night were dropping, and the rain was beginning to turn to sleet. Already they were noticeably weaker. Williams was seized by a violent cold, and then noticed the sores breaking out on his body, and with a sense of horror and revulsion, diagnosed his sickness as the first signs of scurvy. Badcock, one of the tough Cornishmen, was the next to succumb.

Gardiner tried to build a more suitable shelter, securing poles and canvas against a projecting rock, and lighting a fire to keep out the worst of the cold. But poor Gardiner now seemed unable to do anything right; he built up the fire too high, it caught the canvas and poles and quite destroyed this new home.

By March the food problem was becoming pressing. The fishing was as poor as they had found it earlier at Picton, and after they had used up the small amount of powder they had in their flasks, they had to resort to throwing stones at the geese and ducks which abounded along the shore. They rarely hit them. Each day that passed weakened their will to live, and they were overcome by a mental and physical lethargy. They should have busied themselves preparing better quarters against the increasing cold weather, felling trees and building a hut. Instead, they spent most of their time in prayer, or watching the sea for the sign of a sail, or, with a growing dread, the spread of the signs of scurvy.

We have only their diaries and journals to go on, but it appears from these that they were all retiring, uncomplainingly, into their private world of devout contemplation. Their state of mind is summed up in an extract from the journal of Richard Williams, bedridden with the scurvy. 'Our plan of action now,' he wrote, 'is to rough all the circumstances, which it shall please God to permit to happen to us, until the arrival of a vessel.'

Not once during their first eight weeks in Earnest Cove did it seem to occur to any of the party that no rescue vessel would know where they were. Banner Cove was their headquarters. And in the uncertain visibility of these early winter weeks, it was very unlikely that they would even be able to sight, let alone signal, a vessel sailing from the le Maire Strait towards the Beagle Channel. Not until the last week in March did they recognise this danger of being missed; and by then they were also in desperate need of the three casks of biscuit and one of pork which they had hidden on Garden Island.

On 23 March they left the cave and their makeshift hut in the smashed *Pioneer*, and carried the two sick men on board the *Speedwell* for the journey back to the Beagle Channel. It was a cold, difficult and dangerous voyage. The weather was vile all the way, and Gardiner was in a constant state of anxiety about Williams and Badcock, though he did not show it. (It does not appear to have occured to them to leave these two behind in the charge of one other of the party.) They spent one night on shore—Reliance Cove they named the spot—and sighted Garden Island and Banner Cove across the channel on the morning of 25 March.

Only three months earlier, this bay had been a place of hope and endeavour. Now they dreaded their return to it and searched anxiously for signs of Yaghans and canoes. But the main body appeared to have left. There were only a few natives among the wigwams near the cove and they appeared friendly enough. Gardiner even traded a handful of nails for seventy fresh fish, a great boon and some compensation for all that they had lost to their thieving hands in the past. Nor had the casks been discovered. This came as a great relief and surprise, and with full stomachs again, for the first time for weeks, they were seized with new energy.

On a headland sheltering the eastern entrance to Banner Cove there is a rocky cliff some thirty-five feet high and facing east towards the entrance to the Beagle Channel. Except in very poor visibility any vessel sailing up the channel must see it. Working on this cliff with a pot of paint, Gardiner wrote in large white letters: 'GONE TO SPANIARD HARBOUR', and below again: 'YOU WILL FIND US IN SPANIARD HARBOUR.'

Next, on Garden Island they buried three bottles, each containing this message:

'We are gone to Spaniard Harbour, which is on the Main Island, not far from Cape Kinnaird. We have sickness on board: our supplies are nearly out, and if not soon relieved, we shall be starved. We do not intend to go to Staten Island but shall remain in a cove on the west side of Spaniard Harbour, until a vessel comes to our assistance.

N.B.—We have already been two months in Spaniard Harbour, finding the natives hostile here. (Signed and dated March 26, 1851.)'

The news of their return was spreading rapidly, and on the third day in Banner Cove, the shrill sound of Yaghan voices heralded the arrival of the canoes. Soon they were alongside the launch ('very noisy and turbulent' Gardiner described them) and cut adrift the raft Erwin had built to ferry out the casks. They managed to drive them off, and the Yaghans made camp in wigwams on shore a short distance away.

It was another anxious night. Gardiner and Maidment took four-hour watches, and at one o'clock they heard an uproar from the direction of the wigwams as if the Yaghans were working themselves into a frenzy and signalling an attack by beating together lengths of wood. There was not a breath of wind, but Gardiner knew that they must leave without waiting for daylight. He ordered his men to begin rowing. As they pulled out slowly into the Beagle Channel they could see the lights of the Yaghan fires following them in an alarming procession, one to each canoe. The men bent to their oars, knowing that they could not hope to outpace these swift canoes. But, as in their last retreat, they were lucky. Out in the channel they picked up a breeze, hoisted sail and were safely beyond range by daylight.

It is a painful business to read the entries in Williams's journal and Gardiner's diary for the last four months of the mission's life. These were all good men, selfless and brave, concerned through all their worst sufferings with the welfare of the others above their own. No boatload of cold, starving men could have contrasted so strongly with the crew of that other *Speedwell* in these same waters a century earlier. If one appeared more sick than the others, he became the subject of anxious enquiry and extra rations were pressed on him.

We know little of Maidment, except that, like the others, he was a dedicated disciple of Gardiner. He regarded him as a saintly figure with whom he would go anywhere and suffer anything. We can see Erwin a little more clearly. Williams described him as 'a dapper, sprightly, and excellent fellow'; but also told how easily he became fussed and bothered, by contrast with Gardiner's studied calm in adversity.

The picture of Williams himself, struck early by scurvy but proving himself remarkably resilient, is clear-cut. He is a tough character, continuing to write with clarity and grace as he lies for month after month in his sickbed, noting all that he sees, grateful for all that is done for him. He is as devout as the rest, but is a realist, and a good reporter. Months back, on board the *Ocean Queen* as she sailed down the Mersey, when Gardiner had revealed that they would have provisions for only six months, he had told him that this was not enough: a twelve-months supply was what they needed. Eight months later, on 12 June 1851, he wrote in his journal: 'Our diet consists of oatmeal and pease, with rice occasionally. But even of this we have only a stock sufficient to last out the present month, or a very short period beyond this. The weather is very severe, with a deep fall of snow upon the ground. But this is not the worst feature of our case. All hands are now sadly affected. Captain Gardiner, a miracle of constitutional vigour, has suffered the least, and, if I listened to his own words, he is still none the worse; but his countenance bespeaks the contrary. Would it were not so!'

Yet Williams, too, is by now slipping back into the condition of devout, semi-consciousness they had all experienced before the stimulus of action and the temporarily better diet at Picton had revived them. 'Ah, I am happy day and night, hour by hour,' he writes on the same day. 'Asleep or awake, I am happy beyond the poor compass of language to tell.'

The three Cornish fishermen are, unfortunately, faceless figures. They were certainly humble and pious men, with something of the pioneer spirit to have volunteered for this mission and to have left their families for this distant spot of which they could scarcely have heard. We see John Badcock clearly only at the moment of his death, the first to go after three months of suffering. The *Speedwell* had been taken to the estuary of the river a mile and a half away for safety when they returned from Picton, and drawn up on the shore as a sort of land-bound hospital boat. Being decked, it offered better shelter from the snow and gales which raged every few days from early in April, and those who were fit enough took turns to comfort the sick. Erwin had slept with Badcock and Williams on the night of 28 June after Gardiner had visited them on the previous day.

The First Death

Late that evening Badcock knew that he was dying. He had, according to Gardiner, earlier been 'distressed with doubts as to his acceptance before God, but these were entirely removed before the close'. In the cold little cabin of the launch, with the wind whistling through the shrouds and the trees he had called across to Williams in the other bunk, asking if he would join him in singing a hymn. Together the two scurvy-wracked patients sang loudly:

'Arise, my soul, arise,
        Shake off thy guilty fears . . .'

Then the fisherman had died.

Again we notice the curious paradox in their situation: on the one hand, the men's endurance and stoicism through this bitter weather (for it is now mid-winter in perhaps the coldest part of all Tierra del Fuego), on a starvation diet; on the other, their equally remarkable lack of practicality. Lethargy alone cannot entirely account for it. Having come this far, the *Speedwell* could have been navigated without too much difficulty to the Falkland Islands, where there was a small colony. Many people who knew these waters later puzzled over their failure even to consider this course. Then again, there were two expert fishermen left in the party, yet when they fished in the river the blocks of ice racing downstream tore the net to shreds. They repaired it and tried again, with the same result. Their efforts to trap a fox, although eventually successful (it tasted of fish), were extraordinarily clumsy and amateurish. It was not for four months after their return that Gardiner devised some means of attracting the attention of a passing vessel by hanging up a white tablecloth on a tree.

The key to this puzzle is to be found somewhere in the character of Allen Gardiner himself. He had often been unlucky, he had also rather consistently fallen down on his organisation—and yet, before his religious renaissance, he had once been a fine naval officer, highly regarded in the service. He had obviously become habituated to failure, and even unknowingly encouraged it, because he had doubts about himself as a fulfilled missionary—a settled, successful cathechist, making daily converts.

Is it possible that Gardiner was really a missionary *manqué*, his restless, guilt-suffering soul crying out for the struggle—the greater the struggle the more spiritually happy he was—and subconsciously dreading fulfilment, because then the bitter fight within him on which his spirit burned would be extinguished?

Look at the long record of his disasters: twenty years of failure. There has never been anything to match it in the history of missionary work. It is very likely that Gardiner knew that he would never come back from Tierra del Fuego. If this is the truth, then it is very sad that he had to take six others willy-nilly to a martyr's death with him: especially those fishermen—it is over them that one weeps the most.

Gardiner's endurance, which Williams had noted and admired, for a time kept him going while the others weakened. He insisted on remaining in Earnest Cove, driven first from the cave by a gale and freak tide, then from the *Pioneer* and finally into the woods.

From here, like some penitent monk on a pilgrimage, he insisted on making the exhausting trip to the *Speedwell*. There he would join the sick in prayer, and return, usually with Maidment, back to the cove, if it was dry, or to the woods again, where the two men 'united in prayer and thanksgiving for their merciful preservation'.

Their store of food on 28 June, Gardiner's 57th birthday, was half a duck, one pound of salt pork, one pound of damaged tea, one pint of rice, two cakes of chocolate, four pints of peas, and six mice. Yet a month later, he was still active. It was not until 14 August that his strength began to fail. On that day, lying in the bottom of the broken hull of the *Pioneer*, he wrote, 'Today I am from necessity obliged to keep my bed, with little expectation of again leaving it, unless it shall please the Lord in His mercy and compassion to relieve us, and vouchsafe the food which we do much stand in need of.'

The discovery of the missionaries' bodies in Earnest Cove

Others maintained the use of their legs after Gardiner became immobilised, and it was now left to Maidment and Pearce to keep open communications between the two encampments: why they did not combine forces was never satisfactorily explained. This enforced rest conserved the dwindling strength of both Williams and Gardiner, between whom messages were passed. On 25 August Gardiner learnt from Pearce that Erwin was fast failing. On the following day Maidment staggered over to the river and found that the carpenter had died, and that John Bryant could not last much longer. He brought back Williams's prayers for Gardiner.

By 3 September their last food was exhausted and none had the strength even to search for mussels. Of the fishermen, only Pearce was still alive, but so grief-stricken that he could not even bring himself to dig graves for his friends from the little village of Mousehole. He probably died, alone, the next day.

Maidment was now the least weakened of the three who were left, still just able to walk, and when Gardiner tried to raise himself from the bottom of the boat and reach his old friend, Williams, at the river, Maidment managed to cut him a pair of forked sticks to serve as crutches. The two men did not get far. Together they crawled back to the *Pioneer* for the last time, and collapsed into the bottom. During the night, Maidment climbed out again, leaving a small bottle of peppermint water for his leader, and died on the beach.

Gardiner took up his pen, wrote the letter to Williams which never reached him, and began the last entry in his diary. There is no doubt that he died in a state of ecstacy. On 4 September he managed to scoop up some water from the bottom of the boat in a rubber overshoe. 'What continued mercies am I receiving at the hands of my heavenly Father!' he exclaimed. 'Blessed be His holy name!' As he wrote to Williams, he felt no hunger, only a fearful joy.

7

The Fate of the Natives

I F Gardiner had sailed his two launches a further fifteen miles west up the Beagle Channel, he would have reached the end of Navarin Island and off his port beam he would have seen one of the most spectacular channels in Tierra del Fuego. It is called Canal Murray after the intrepid officer in Fitzroy's first expedition who discovered the Beagle Channel in 1830. It runs north-west south-east for six miles, between high mountains on both sides,

The *Beagle* in Canal Murray

narrow all the way, and at one point is less than a half mile wide. The whole length is an ornithologist's paradise, for every breed of seabird seems to be represented amongst the audience on the tiers and terraces as a rare boat passes, its bows cleaving through more gulls and skuas too bloated with fish to bother to move aside. Ahead, schools of seals show off their speed, thrusting themselves out of the water, remaining half-airborne for an unnatural time before slipping below again. Groups of tidy penguins, like midget men at a stiff stag party, stare out with red eyes, heads turning together as the boat passes; but they have nothing to say. Only the steamer ducks appear nervous, their vast bulk half concealed by the frenzy of spray set up as their pathetic stumps of wings beat the water, accelerating their skimming retreat to a good twelve knots.

No vessel would dare approach the pace of the steamer ducks through the Canal Murray; four knots is about the safe speed, so swift and variable are the currents racing to and from the deepest recesses of the archipelago to the Atlantic and Pacific Oceans and the Drake Strait to the south. Judged on the standards of seamanship Gardiner and his fishermen practiced in the Beagle Channel, they would have been lucky to pass safely through the Canal Murray and into Ponsonby Sound in the extreme north-west of Bahia Nassau.

Half way down the west coast of Navarin Island, protected from the westerly winds by a round sugar-loaf island and a group of islets, there is a stretch of some twenty acres of natural flat pasture land cut from the forest-lined shore. Today three tin-roofed huts form a sheep station and a Chilean navy outpost. This is Caleta Wulaia, or Woollya Cove as Fitzroy wrote it. From the edge of the wood above this fertile oasis you can see to the west across the sound to Button Island guarding the entrance to Canal Murray, and on a fine day to the Dumas Peninsula, one of Hoste Island's many eccentric peninsulas, and its snow-capped mountains. You are looking towards the heart of the archipelago's wildness, where the land's vertical and horizontal configurations were formed when nature was in a wild rage.

Twenty years before Gardiner disembarked from the *Ocean Queen*, Wulaia was usually occupied by Yaghan families, who spread their wigwams along the grassy shore. It was as near a home base as any of them ever had, and a favourite haunt of the best-remembered of all Fuegians, Jemmy Button.

Jemmy Button was one of four natives brought back by Fitzroy

Wulaia

from his first cruise, three of them as retained hostages against
the theft of a whaler, while Button was bought from his supposed
father for, needless to say, a button—though a large shining
mother-of-pearl one. As it turned out, Button was an appropriate
name for this bright-as-a-button Yaghan lad of thirteen; shrewd,
quick minded, a lively laughing opportunist, in strong contrast
with those dour, irascible tribesmen who were to drive Gardiner
from Banner Cove.

Even to a humane and cultivated man like Fitzroy there was
nothing improper in acquiring specimens in this way, nor was
there anything coy in naming them Jemmy Button, Boat Memory,
York Minster, after the ecclesiastically architected cliff Cook had
discovered on one of the western islands, and Fuegia Basket after
the basket-like canoe by which the whaler's party returned to the
Beagle after their boat had been stolen.

Jemmy Button's family was one of those who were often based
near Wulaia and the island which will always carry his name. All
but Button were Alakalufs, Boat Memory an agreeable, mild lad
of around twenty years, Fuegia Basket a pert, joyful, vain little
tubby girl of about eight, York Minster a glowering, quick-

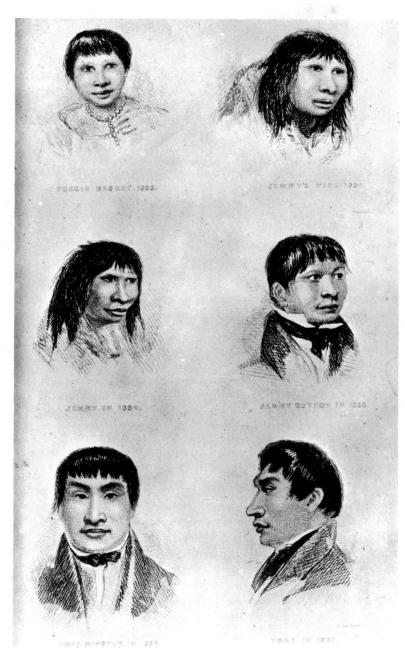

FUEGIA BASKET 1833.   JEMMY'S WIFE 1834.

JEMMY IN 1834.   JEMMY BUTTON IN 1833.

YORK MINSTER IN 1833.   YORK IN 1832.

Fitzroy's Fuegian captives

Robert Fitzroy

tempered brute, as strong as any two of the *Beagle*'s seamen, whom
Fitzroy (never a one to mince his words) described as 'a displeasing
specimen of uncivilized human nature'. It was easy to imagine
him as the ringleader in a cannibalistic orgy, and he was always
treated with circumspection.

On his way back to England, Fitzroy addressed a letter of
explanation of the whole business to his commanding officer, who

had no idea that the *Beagle*'s company had been increased by four.
I have maintained them entirely at my own expense, and hold
myself responsible for their comfort while away from, and for
their safe return to their own country: and I have now to request
that . . . you will consider of the possibility of some public
advantage being derived from this circumstance; and of the
propriety of offering them, with that view, to His Majesty's
Government.

If you think it proper to make the offer, I will keep them in
readiness to be removed according to your directions . . .

Fuegians in England

The experiences of Jemmy Button and his three fellow-Fuegians
in England were mainly surprising and confusing. The sights
were strange enough: one of the first an early steamboat outside
Falmouth Harbour in Cornwall, or the inside of a stagecoach, or
the shops in the Regent Street in London. But it was their treatment that was the most bewildering, for they were treated in turn
as if they were new specimens for the Zoological Gardens, prophets
of some new cult, or visiting royalty. In fact, they were received
at court privately, and thus became the objects of envy as well as
even greater curiosity by society. Queen Adelaide took a special
fancy to Fuegia Basket, whom she found a fetching little thing:
and Fitzroy who presented his party, later told how the queen
'left the room in which they were, for a minute, and returned
with one of her own bonnets, which she put upon the girl's head.
Her Majesty then put one of her rings upon the girl's finger, and
gave her a sum of money to buy an outfit of clothes when she
should leave England to return to her own country.'

Boat Memory had come down with the smallpox soon after his
arrival in England, and died a few days later. The others
flourished, learned the language (York Minster was a reluctant
and slow linguist) and took readily to wearing clothes, especially
the youngsters. Jemmy Button was the most vain, and loved to
dress himself extravagantly and admire himself in the glass; but
Fuegia Basket could sometimes be surprised pirouetting in front
of Button and Minster, too. A shrewd eye would have noticed
that this big brute was beginning to eye little Fuegia with a hungry
expression.

Fitzroy persuaded the Church Missionary Society to take over
his charges, and they were sent to be educated and refined further
to a willing volunteer not far from London, the Rev. William

Wilson of Walthamstow. In this quiet Essex village they were taught comportment and manners, better English, and the Scriptures: especially the Scriptures, for already the idea had formed in Fitzroy's mind that the three survivors of his experiment would make admirable missionaries who could be sent back to their homeland 'with as large a stock as I can collect of these articles most useful to them, and most likely to improve the condition of their countrymen, who are now scarcely superior to the brute creation'.

The Rev. Wilson did his work well in his 'attempt to teach them such useful arts as may be thought suited to their gradual civilization'; but was less successful with York Minster, who was not really a ripe subject for Fitzroy's bizarre experiment and gave every evidence of greater interest in Fuegia Basket than the Psalms. Jemmy Button was growing into a strutting, cocky little fellow, almost precociously bright, an excellent mimic, like most Fuegians, but now in dandy's garb appeared far removed from one of his seal oil-coated brothers shrieking 'yammerschooner!' and waving a fishing spear. Even the most optimistic evangelist could not see any of this trio preaching the word of the Lord successfully without professional support, and the Missionary Society wisely decided to search for a volunteer to return to Wulaia with them.

Richard Matthews was the unfortunate young man destined to become, briefly and disastrously, the first Anglican missionary to go out to Tierra del Fuego. He was, unlike Gardiner, no fanatic, 'rather too young, and less experienced than might have been wished', as Fitzroy described him; but an honourable, upright fellow. It was the first time he had set foot on a deck.

After twelve months, and a rather rushed education, the three Fuegians re-embarked in the *Beagle*, which left England on her second scientific and exploratory voyage on 27 December 1831, this time with the 23-year-old Darwin on board. Besides her regular supplies, and the instruments and implements for her special work, the *Beagle* carried many donations and contributions by the Missionary Society's supporters—embroidered tablecloths, table napkins, tea and coffee sets, decorated chamber pots (a number of these), tea trays and quantities of clothing of all kinds, for missionary societies had for long believed that their catechists were able to work better when their flock was covered.

On the long voyage out, with stops for scientific work *en route*, the Fuegians settled in to the routine of shipboard life. Jemmy

Button was especially popular, full of pranks and endearing ways, the butt of many jokes about his smart clothes. Fuegia Basket was the *Beagle*'s only female. She was still only ten but already formally betrothed to York Minster and had her own quarters and was chaperoned everywhere: while her fiancé became increasingly jealous of her, and was also watched carefully, for a different reason: his black moods always looked as if they might become dangerous.

Jemmy Button's Homecoming

The *Beagle* did not reach Wulaia until 23 January 1833. By then they had already made contact with a number of other tribes, whose antics and primitive manners had discomfited Jemmy Button. It was a difficult and embarrassing time for him. He explained them away by saying that they were a low lot by contrast with his own, whose superiority was increasingly extolled as they neared his region. His family were not long in appearing after the *Beagle* anchored offshore, arriving by water in an overloaded small canoe. 'When it arrived,' Fitzroy described this moment, 'instead of an eager meeting, there was a cautious circumspection which astonished us. Jemmy walked slowly to meet the party, consisting of his mother, two sisters, and four brothers. The old woman hardly looked at him before she hastened away to secure her canoe and hide her property, all she possessed—a basket containing tinder, firestone, paint, and a bundle of fish. The girls ran off with her without even looking at Jemmy; and the brothers (a man and three boys) stood still, stared, walked up to Jemmy, and all round him, without uttering a word.'

The nature of the reunion was unexpected. Fitzroy's surprise was matched by Jemmy Button's mortification, for besides the humiliating contrast between his own smart appearance and the greasy, unkempt near-nakedness of his family, he discovered that he had forgotten the Yaghan language, and although he could understand most of what was said to him, he could not speak a word back.

For York Minster and Fuegia Basket, the arrival at Wulaia was a much more satisfactory experience. They liked the look of the place and decided at once that they would stay, rather than return to the desolate western islands where they had been brought up, and help Matthews with his mission.

The Beagle Channel in mellow mood.

During the first days after the *Beagle*'s arrival, Wulaia was a bustling and happy spot. The weather was fair, and the Yaghans who had congregated in large numbers all seemed anxious to help settle Matthews into his new home. Jemmy Button was soon able to talk freely again in his native tongue, and saw to it that his family were all decently clothed. Wigwams were built for the mission, and the natives helped with these and even with the unfamiliar task of digging the soil and planting seeds for Tierra del Fuego's first-ever crop of potatoes, carrots, turnips, beans, peas, lettuce, onions, leeks and cabbages. Matthews's stores were buried under the floor of his large and rather superior wigwam, or placed in a rough sort of attic under the roof.

Towards the end of the month, Fitzroy and Matthews both felt so confident about the situation, that they agreed that the mission should be given a trial period to run on its own. Matthews appeared quietly confident, 'betraying no symptoms of hesitation' as Fitzroy described him; and it really looked as if Wulaia was on the road to civilisation.

Fitzroy was not away for long. He returned south down the Canal Murray on 6 February, anxious to see how Matthews had fared alone. The first signs were not hopeful. On the shores of the narrow channel they caught sight of groups of Yaghans among the trees, all sporting linen tablecloths or lengths of tartan cloth, which could only have come from Matthews's store, and when Wulaia hove into sight with its wigwams spread out over the pasture, it appeared to be in a state of some agitation, and everyone had dressed themselves in torn strips of colourful clothing as if to flaunt their emancipation.

Fitzroy hurried ashore and was met by a distraught Matthews. The plundering and bullying had begun soon after they had left. He had been teased and threatened and then assaulted. One man had forcibly held down his head, Matthews told Fitzroy, another had begun to pull out the hairs of his beard, and many of his stores had been broken open and ransacked. York Minster had apparently stood aloof from this rioting: Jemmy Button had remained loyal and done his best to defend the wigwam, but he, too, had suffered the loss of most of his goods. These pillagers, Jemmy Button was quick to explain, were not from his tribe: they were no good men. The vegetable garden, too, had been ruined, and for this Jemmy Button had to admit to the guilt of his own people. 'My people very bad; great fool; know nothing at all; very great fool.' He was ashamed and crestfallen.

Button Island

Matthews had had enough, and asked to be taken back on board the *Beagle*. The only religious ceremony he had been able to conduct, after all the high expectations of the London Missionary Society and his arduous year-long voyage to the south, had been the marriage of Fuegia Basket to York Minster. He eventually left the *Beagle*, nearly three years later, in New Zealand, where he joined his missionary brother working in a less hostile region.

A New Missionary Assault

Although Wulaia's vegetable garden, along with the mission, had been a disaster, it was believed for many years that at least the seed of Christianity had been planted, and might perhaps be flourishing, in Tierra del Fuego. There was still reason for faith and confidence, even if they rested in the soul of one Yaghan lad. Anyone who had seen Jemmy Button on board the *Beagle*, or driving through London in a carriage, or kneeling at prayer with the Rev. Wilson at Walthamstow—the bright, intelligent, good-natured boy whose only weakness was for rather vulgarly-bright clothes—must believe that Fitzroy's extraordinary experiment

had succeeded, and that future missionaries in the south could be-
certain of his support. They were not so sure about the lusty,
moody York Minster; and Fuegia Basket was just a chit of a girl.

Allen Gardiner had wanted to be left in Button country, but
no captain would take his ship so deep into the heart of the
archipelago. When he was driven from Banner Cove, he had tried
to take his launches west up the Beagle Channel to Wulaia to find
Jemmy Button; but the wind had driven him eastwards instead,
and he never got farther west than Blomefield Harbour.
    After the Allen Gardiner tragedy (and it caused a national
shock with many recriminations and accusations against this
small-scale amateurish missionary work) there was a short period
when the uttermost south was given up for lost. Only George
Pakenham Despard kept his faith and resolution, and the Patagonian Missionary Society did not die. Amongst Gardiner's papers
that were discovered, wet and torn, along the beach of Earnest
Cove were his plans for the next missionary attack. His idea to
carry off young Yaghans to the Falkland Islands, learn their
language, and create from them a sort of elite corps of salvationists,
to join with Jemmy Button in a new Fuegian crusade, was a
perfectly serious one; moreover, Despard, to whom Gardiner had
been only one step away from Christ, determined to put this plan
into operation. It was the least that could be done in memory of
the man and his martyr's death.
    Gardiner's widely-reported death had brought the Patagonian
Missionary Society contributors as well as calumny. With their
new wealth they bought a grant on one of the Falkland Islands
on which to make their missionary headquarters and an eighty-
eight ton schooner which they named the *Allen Gardiner,* just the
vessel the man after whom it was named had needed. This time
there were no hitches. She had on board prefabricated buildings,
proper provisions, plenty of gunpowder, tools, and any number of
tempting gifts. The organisation and material appeared faultless,
and this new assault seemed certain of success. The *Allen Gardiner*
would sail to Wulaia, seek out Jemmy Button, and see what
progress he had made, then ask him to come to the Falklands for a
refresher course, bringing some of his friends with him.
    Despard had made only one mistake, and it was to prove fatal.
He gave the command of the schooner to a Captain W. Parker
Snow, a devout enough seaman with a good reputation as a
navigator, but not nearly dogged nor diplomatic enough for the

operation. He became querulous and edgy when things went badly, showed his anxiety, and then defiantly attempted to justify himself. His wife went with him, and this seemed to fuss him further. The voyage was a dreadful failure. Jemmy Button's missionary zeal had been short-lived. His appearance was not a total surprise, for Fitzroy had found him looking decidedly scruffy when he had revisited Wulaia before leaving Tierra de Fuego. Now, twenty years later, he was indistinguishable from his fellow Yaghans, a naked, dishevelled heretic, stinking of seal oil. When Captain Snow located him, he was with his family in a canoe off Button Island. He had married soon after Fitzroy had left and had three sons, the eldest almost a man. He had retained a few words of the English language, and a little of the self-consciousness he had absorbed during those impressionable childhood years. When the canoe was paddled alongside the *Allen Gardiner* and he saw Mrs. Snow looking down from the deck, he called out in halting English for a pair of trousers and then a pair of braces to hold them up before coming aboard.

But the deck of the anchored schooner was as far as Jemmy Button would come. He made it clear that he had finished with missionary life for ever. No other young Yaghans would come either, so without wasting any more time, Snow sailed back to the Falklands to report his failure.

Months later, when Despard heard about this feeble effort, he deprived Snow of his command and himself sailed out to the Falklands with his entire family—three daughters and two sons of his own, and two adopted sons. Besides this powerful contingent there were several fresh young catechists in whom the light of evangelism burned brightly, and Gardiner's son, Allen W. Gardiner, who had come to visit his father's grave and do what he could to carry out his father's intentions.

During the following three years, the first stage of the late Allen Gardiner's plan was completed. Yaghans from the Wulaia area 'were induced to leave for instruction at the mission'. None of the missionaries satisfactorily explained what sort of pressure was brought to bear on these native lads to make them leave their families, but one hopes it was all done by kindness. Jemmy Button was this time persuaded to come with his family for a while, and they all had a good time. There were many prayers and much religious instruction, and there was also practical work, too, like carpentry which would be useful back home. But the main task was the exchange of languages. As good mimics, all the Yaghans were adept at picking up English. In the mission, now a self-sustaining little Anglican community, one of Despard's adopted boys, Thomas Bridges, who was only thirteen when he left England, was by far the quickest, and in about 1858 began work on a Yaghan dictionary, the first and only one ever compiled.

By October 1859 all the groundwork appeared to have been completed for the carrying out of the second stage. Nearly thirty years had passed since Jemmy Button had been taught the catechism at Walthamstow, seven years since Gardiner had knelt on the beach at Banner Cove to pray for the souls of those bent on his murder. A nucleus of native converts—mostly young men—had been deposited back at Wulaia, decently clad, each with a Bible and a smattering of English. Now at last Wulaia and its environs appeared ripe for all-embracing Christianisation.

The Affair at Wulaia

The *Allen Gardiner* and her captain with his company of seven including Garland Philips, the leading catechist, a big Swedish sailor named Agusto, and the cook, Alfred Cole, as well as three

Wulaia

Yaghan families who had completed their instruction, made a successful passage back to the familiar cove by the end of the month, and anchored offshore. Wulaia was more crowded than ever, and before they stepped ashore for the first time, some three hundred more Yaghans appeared from the creeks of Canal Murray, Button Island and the neighbouring islands, all paddling determinedly towards the schooner, eager for a look and for loot.

This was the same intimidating scene that every missionary vessel had had to face, one that had caused the bold Fitzroy a moment of anxiety, even with the brass cannon of the *Beagle* loaded and ready to discharge.

The *Allen Gardiner*'s captain was ready for trouble. It began, not among the swarming natives (and this was unexpected as well as disappointing) but among the new converts from the Falklands disembarking to return to their families. The captain heard from his crew that some of their property was missing, and insisted on examining the natives' bundles before they went ashore. They were not pleased at this especially as they were now formally baptised Christians, one of them with the name Scheymuggins, since corrupted to Squire Muggins. It was this fellow who took the most violent objection to the search, hurled himself at the captain and tried to strangle him. The captain, a muscular seaman, threw Squire Muggins violently aside, and then discovered in this native's bundle some of the missing goods.

Here was a bad start to the enterprise. Instead of sending ashore as a vanguard a party of friendly Christian Yaghans, anxious to help spread the word of God, three families of properly dressed but sour and resentful natives were returning to their wigwams. It was almost as if at the first sight of their homeland and their fellow tribesmen, the past six months' of friendly religious instruction and regular meals, with grace before and after, had been struck from their memories.

Nor were the following days much more auspicious. In almost constant rain, the missionaries ferried ashore the prefabricated sections of their huts, put them together and built a fence about their compound in the same place where Matthews's wigwam had earlier been erected. They were offered no help. On the contrary, they were constantly molested, and among the most importunate was Jemmy Button himself, now no better than a naked middle-aged renegade, as dirty as ever and more resentful still because he felt, as a twice-civilised savage, that he was entitled to special treatment.

The party attempted to conceal their fear and disappointment from their flock, and from one another, the spirit of Allen Gardiner driving them on to complete their establishment. The morning of 6 November 1859, dawned bright and clear, the cove had never looked lovelier, their mission buildings were erected. It was a Sunday, and Garland Philips determined that today they would hold their first service and give thanks to God. The captain ordered out the longboat, and leaving only Alfred Cole on board, the party went ashore with their Bibles. The service was held outside in the sunshine, and the congregation that gathered was not less than three hundred. It was a scene that Allen Gardiner must have dreamed of witnessing many times when he was preparing his own plans.

The service began with a hymn, but got no further than the first lines. Cole watched with horror as a mass assault began with terrifying speed. Suddenly spears and stones were being hurled, and the sound of the confident singing voices of the white men was drowned by shrill shrieks. It was a premeditated and well-organised attack. One group of natives raced to the longboat, cast it adrift and took away the oars. When Agusto and Philips succeeded in breaking through the throng and raced to the beach, they were cut off. The Swede was clubbed to death, Philips waded out to the drifting longboat amidst a hail of missiles and got his arms over the gunwale before a stone struck him on the head and knocked him unconscious into the water. Within a few minutes all seven men were dead.

Cole had already leaped into the dinghy and was rowing frantically towards a headland north of Wulaia cove. Canoes put off in pursuit and had almost caught him when he reached the rocks. Stones whistled about him as he fled into the forest and got clear amongst the dense beech. Like Gardiner and his party, he lived for a short time a precarious nomadic existence among the forests and along the shore, tearing mussels and limpets from the rocks and sleeping under what shelter he could find. But he was soon discovered, so weakened now that he was captured and brought back to the scene of the massacre.

Alfred Cole survived. In their turn, the Yaghans tried to make a convert of him, plucking out his beard (always a sign of dirt and degradation among the Fuegians), and stripping him of his clothes. He was made to conform to the group, and was expected to find his own food and look after himself. Like many other before him stranded among the natives, only the women took any pity on him; without the food they secretly shared with him he would never have lasted until rescue arrived.

After five months of silence, Despard had become increasingly anxious for his missionaries and sent a second vessel for news. Wulaia looked as it had when Fitzroy and Darwin had first seen it, and had agreed on how primitive, savage and dangerous the natives appeared; and doubtless the scene had been no different two thousand years before them. There were wigwams, each with its fire burning inside, scattered higgledy-piggledy in sheltered nooks and along the shore of the cove, and a constant and seemingly purposeless to-ing and fro-ing of canoes trailing their smoke. There was no sign of the huts that were to have been erected on the shore of the cove, nor of the vegetable gardens that should by now have been flourishing. The only evidence that civilised man had been here was the schooner, dismasted, ransacked of everything that could be moved, a mere floating hulk.

Most disquieting of all was the unctuous friendliness of the natives when they went ashore. They had never before been known to behave like this. What could they do to help? Did the great ship need water? Wood? These people were as afraid and guilt-stricken as children surprised after some act of vandalism. Then from the crowds there appeared the figure of Alfred Cole, stripped of his beard, moustache and eyebrows, almost naked in the bitter winter air, and covered in boils. He poured out his terrible tale.

It was not until five years later that the missionaries' bodies were found, carefully laid out in a row in a catacomb, just like the bodies Magellan's men had discovered on that first-ever Fuegian landing.

The Missions Established

This is not the end of Jemmy Button, nor of all missionary efforts in Tierra del Fuego; although faith in the cause, as well as that old renegade Yaghan, came near to death. Jemmy Button, inveterate liar too, claimed that the massacre was the work of the Onas from across the Beagle Channel, out on one of their raids. This was discounted at once. Besides, he and one of his sons had been seen by Cole, throwing stones with the rest, on that November morning. Despard considered a punitive raid against Wulaia, and then, his spirit at last utterly broken, went home with all but one of his family. Only his adopted young son, Thomas Bridges, insisted on remaining.

Bridges was very different from poor Gardiner. He was a well-organised young man, patient, clever and by contrast with that martyr, an extrovert. He had by now mastered the Yaghan tongue, and believed that the events at Wulaia marked the end of violent native hostility to the missionaries in Tierra del Fuego. Still too young to run the Falklands' mission on his own, he was joined by the Patagonian Missionary Society's new secretary in England, the Rev. Whait H. Stirling.

With a small body of helpers, these two succeeded during the 1860s in completing Allen Gardiner's long-delayed plan. Back in 1852, when Gardiner's half-decipherable notes had been picked up from the corpse-strewn beach of Earnest Cove, they had read like the crazy emanations of a mind that had reached the end of its tether. As a man of action, Gardiner had brought death to himself and his companions; but no one can deny him his visionary powers.

The shuttle service of natives between the Fuegian islands and the Falklands was re-started and one of the most promising recruits was Threeboys, the last of Jemmy Button's three boys. Now there was someone who could talk to them in their own language, and this, as much as Bridges's love and devotion to his cause, slowly produced results. Avoiding the soiled beaches of Wulaia, a settlement was established first on the south side of the Beagle Channel, and then at Ushuaia, set in a deep bay almost opposite. A simple form of agriculture was begun, baptisms conducted in the wooden church, and for the first time in their history Yaghans, decently clothed, settled permanently into their wigwams or into new wooden huts.

It was the end of their precarious nomadic existence, afloat for much of the time, forever searching from inlet to river mouth to sheltered cove for fish and mussels, the occasional seal or otter, or, rarest prize of all, a guanaco. Back in England, Darwin expressed his warm approval. 'I could not have believed,' he wrote, 'that all the missionaries in the world could ever have made the Fuegians honest.' And he actually began contributing to the South American Missionary Society (Gardiner's old renamed mission); although he had disapproved of missionaries almost as strongly as of Yaghans. But for a few more decades, families of Yaghans and Alakalufs still remained beyond the reach of this furthest outpost of the Anglican church; and by an ironical stroke of fate, their chances of survival remained higher than those of the converts, for all their regular meals and rain-proof homes.

The white man, who for 350 years had passed through or sailed round these islands for convenience, exploration or the conquest of other lands, had now come to stay. And this meant not just the destruction of a way of life, but of human life itself. As in the Pacific, and Africa, and so many other parts of the world, disease and greed began to take their toll with the arrival of the word of God. The missions were not the only source of the decimating plagues that wiped out thousands from the 1860s, though the germs of European diseases brought with every consignment of clothes and blankets probably began the process of destruction. The first epidemic followed the Wulaia massacre, and doubtless originated from the looted supplies, though it was regarded locally as the result of the wrath of the white man's God, and also created more fear than Fitzroy's cannon or the fire of Sarmiento's muskets.

A second and more terrible epidemic followed sixteen years after the Ushuaia settlement was founded. In September 1884 three steam-driven warships flying the Argentine flag arrived off the little jetty, creating consternation among the Yaghan farmers and the missionaries. Such a show of strength had never before been seen in the Beagle Channel. The Argentine republic was confirming its claim to its most southerly region, intent on setting up a sub-prefecture in its share of Tierra del Fuego, which had recently been agreed with the Chilean republic by drawing some lines on a map. It was a peaceful enough occupation. The mission's flag, just dissimilar enough to the Union Jack to avoid any imperialistic misunderstandings, was hauled down, the Argentine flag raised in its place; and a salvo of twenty-one guns echoed across the channel from the Montes Martial to the Navarin mountains across the strip of water.

The Argentine expedition's leader, a Colonel Augusto Lasserre, was understanding and realistic and promised his government's support. But the measles germs these sailors brought with them soon reduced the number of natives to govern, or the missionaries to baptise. The disease raged from hut to hut, and extended outside the settlement and along the coast. Bridges and his little party could not dig graves fast enough to keep pace with the deaths, and bodies piled up outside the wigwams.

All through the holocaust, the Alakalufs on Desolation Island far to the west continued to fish and search for mussels and paddle from bay to bay in their canoes, untouched by the white man's plague. But their days, too, were numbered.

Next came the gold prospectors, a mixed bunch from eastern Europe, Spain, north America, the Argentine. The arrival of the first two on horseback at Ushuaia after an adventurous ride clear across the main island lasting three months, set the character of the minor Fuegian gold rush in the 1890s. They had shot every Ona they had seen on the way. Others followed them by schooner, gathering in rough settlements on the north shore of the Beagle Channel, up the east coast of the main island as far as the Rio Grande river, and on Lennox and New islands, and on Dawson Island to the west. These were robust as well as ruthless men, for the best deposits were found on the most exposed beaches, where the heaviest seas and tides helped to pan the gold particles mixed with the magnetic black iron sand from its overburden of gravel.

By way of trade for guanaco flesh, or by theft, the gold miners' guns got into the hands of the Onas and became a new unbalancing influence in the natural cycle of life and death. With their superb eyesight, the Onas proved themselves deadly shots. The guanaco soon became extinct, and family vendettas, once little worse than a dangerous sport, developed into tribal annihilation. At this time, too, the first sheep farmers were crossing the Magellan Strait and taking over more and more of the main island's grazing land. Sheep provided the Onas with an easier prey than guanaco, and in reply the farmers shot the Onas whenever they saw them, and later hunted them down in packs on horseback across the pampas and up into the central mountains.

A few of the fierce Onas were preserved for a while from this genocide by another mission, the first southern Fuegian Catholic mission, which was established in Patagonia in 1879. This Silesian Order gradually extended its work south, across the entrance to the Magellan Strait. As the Onas' hunting life was over, a hundred or so were packed into a ship and taken west to Dawson Island, to a new climate and a strangely different way of life. Here the same Order had established a settlement for Alakalufs of the west close to the point where nearly four hundred years earlier Magellan, Serrano and Mesquita had separated on their exploratory probes into the channels in search of the *Mar del Sur*.

At Harris Bay a hundred little Alakalufs, descendants of Fuegia Basket, Sarmiento's captives, Francisco and Juan, and the naked canoe natives who had traded fish for Anjou cloth with Francis Drake, worked side by side and pronounced their Ave Marias with the tall men from the east—unseen neighbours for thousands

Above: Ona warrior
Below: Ona hunters

Reprisals

of years. The men and women were taught new skills: forestry work, gardening and sheep shearing for the men, spinning and weaving for the women. But constitutions that could withstand the freezing summer rains of Desolation Island and the snow and the gales of the Sierra Beauvoir in the centre of the main island, were no proof against the germs brought in by the wool and provision ships, and the Italian priests and nuns who ran the mission. Measles, typhoid and pulmonary diseases soon began to kill off the new converts. A stout young native, brought up naked in the outer reaches of the archipelago, might go up into the hills behind Harris Bay to bring in the sheep, the rain would soak his clothes and he would come back shivering and be dead of pneumonia within days. A good thick layer of seal oil would have saved that Alakaluf.

The end of the nineteenth century marked the end of innocence or the end of freedom for the remaining Fuegian natives from Cape Desire to the le Maire Strait. The last of the Onas had been hunted down (some farmers paid a pound a head) or herded into a missionary settlement. Thomas Bridges's son, Lucas, visited them at this time at Harris Bay. They were ' "decently clad" in discarded or shop-soiled garments, generally some sizes too small for them', he remarked. 'I could not help picturing them standing in their old haunts, proud and painted, armed with bows and arrows and dressed, as of yore, in ... head-dress, robe and moccasins.'

Not that the scenes at the Bridges's Ushuaia Anglican mission had been much happier in its last days. The Argentines had set up a penal settlement on Staten Island. The convicts could hardly be blamed for rising up and murdering their guards to escape from this dreadful place. After most had been rounded up, the government moved the prison to Ushuaia. This brought an end to the mission. In 1888 another terrible epidemic had broken out, killing every Yaghan in a thirty-mile radius.

With bitter truth it could now be said that Gardiner's vow to bring into the fold of the Anglican Church every living Yaghan had been fulfilled fifty years after his death. There were still a few families left (170 was their estimated population in 1908) in the deeper recesses of Hoste Island and the Wollastons down to Cape Horn, and for a short time Thomas Bridges's assistant, Leonard H. Burleigh, ran a tiny station on Bayly Island, 27 miles from Cape Horn, the most remote and outlandish settlement in the world. After one year's operation here, Burleigh's weather chronicle read, 'Three hundred days continuous rain, twenty-five storms, the other days neither fine nor wet.' This Anglican remnant moved north again, to the southern shores of Hoste Island, where Burleigh was drowned in a sudden gale in 1893.

By then the Bridges family had long since moved from Ushuaia and given up formal missionary work. East along the shores of the Beagle Channel, near Blomefield Harbour, they built a homestead and began a new farming life, for their work was done. Their descendants are still there today, the last links with those early Fuegian missionary disasters.

Chile takes Possession

The same pattern of missionary endeavour, of civilised and uncivilised infiltration from outside, began to break up the world of the Tehuelches of the north before the middle of the 19th century. The explorers and scientists from England, France and Italy charted the coastline, noted the wildlife and geology, measured the mountains and rainfall, Fitzroy and Darwin spent as much time in the Magellan Strait as in the southern channel. The missionaries soon followed, then the gold prospectors and sealers with their cheap gin and firearms, the sheep farmers and

Above: Civilised Fuegian natives working on the Silesian Mission
Below: The process of conversion

the convicts. Religious conversion, corruption, exploitation, and disintegration of the old way of life can be marked out in parallel in Tierra del Fuego's two main passages linking Atlantic and Pacific.

Port Famine, that rich-looking river estuary land where Sarmiento had built his doomed city, where Cavendish counted the corpses of the colonists, where countless mariners had anchored below the sheltering summit of Mount Tarn, appropriately marked the setting of the end of the old life of the north. It added to its reputation for gloom and disaster even in Fitzroy's time. He was there during the winter of 1828, and had good reason to marvel at the endurance of those old-time Spanish colonists. In spite of first-class provisioning and organisation, his men suffered sorely from scurvy and hunger. The captain complained of the 'gloomy appearance of the country, and the severity of the climate'; and was relieved to get away. Darwin reported it in the same terms six winters later. 'I never found a more cheerless prospect,' he wrote in his journal. 'The dusky woods, piebald with snow, could be only seen indistinctly through a drizzling hazy atmosphere.'

The missionaries came close on the heels of these disappointed scientists and naturalists. Here the Catholics were first, building a tiny nucleus of a settlement, and making a handful of converts among the Tehuelches. In less than a year, a surprise assault led to the massacre of every priest and convert, and the total destruc-

The Magellan Strait

tion of the wooden encampment. It had not even lasted as long as the city of Don Felipe.

Who could ever want the place? Yet, a few years later, in 1843, this curving strip of land—now no more than a graveyard of lost causes and the bodies of white men—was once more claimed in the name of a European power. Over the centuries Spanish, Dutch, French and English navigators had raised their national flags and read their gradiose proclamations. On 22 September it was France's turn again. The man-of-war *Phaeton* landed a party for wood and water and prepared for the ceremony. Before it could be performed, a small schooner appeared, flying an unfamiliar flag. The Chileans had already been there, just three days earlier. Their new independent republic was only ten years old, and they had hardly had time to find out what belonged to them. But General Bulnes, Chile's soldier-president, understood the strategical importance of the Magellan Strait, and had heard that the French might be trying to stake their claim to it.

The commander of the little schooner *Ancud* told the *Phaeton's* commander that he was trespassing on Chilean soil, and pointed to the Chilean flag already flying on shore. The proclamation of occupation had been read out:

VIVA CHILE !

Complying with the orders of our Superior Government upon this 21st day of September 1843 we Citizen Captain Don Juan Williams . . . DO HEREBY TAKE possession, with all customary formalities, of the passages of Magellan and its territory in the name of the Republic of Chile, to whom it belongs . . .

For the first time the uttermost south really belonged to someone. With the departure of the *Phaeton*, which could have blown the little *Ancud* and its company out of the water in a few minutes, the right to sail through Magellan's strait, and the possession of all the land he had seen after passing Cape Virgins, justly passed into the hands of a Spanish speaking nation.

M. BOUGAINVILLE *hoisting French Colours on a small Rock, in* MAGHELLAN STREIGHTS

8

The Uttermost South Today

Before starting to write this book, I travelled the uttermost south, from southern Patagonia, along the Magellan Strait, and through the channels to Cape Horn itself, and beyond. Few people could tell me about Tierra del Fuego today, and I could find no one who had been far south of Punta Arenas before I completed arrangements for my wife and me to make the journey. Unless you are immensely rich and have all the time in the world, there are too many obstacles against making the journey through the islands independently. Even the occasional British and American naval vessels which find themselves in this area must have an experienced Chilean pilot on board, and the weather is so unpredictable that you may find yourself held up, expensively and uncomfortably, and even dangerously, in some obscure anchorage for many days. I finally discovered that I must be dependent on the hospitality of the Chilean and Argentine navies, which have one or two minor naval bases in the area, for serving the few settlements, showing the flag, and maintaining navigational aids. When they understood the purpose of my journey, the naval authorities of both these nations promised a warm welcome and the offer of all possible assistance.

There is only one base from which you can explore Tierra del Fuego. Punta Arenas is not only still the most southerly town in the world; it is the only town in the whole area. It is accessible from any of the big cities of Chile, and when weather permits, there is a jet service from Santiago thirteen hundred miles to the north. On the day in January when my wife and I flew in from the heat of Santiago, the sky was clear, and after reading so much about the *paso* and Tierra del Fuego and carrying for so long in my mind the nature and the configuration of the area, it was rewarding and moving to see so much of it spread out below: the reality of the maps and charts I had been studying for so long.

The aircraft's circuit took us over the main island of Tierra del Fuego, grey, flat and lake-splashed, near the shoreline. Already my eye was identifying features of the landscape below with events in the country's past. Far to the north was the second narrows, which had revealed the southerly course and the welcoming widening of the strait to so many of the early navigators; and close to the exit from these narrows, the long shape of Elizabeth Island—today still chock-a-bloc with penguins—where Pigafetta had found 'there were many sea wolves and large birds', and Drake had killed three thousand penguins in one day for salting down. And somewhere below the dipping starboard wing of the Caravelle, Magellan's men had found those thatched barrows concealing the corpses of some two hundred Ona natives.

Sixty miles to the south we could just make out the snow-capped peaks of Dawson Island, dividing the narrowing strait where it begins to curve south-west towards Cape Froward, and the wider channel taken by treacherous Gomes in the *San Antonio*.

The drive from the airport took us along the only metalled road in southern Patagonia to the only modern hotel, the Cabo de Hornos, a multi-storied structure dominating the central square with its fine statue of Ferdinand Magellan peering out over his strait.

Punta Arenas was set up as a township, a sheltered roadstead, and a penal settlement in 1850. It was at first a rough-and-ready shanty town of hutments hastily constructed from local timber. It was also to serve as the administrative headquarters of Chile's new territory of Magallanes, whose first Governor was Colonel Mardones.

Set mid-way between the strait's two climates and with plenty of grazing in the hinterland, there seemed to be a good chance that at least a basic form of agriculture—sheep, cattle, some winter vegetables—might flourish. By the southern winter of 1851 the township was complete and appeared well-settled and secure to the three hundred colonists and the soldiers in command of the convict settlement.

The first Punta Arenas lasted no longer than Sarmiento's Don Felipe two hundred and seventy years earlier, and again hunger, violence and treason were the causes of destruction. On 16 November 1851 the convicts arose and overcame their guards. It had been a bitter winter, food had run short, a further batch of three hundred convicts had been landed, and the new governor who had taken over from Mardoñes, Munoz Ramero, was a weak man. The governor and guards were murdered and the township looted and almost levelled. The convicts seized horses and arms and scattered north into Patagonia.

The Chilean government persevered, Punta Arenas was rebuilt, roads were laid out, the fort reinforced, the prison secured. Then for more than twenty years the little place prospered. In 1877 there was another uprising. The guards hated the place as much as their charges, and conspired with them to overthrow the governor. Again there was much bloodshed and destruction before the convicts and their guards made off north for Argentina. The government tried again and the place was rebuilt. And now the worst was over. The heyday of Punta Arenas lasted until the opening of the Panama Canal in 1914. During this time it developed into a wool centre for the *estancias* of southern Patagonia and the main island of Tierra del Fuego, and a port for the sealers. While the clipper ships from Australia and San Francisco preferred to risk 'the blind Horn's hate', marking a final glorious era in the age of sail, steamers used Magellan's *paso*. Punta Arenas became an important coaling station.

Three hundred and fifty years later, the Iberian vision of the strait as a regular trade route to and from the east became a reality; and mid-way between Sarmiento's two doomed cities, the Spanish-speaking colony of Punta Arenas flourished. By 1912 the population was over 10,000—merchants, traders, naval and military personnel, tradesmen and workers at the sawmills, administrators and port officials. There were always several steamships tied alongside the three wooden piers, unloading imports of coal and loading exports of wool and meat. The place had an international flavour, in keeping with the multi-nation effort of Fuegian exploration. There were many Yugoslavs, refugees from conscription and the Balkan troubles, most of them disappointed gold prospectors; Germans and English, who owned the largest *estancias*; Italians, Greeks, a scattering of Swedes, besides Chileans from the north, many of whom bred with the last of the native survivors. Like a miniature Singapore, the Europeans had their clubs, and kept themselves to themselves. The Panama Canal, and the First World War, did not quite destroy Punta Arenas, but its strategical importance, and its value as a coaling station, were greatly reduced.

Punta Arenas is wet for much of the year, snow-covered for most of the winter, and in summer sunshine warm only in corners sheltered from the daily winds—they start at about 10 a.m.—sweeping up the strait from the west. There are five times as many people living here as in 1912, but it is mainly bureaucratic and naval growth, and the discovery of oil in Tierra del Fuego, that has caused this. It still seems an unfinished sort of place, a pioneer town that has never quite found its way and doubts its future. Most of the houses are of galvanised iron, seemingly knocked together by the dark mixed-breed inhabitants with a do-it-yourself book in one hand. But a defiant civic pride beats in the heart of the town, where some tough wind-swept gardens are laid out between the more permanent looking government buildings. Punta Arenas continues to grow. But just as the early navigators had to impress their crews, or offer them double pay to sail south, so the Chilean government still has to offer special tax concessions to persuade people to come and live here.

From the south-facing windows of the Hotel Cabo de Hornos you can see across to the flat coastline of Tierra del Fuego in most weathers. But the visibility seems always to be changing. It takes only a few minutes for a black sky far to the west to sweep overhead and release squalls of near-horizontal rain. The strait changes its shade—dark grey, light grey, Mediterranean blue, through green, dark green to pitch black—every few minutes. Mid-summer sun steams dry the uneven sidewalks of the town a dozen times in a morning. It is like a parody of the climate of Scotland.

On our second day we made our way north of the town along the coast, following the route Viedma and his handful of survivors had taken from Don Felipe in January 1587. It appeared remarkable that anyone could survive off this seemingly endless stony flat beach or the bleak hinterland of scrubby grass, and without shelter from the wind. Where did they lie at night? And there were many miles without sign of fresh water. The going was rough, the shoreline heavily indented, making necessary diversions round marshes and pools. A six-hours-long walk would not seem to bring any nearer the gap, marking the exit from the second narrows, between the north-western tip of the main island and the southern extremity of Patagonia. Here, in this bleak spot, Sarmiento had once made captive his 'giant' and named him after his King; and later had been waylaid by natives who might have been Felipe's relatives.

It was easier to understand the glowing nature of Sarmiento's and Drake's reports on the *paso* when we made our way by land south of Punta Arenas towards Cape Froward. The weather was at first sunny and the summer flowers on both sides of the track leading to Santa Ana Point were in full bloom. This looked 'a good and pleasant land'. The clearings in the forests appeared rich and warm enough for vine-growing, and in the ravines cut into the side of the low hills 'the sweet streemes' reported by Cavendish and his contemporaries flowed into the strait every few miles. Yet there was no cultivation, and we saw only a few hardy sheep.

Our destination was Fort Bulnes and Port Famine. After Chile, the last of so many claimants, had formally taken possession of the *paso* and the islands of Tierra del Fuego in 1843, a fortified settlement had been built at the head of Santa Ana Point. Named after the new republic's military President, Fort Bulnes overlooked the site of Sarmiento's city and was almost a replica of the city of Don Felipe, with log cabins, storehouses, a chapel, an armoury, surrounded by a spiked stockade and protected by cannon which could also fire at any unauthorised vessel sailing through the strait. Like Don Felipe before it, and the first Punta Arenas which was to replace it as the Chilean capital of the south, Fort Bulnes had a short life, in keeping with the destructive tradition of Port Famine. The Chilean government, like the Argentines later, unwisely used their most southerly outpost as a prison for some of their more desperate criminals. One night the convicts arose against their guards, murdered the Governor and all the colonists, seized the ships at anchor in the bay, and set sail as pirates. It was some time before they were all recaptured and hanged.

Fort Bulnes was destroyed when the move was made north to Punta Arenas, but a facsimile of the settlement and fort stands on the site today, complete in every detail, as a memorial to those Chilean pioneers, the last of so many who had failed to settle Port Famine.

I stood for a long time beside one of Fort Bulnes's cannons, looking over the spiked stockade towards the broken coastline south of the *paso*. The sky was black and many shades of dark grey and light grey, with breaks where the sun slanted down in narrow beams onto the water. But the air was clear, and I could see the jagged white peaks rise up higher and higher into the southern distance. Here the islands are crammed so closely together, like ill-fitting pieces of a jig-saw puzzle, that it is easy to understand why for so long Tierra del Fuego was believed to be northernmost *Terra Australis*. When you knew that round the next headland in the strait, at Cape Froward, you would be on your way north-west towards the *Mar del Sur*, a mere 170 miles distant, there would be no curiosity to explore down those dangerous looking inlets and channels. Above all, you wanted to leave the place. It had taken that monstrous storm of 1578 to reveal involuntarily to Francis Drake that this was not a southern land mass extending clear to the South Pole, but only a multitude of ragged islands and islets, fining down to a tip at the Horn.

There is a memorial to Pedro Sarmiento at Santa Ana Point. I wonder if he deserves it. You can forgive him for being deceived by the seeming hospitality of this wide bay, its safe anchorage, and the pure waters of the River San Juan; and you must admire his tenacity and his single-mindedness. He did, after all, and after a fashion, fortify the strait. He brought the cannon here, and force-marched the soldiers overland to man them, even if he did leave them to die 'like dogges in their houses'. I should like to see another memorial to poor Viedma, who was left to continue the struggle. I had already seen that bleak shore to the north where he had sighted the sails of Cavendish's ships, and now I followed for a short distance the start of that last march, around the rocky headland. Like the members of his mixed party, I found few mussels or limpets and little shelter from the wind and squally showers; and I realised how they must have hated the sight of the endless slippery kelp, draped over the rocks at low tide and blackening the water with its waving strands. It was uncomfortably cold in thick clothing in mid-summer, and those last colonists had already endured three southern winters, keeping themselves alive by what they could find in the forests and along this hostile shoreline. Now I was more than ever puzzled to know how they survived.

With Darwin, and all those who had experienced the false promise of Port Famine, I was glad to leave this bay a few miles from the end of America's land mass. Like the fields of Picardy, the stony beach and the coarse grassy hinterland and the thick antarctic beech forests beyond, have known too much grief and suffering.

The next day, at dawn, we saw Santa Ana Point from the middle of the Magellan Strait. At midnight we had boarded at Punta Arenas a Chilean navy armed patrol ship, the *Lientur*, a 534-ton ex-United States coastguard vessel, built in 1944, and brought by Chile, along with two sister ships, for the exclusive purpose of servicing the navigational aids of the intricate channels among the islands south of Valparaiso, and of the Fuegian archipelago. The *Lientur* is ideal in size and manoeuvrability for this delicate and sometimes dangerous work: a third vessel was recently wrecked carrying out these tasks. We carried on board drums of oil, food supplies, livestock for some of the remoter Chilean outposts, and a number of acetylene cylinders to fuel the unmanned navigational lights which mark the worst hazards of the channels south of the Magellan Strait. The *Lientur*, we learned, had a complement of some thirty-five sailors, two junior officers, and was commanded by Lieutenant-Commander Renaldo Rivas.

Our captain, a tall, handsome, conquistador-like figure, soon became, in the cramped quarters below and on the diminutive bridge, our friend, guide and adviser. He knew every cable-length of the channels, all the vagaries of the climate, from a Magellanic williwaw to a flat calm. He loved the beauty and loneliness of the islands, and in the throes of the most delicate navigational situation could still point out a group of penguins, a leaping seal, or a pair of steamer ducks.

The attractions of Port Famine were even more evident from the sea. It appeared a perfect haven as an anchorage, with all that a weary crew needed for refreshment on shore. An hour later we sighted Cape Froward, a dark, lowering cliff face, looking less high than I expected, because it was dwarfed by the 3,000-foot peak of Mount Victoria towering above. Together they make a fitting signing off mark to the American mainland and entrance to the narrow steep-sided north-west leg of the *paso*. That was the way Magellan himself had gone with the *Trinidad*, to the Bay of Sardines; we were following old John Serrano in the *Concepción*, on both sides the cliffs rising in every style and angle, through beech forests to bare rocky slopes, to the snowline; ahead of us, crystal clear in the morning sun, its twin summits topped by an inverted saucer of cloud, stood Mount Sarmiento. But most of the names on our charts originated with Fitzroy's surveys, especially the islets scattered by the hundred in every channel through which we passed—Darwin Island and Fitzroy Island, of course, though neither of any distinction, Chair Island for its shape, Burnt Island, Smoke Island, London Island. No islets could be more un-English than these, and it was just as curious to examine some deep inlet, full of the most foreign bird life, perhaps with a group of penguins on a rock and the blue-white face of a glacier entering it at the far end, to find it named prosaically after some English place or explorer.

The Magdalena Channel turned, at Cape Turn, west beneath the glacier face of Mount Sarmiento, and became Cockburn Channel; the sun blazed down at noon; and the only mark on the waters was the *Lientur*'s own wash. Captain Rivas noted our surprise. 'It is not usually like this,' he said. It was a comment we were often to hear. But later in the day we felt the first distant pulse of the ocean, the islands became lower and thinned out, and we caught the first glimpse of the Pacific. It was not the way Magellan had come—Serrano had turned back to rejoin his Captain-General many miles before this point—and there was no Cape Desire to mark the entrance to the *Mar del Sur*. But the first sight of the southern sea from the Canal Cockburn is charged with emotion, even if you have come most of the way by jet. We came out at Meteor Island, glimpsing briefly the rock-strewn lee shores of the outer archipelago along which Drake had been driven, and we rolled and pitched heavily before heading for the shelter of the islands and channels again.

Somewhere along here, perhaps behind Stewart Island or at the entrance to the Canal O'Brien, the *Golden Hind* had experienced a short respite, had taken on water, before being driven south again. Our progress was more stately, tracing in reverse the course of the *Adventure* and the *Beagle*, through channels so narrow that I could photograph the birds on the shore without the aid of a telephoto lens.

The range and density of the bird life was an unexpected bonus on this voyage. We had read our Darwin, and the books of other naturalists, but were surprised by the ornithological profusion and variety. The shyest were the flightless steamer ducks, often reported as extinct, which left a long white wash behind them as they thrust their way along like hovercraft, stump wings beating the water frenziedly. They weigh up to thirty pounds and could match our maximum speed of eleven knots.

On the kelp-strewn rocks there were scores of oyster-catchers, black-and-white kelp geese and cormorants; white, dainty Antarctic terns flashed from side to side of the channels; big Magellanic gulls, gorged with fish, rose reluctantly only seconds before our stem would have tossed them aside, and settled again at once; great skuas, with eight-foot wing-spans and a predatory gleam in their eyes, followed astern for any scraps. If a gull got there first and was not quick to swallow, he would be forced to drop the morsel by a harassing and suddenly very nimble skua which would retrieve it in mid-air. This act of theft was mis-construed by early mariners, who reported a breed of bird that consumes the excreta of its mate.

We entered the Beagle Channel at dusk, and on a windless clear night watched the glaciers pass by, deep blue in the full moonlight, the most spectacular of them sweeping down almost from the peak of Mount Darwin more than seven thousand feet above. Our narrow world was all blue and white until, shortly before dawn, the channel perceptibly widened and we passed north of Navarin Island and anchored off the little Chilean naval base at Port Williams.

During the days that followed, as we made short voyages up and down the Beagle Channel to the nearby islands, I was able to follow every mile of the last sad journeyings of Gardiner and his party. The almost continuous fine weather made this a mainly comfortable business, and with the Beagle Channel as still and sunlit as a Pacific lagoon, it was hard to imagine the *Speedwell* and the *Pioneer* battling their way up the Channel in search of Blome-field Harbour, every wave threatening to swamp them.

We were rowed ashore in a whaler to Gardiner Island, struggling all the way with the kelp. Gardiner originally named this Garden Island, but the reality was very different from such an im-plication . Cormorants nested head to tail up the cliffs and windswept antarctic beeches leaned precariously over the brink. We saw a pair of condors sweeping to and fro, watching us hungrily as we struggled into the forest. We did not get far. Piled up trees fallen into the marshy ground made progress impossible, and we wondered how Gardiner's party had hurried from this place, pursued by screaming Yaghans. We felt again the chill deadness of these Fuegian forests. There was no sound except the sawing of branches against branches, no birds, no animals, no visible insects, and very little light. By contrast, the cliffs and rocky northern shore swarmed with kelp geese and duck, oyster catchers, gulls and more cormorants. There was an open grassy area on the west side of the island, and this was the place where the missionaries had planted their garden, hoping for tulips and a fine crop of vegetables when they returned. In Banner Cove, too, we found the smooth rock cliff, facing the entrance to the Beagle Channel, on which Gardiner's party had painted that last *cri de coeur*, GONE TO SPANIARD HARBOUR. The letters had long since faded away, although they were repainted in Gardiner's memory every year by later missionaries until the turn of the century.

We could not land at Spaniard Harbour, or view that sombre cavern and the missionaries' graves, and could only examine it through binoculars from the sea. It looked as gloomy a refuge as Banner Cover had been an uninspiring missionary headquarters, and I wondered again at the strength of spirit of these men who had remained cheerful to the end. Even Port Famine was a better place to die in than that hopeless shore.

Wulaia, on the other hand, had a feeling of cheerfulness about it, although here as many men had died violently as had died quietly of starvation at Spaniard Harbour. We had followed Gardiner's route to Lennox Island, thence along the southern shores of Navarin, through Ponsonby Sound, arriving at Wulaia at dawn and anchoring offshore. It was a brilliant sunrise, the rays catching first the jagged white peaks of the mountains on the Dumas Peninsula, then throwing long shadows from the scattered islets across the lagoon. One hundred and twenty years ago, before the missionaries got them organised, Wulaia cove and the shoreline of Button Island across the water, would have been thick with the smoke from hundreds of fires and the women would have been out in their canoes with their children and dogs after fish. At the sight of our anchored vessel, the men would have reached for their paddles, too, and we should have been assailed by the cry of 'Yammerschooner!' as they swarmed over the rails. Now a single figure met our whaler at the little landing stage, pleased to see us, glad to have the stores we brought, but evidently quite content with his life in this lonely spot. Perhaps our crew would come for a game of football?

We followed the route the unfortunate cook, Alfred Cole, must have taken, up the hill and into the forest, with screaming Yaghans in hard pursuit. It was an exceptionally clear morning, and from high up the slopes of the hill we could see Mount Darwin to the north-west, deep into the heart of wild Hoste Island, and to the south we could make out the Hardy Peninsula, a roughly-clipped grey shape set close to the end of the archipelago.

On only one or two days in a year is Tierra del Fuego as bright and serene as this. 'It is not usually like this,' said our Captain again when we returned to the ship. He explained that we were going down to a sheltered anchorage behind False Cape Horn, from which we hoped to make a dash to the Diego Ramírez islets. 'They need food badly,' Commander Rivas told us. There is a weather station on one of the islets, the loneliest Chilean outpost of them all, and the two men were long overdue for relief. The most important duty during this voyage was to make a landing on Diego Ramírez. But our captain knew how tricky these islets could be, for there is no proper shelter from the Cape Horn winds and only one beach on which a whaler can be got ashore. Rivas handed me a long signal the *Lientur*'s radio had just picked up from an American nuclear-powered aircraft carrier, one hundred times our size, which had just doubled Cape Horn. 'I cannot understand all this English,' he said. The message told of very high winds and forty-foot waves, and generally suggested that they were having a rough time of it.

'We will hole up in Orange Bay,' said the captain, proud of his colloquialism. 'If we wait long we shall have gunnery practice.' Target practice is simply arranged in Tierra del Fuego: you just pinpoint some landmark on any cliff face or mountainside and blast away. Only the birds are disturbed.

Commander Rivas had also picked up the phrase 'take the calculated risk', and he used it with relish that night when we anchored in Orange Bay. 'At midnight I shall go out and smell the sea. If I like the smell I shall take the calculated risk.' This meant breaking out of the archipelago into the Drake Strait and steaming some seventy miles south-west, following the track of the Nodal brothers. Suddenly I realised that, by a happy coincidence, it was 350 years to the week since Gonzalo and Bartolomé had first sighted the islets they named after their cosmographer. I hoped that our passage would be smoother, for our ship was little bigger than theirs.

In the early hours of the morning we were awoken by new sounds, and realised that Rivas had taken his risk. Bulkhead doors were banging, the old hull was creaking at every joint, and everything unsecured was sliding about the decks. Our husky dogs were howling with fear, and there was a new urgency in the pace of the feet on steel decks and gangways. We were Cape Horners at last.

Every dawn had brought us a splendid new sight, but none would be more memorable than this one. We were hove to, rolling and pitching moderately half a mile from a green-capped islet that rose up to a summit some 500 feet above the sea. The full weight of the Pacific rollers was beating against the western shore, sending spray over the top of the cliffs. For most of the year, Rivas told us, the spray covered the islet, freezing as it fell. The *Lientur* derived some shelter from a smaller islet, only a few hundred yards long and two or three hundred feet high, little more than a grass-capped big rock. Many more lethal-looking rocks stuck up out of the sea to the north, and farther north, a mile away, was Bartolomé, the only other big islet, a long, and inaccessible shapeless rock, half covered with the same tussock grass, the only vegetation on Diego Ramírez.

The first of our whalers had already been lowered and was loading barrels of oil. We could just make out the beach, perhaps twenty feet wide, and the track up the cliff face leading to three steel huts, a pole flying the Chilean flag, and a primitive-looking radio aerial. 'Yes, they are lonely men,' Rivas replied to my predictable question. 'But they have the psychological test and their appendix removed before they come.' He said we could go ashore, and smiled at my wife. 'You will be the first woman.'

We clambered over the side and dropped into the second whaler. There were a dozen sheep in the bottom, legs tied and apparently dead, though in fact they were only stunned by seasickness and shock. We sat on them, for there was no other place. Besides the sheep we had two dozen sacks of small coal, already sodden, cans of apricots, from Bulgaria of all unlikely places, more cans of meat, condensed milk from Switzerland, and several crates of a potent white alcohol like crude brandy, which was appropriately called 'firewater' in Spanish.

The ship's launch towed us for part of the way, and turned back to the *Lientur* when we reached the kelp. The first whaler had already been half swamped, and the young lieutenant in command was having a hard time getting her through the breakers and the kelp. Our crew got a stern anchor out in time, and we waded the last dozen yards to the beach with sacks of sodden coal on our backs. We next dumped the sheep on the shelving beach, cut their bonds, kicked them into consciousness. They at once wandered off and cropped the nearest tussock grass as if Diego Ramírez was just another meadow in their lives.

My wife had wandered off, too, with my camera. She had found her first Magellanic penguins, the burrowing breed with the great yellow rings round their eyes, and a screaming voice which has sent many a mariner off in retreat. But they were quiet today, weary and gloomy in mid-moult. The firewater bottle was passed round after we had unloaded the whaler. The spout tasted salty from the palm that had just wiped it, and the thick colourless liquid at once sent a glow of warmth all through my body. We climbed the cliff track together, and the sailors could not understand why we were not joining them in the hut, to drink more firewater and talk football. This was no place for walking, they suggested.

Although this station had been here since 1951, we soon realised that none of these sailor-meteorologists had ever ventured more than a few yards from the huts. Down to the storehouse above the beach, and up to the radio mast, was their limit. Neither the climate nor the terrain invited volunteer explorers.

Fitzroy had failed to land here, like all the naturalists and scientists since, but he had plotted the islets from the tip of Horn island, and we wanted to climb high to try to see the Cape. Unfriendly hawks prevented this. They were big brown Austral Caracara, previously believed to be found on only a part of the Falkland Islands. About a dozen pairs were nesting on the exposed western cliff tops, and attacked us from above as we approached, quite undeterred by the rocks we hurled at them (we were quite alarmed) before we fled, covering our eyes. Those sheep, we felt certain, did not have long to live. The hawks would clutch the wool of their heads, just as they were after our hair, and peck out their eyes, and eat them after they had crashed blindly over some outcrop or cliff. I discovered later that sheep had been landed here before, but had always mysteriously disappeared.

It was difficult to hurry. Above the cliffs the islet consists of hundreds of criss-crossing muddy runnels between the tufts of tall coarse tussock grass, which we clutched to drag ourselves along, always up to our ankles in mud. The rest of the bird life was profuse and friendly. Grey-headed albatross were nesting in their hundreds on the sheltered side of the island, one protesting, clacking giant chick to each nest raised into a saucer-topped platform above the wet ground. The fully grown birds stretched their huge wings and nodded what we supposed to be approval of their children and of our visit.

We knew that Commander Rivas's calculated risk allowed for only an hour or two before this spell of comparative calm would break. The football talk in the warm hut must soon end, and the *Lientur* must hasten back to the archipelago, for she was never built for real Horn weather. But we could not leave without briefly exploring the eastern shore. We slithered and clambered down a wet cliff face, leaving behind the clacking albatross chicks. The cove we were entering was like a giant auditorium, and it was a full house. The stage was the choppy, briefly sunlit, waters of the Drake Strait; the audience ten thousand Rockhopper penguins, mostly in full moult, as if they had hired their dinner jackets from

a store that had known better days. They were neither friendly
nor hostile, hopping reluctantly away from their perches as these
two burly late-arrivers bustled along the aisles photographing the
celebrities. Then they refocused their attention on the sea show.

But out at sea there was real activity for once. The *Lientur* was
sounding her siren, and the blasts were becoming increasingly
impatient. We took some last photographs and dragged ourselves
back up the cliff. We spotted some rodent—a guinea pig we
thought—an Antarctic peewit, a blackbird: and that was our sum
total of findings as amateur naturalists on Isla Gonzalo. But at
least we had done better than Darwin and the other naturalists,
and had landed when even the brave Nodal brothers had been
driven south before they could get ashore.

There are reports of landings, of watering from the single
stream that trickles down beside the landing beach. And a stone
plaque above it tells of an eighteenth century English mariner,
drowned on these shores—just one of a number shipwrecked on
Diego Ramírez.

Our departure was undignified. It was a waist-deep struggle to
the whaler, a fight through the kelp in the rising seas, and every
man was on deck to drag us up the *Lientur*'s side. We were under
way before we had squeezed out our clothes, the sky was turning
dark, and wind getting up, and the receding islets—manned for
another five months by two new lonely men—were looking more
as the Nodals had seen them for the first time 249 years, 364 days
earlier.

Our wonderful luck stayed with us for another 65 miles. The
Lientur kept ahead of the worst of the bad weather coming in from
the Pacific, and we caught our first sight of the Horn in misty
evening sunshine. The Hermite Islands were grey against a
white-flecked blue sea, False Cape Horn no more than a smudge.
Even under these benign conditions, Schouten's Cape itself lived
up to every expectation. No other landmark in the world can
match the grand finality of this turning point of the American
continent, soaring 1300 feet straight up from the battered rocks
at its base, arrogantly, menacingly terminal.

I was allowed to take the *Lientur* to within a mile, then a more
competent steersman took over, and we doubled Cape Horn with
the sun low, and headed north-east with Deceit Island to port, and
the Barnevelt rocks to starboard. With a 25-knot wind astern, and
a 1500-horsepower diesel pulsing away below the decks, it had
been an exhilarating experience. But again we puzzled how had

they done it, Drake and Schouten, Brouwer, the Nodals, and the rest, in 100-ton tubby galleons, incapable of sailing close to the wind, but with the wind always against them, three months out from Europe with water, wood and provisions low, and scurvy probably claiming its first victims? Many had given up after fighting the wind and currents for weeks. Others had been wrecked. But some had made it to the *Mar del Sur*, round this final climax to the archipelago's break-up, or through the *paso*, and came home millionaires.

We steamed back into the channels, which were now in a dark mood, with freezing drizzle by day and snow at night. Before flying north, we noted again their solemn grandeur and mystery. But the hostility of the uttermost south is as strong today as ever, and you can understand how those courageous mariners of the 16th, 17th and 18th centuries sometimes succumbed to the influence of black powers, or kneeled down in prayer to their vessel's patron saint. Now that there are no natives left, the sterility of the place is more evident than ever. Even in the last hundred years, every attempt at exploitation has been, more or less, a failure—the fishing, the gold, the coal they once found near Punta Arenas which promised so well, the timber, the agriculture. The oil has not come up to expectation, sheep farming on the islands is hardly profitable, and it is mostly man-made fibres that are wanted today anyway. Christianity arrived bravely, but too early and too late; for the missionaries were blinded by prejudices and ignorance almost as old as the way of life of those they came to save, and were followed by men who were more savage than the natives they hunted down and corrupted.

The longer you cruise the Fuegian channels and wander the islands, the more strongly you feel that, in spite of the courage that man has shown in his attempts to explore and tame the uttermost south, his only real accomplishment has been the destruction of man.

Main Source References

CHAPTER 1

The most important source reference on Magellan must always be Pigafetta's Journal, from which I have frequently quoted. I have used the Stanley translation in *The First Voyage Round the World by Magellan*, published by the Hakluyt Society in 1874.

Benson, E. F. *Ferdinand Magellan* (London, 1929).

Correa, G. *The Three Voyages of Vasco da Gama* (Hakluyt Society, 1869).

Guillemard, F. H. H. *The Life of Ferdinand Magellan* (London, 1890). Quoted on pp. 41, 55-7, 65.

Parr, C. M. *So Noble a Captain: the Life and Voyages of Ferdinand Magellan* (London, 1955).

Zweig, S. *Magellan: Pioneer of the Pacific* (London, 1938).

CHAPTER 2

The Hakluyt Society's *The World Encompassed by Sir Francis Drake* (1854), edited by W. S. W. Vaux, with Fletcher's Narrative is the main source reference. There are frequent and easily identifiable quotations from Fletcher.

Benson, E. F. *Ferdinand Magellan* (London, 1929). Quoted on p. 87.

Corbett, J. S. *Drake and the Tudor Navy* (ii vols., London, 1898). Quoted on pp. 82, 83, 87-8, 91-2, 99.

Markham, Sir C. (Trans. and Ed.) *Early Spanish Voyages to the Strait of Magellan* (Hakluyt Society, 1911).

Somerville, B. *Commodore Anson's Voyage into the South Seas and Around the World* (London, 1934). Quoted on p. 79.

Williams, G. (Ed.) *Documents relating to Anson's Voyage round the World 1740–44* (Navy Records Society, 1967). Quoted on pp. 79-80

CHAPTER 3

Narrative of the Voyages of Pedro Sarmiento, published in 1895 by the Hakluyt Society, is the most important source in the English language, and I have drawn freely, and quoted freely, from this volume.

Barclay, W. S. *The Land of Magellan* (*London, 1926*).
Cunningham, R. O. *Notes on the Natural History of the Strait of Magellan* (*Edinburgh, 1871*).
Hakluyt, R. *The Principal Navigations, etc.* (*iii vols., London, 1598–1600*). Quoted on pp. 149-50, 153-4.

CHAPTER 4

Burney, J. *A Chronological History of the Voyages and Discoveries in the South Sea or Pacific Ocean* (*v vols., London, 1813*).
Harris, J *Complete Collection of Voyages and Travels* (*ii vols., London, 1745–48*).
Markham, Sir C. (Trans. and Ed.) *Early Spanish Voyages to the Strait of Magellan* (*Hakluyt Society, 1911*). Quoted on p. 170.

CHAPTER 5

The three most important source references are Byron's, Bulkeley and Cummins's, and Campbell's Narratives (listed below), and quotations from these volumes are readily identifiable.

Bulkeley, J. and Cummins, J. *A Voyage to the South Seas in the Years 1740–41* (*London, 1743*).
Burney, J. *A Chronological History of the Voyages and Discoveries in the South Sea or Pacific Ocean* (*v vols., London, 1813*).
Byron, the Hon. J. *The Narrative of . . . . . , containing an Account of the Great Distresses, etc.* (*London, 1768*).
Campbell, A. *The Sequel to Bulkeley and Cummins's Voyage to the South Seas* (*London, 1747*).
Charnock, J. *Biographia Navalis* (*London, 1797*).
English Historical Review (*Vol. IV*). Quoted on p. 185.
Lloyd, C. *The Health of Seamen* (*Navy Records Society, 1965*).
Lloyd, C. and Coulter, J. L. S. *Medicine and the Navy* (*iii vols., London, 1961*).
Somerville, B. *Commodore Anson's Voyage into the South Seas and Around the World* (*London, 1934*).
Walter, R. *Anson's Voyage Round the World* (*London, 1928 edn.*). Quoted on pp. 189, 193-4, 196, 198.
Williams, G. (Ed.) *Documents relating to Anson's Voyage round the World 1740–44* (*Navy Records Society, 1967*).

CHAPTER 6

Burney, J. *A Chronological History of the Voyages and Discoveries in the South Sea or Pacific Ocean* (*v* vols., London, *1813*). Quoted on pp. 251-3.

Darwin, C. *Journal of Researches into the Natural History and Geology of the Countries Visited during the Voyage round the World of H.M.S. Beagle* (*London, 1890 edn.*).

Falkner, T. *A Description of Patagonia, etc.* (*Hereford, 1774*).

Hamilton, J. *A Memoir of Richard Williams* (*London, 1854*).

Marsh, J. W. *A Memoir of Allen F. Gardiner* (*London, 1857*).

Marsh, J. W. and Stirling, W. H. *The Story of Allen Gardiner* (*London, 1857*).

Riesenberg, F. *Cape Horn* (*New York, 1939.*) Quoted on p. 247.

Weddell, J. *A Voyage towards the South Pole* (*London, 1825*).

CHAPTER 7

Barclay, W. S. *The Land of Magellan* (*London, 1926*).

Bridges, E. L. *Uttermost Part of the Earth* (*London, 1948*).

Narrative of the Surveying Voyages of His Majesty's Ships Adventure and Beagle (*iii* vols., *London, 1839*).

Select Bibliography

Barclay, W. S. *The Land of Magellan* (London, *1926*).

Benson, E. F. *Ferdinand Magellan* (London, *1929*).

Bridges, E. L. *Uttermost Part of the Earth* (London, *1948*).

Bulkeley, J. and Cummins, J. *A Voyage to the South Seas in the Years 1740–41* (London, *1743*).

Burney, J. *A Chronological History of the Voyages and Discoveries in the South Sea or Pacific Ocean* (*v* vols., London, *1813*).

Byron, the Hon. J. *The Narrative of . . . containing an Account of the Great Distresses, etc.* (London, *1768*).

Campbell, A. *The Sequel to Bulkeley and Cummins's Voyage to the South Seas* (London, *1747*).

Charnock, J. *Biographia Navalis* (London, *1797*).

Corbett, J. S. *Drake and the Tudor Navy* (*ii* vols., London, *1898*).

Correa, G. *The Three Voyages of Vasco da Gama* (Hakluyt Society, *1869*).

Cunningham, R. O. *Notes on the Natural History of the Strait of Magellan* (Edinburgh, *1871*).

Darwin, C. *Journal of Researches into the Natural History and Geology of the Countries Visited during the Voyage round the World of H.M.S. Beagle* (London, *1890* edn.).

English Historical Review (Vol. *iv*).

Falkner, T. *A Description of Patagonia, etc.* (Hereford, *1774*).

Frezier, Mons. *A Voyage to the South Sea etc.* (London, *1717*).

Gallagher, R. E. (Ed.) *Byron's Journal of his Circumnavigation 1764–66* (Hakluyt Society, *1964*).

Geographical Journal (Vol. *xxi*).

Guillemard, F. H. H. *The Life of Ferdinand Magellan* (London, *1890*).

Hamilton, J. *A Memoir of Richard Williams* (London, *1854*).

Hakluyt, R. *The Principal Navigations, etc.* (*iii* vols., London, *1598–1600*).

Harris, J. *Complete Collection of Voyages and Travels* (*ii* vols., London, *1745–48*).

History of a Voyage to the Malouine (or Falkland) Islands made in 1763 and 1764, etc. Trans. from Dom Pernety's Historical Journal written in French (London, *1871*).

Lambert, J. C. *The Romance of Missionary Heroism* (London, *1907*).

Lloyd, C. *The Health of Seamen* (*Navy Records Society*, *1965*).

Lloyd, C. and Coulter, J. L. S. *Medicine and the Navy* (*iii vols.*, London, *1961*).

Markham, Sir C. (Trans. and Ed.) *Early Spanish Voyages to the Strait of Magellan* (*Hakluyt Society*, *1911*).

Marsh, J. W. *A Memoir of Allen F. Gardiner* (London, *1857*).

Marsh, J. W. and Stirling, W. H. *The Story of Allen Gardiner* (London, *1857*).

Mason, A. E. W. *The Life of Francis Drake* (London, *1941*).

Miller, A. W. *The Straits of Magellan and Eastern Shores of the Pacific Ocean* (Portsmouth, *1884*).

Narrative of the Surveying Voyages of His Majesty's Ships Adventure and Beagle (*iii vols.*, London, *1839*).

Narrative of the Voyages of Pedro Sarmiento (*Hakluyt Society*, *1895*).

Riesenberg, F. *Cape Horn* (New York, *1939*).

Robinson, C. H. *History of Christian Missions* (Edinburgh, *1915*).

Snow, W. P. *A Two Years' Cruise off Tierra del Fuego, etc.* (*ii vols.*, London, *1857*).

Somerville, B. *Commodore Anson's Voyage into the South Seas and Around the World* (London, *1934*).

South America Pilot, Part II, (*Eleventh Edn.*, London, *1916*).

Stanley of Alderley, Lord (Trans. and Ed.) *The First Voyage Round the World by Magellan* (*Hakluyt Society*, *1874*).

Vaux, W. S. W. (Ed.) *The World Encompassed by Sir Francis Drake* (*Hakluyt Society*, *1854*).

Voyage Round the World in H.M.S. Dolphin by an Officer (Dublin, *1767*).

Walter, R. *Anson's Voyage Round the World* (London, *1928 edn.*).

Weddell, J. *A Voyage towards the South Pole* (London, *1825*).

Williams, G. (Ed.) *Documents relating to Anson's Voyage round the World 1740–44* (*Navy Records Society*, *1967*).

Zweig, S. *Magellan: Pioneer of the Pacific* (London, *1938*).

Index

Bold type figures refer to illustrations

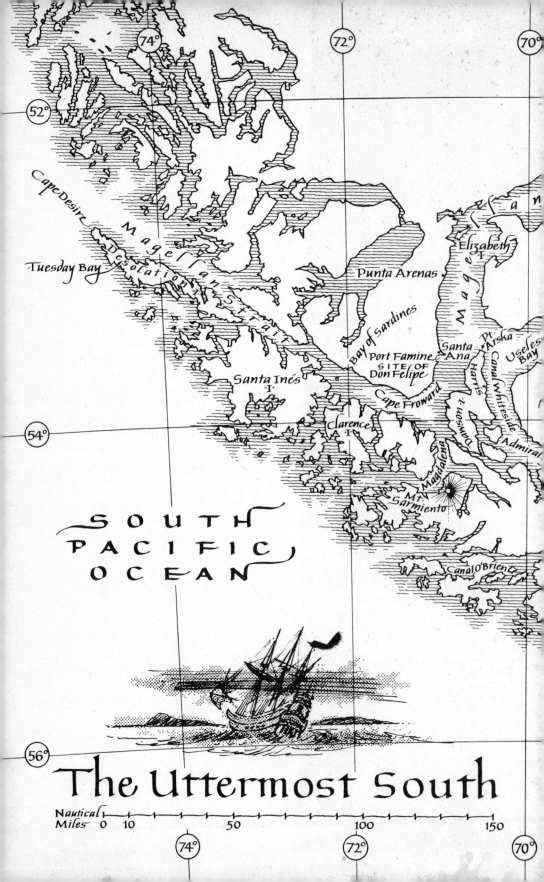

The Uttermost South